New Trends in Cor
Language Lea

C000017263

Corpus linguistics provides the methodology to extract meaning from texts.
Taking as its starting point the fact that language is not a mirror of reality but lets
us share what we know, believe and think about reality, it focuses on language as a
social phenomenon, and makes visible the attitudes and beliefs expressed by the
members of a discourse community.

Consisting of both spoken and written language, discourse always has historical,
social, functional, and regional dimensions. Discourse can be monolingual or
multilingual, interconnected by translations. Discourse is where language and
social studies meet.

The *Corpus and Discourse* series consists of two strands. The first, *Research
in Corpus and Discourse*, features innovative contributions to various aspects of
corpus linguistics and a wide range of applications, from language technology
via the teaching of a second language to a history of mentalities. The second
strand, *Studies in Corpus and Discourse*, is comprised of key texts bridging the gap
between social studies and linguistics. Although equally academically rigorous,
this strand will be aimed at a wider audience of academics and postgraduate
students working in both disciplines.

Research in Corpus and Discourse

Conversation in Context
A Corpus-driven Approach
With a preface by Michael McCarthy
Christoph Rühlemann

Corpus-Based Approaches to English Language Teaching
Edited by Mari Carmen Campoy, Begona Bellés-Fortuno and Mª Lluïsa Gea-Valor

Corpus Linguistics and World Englishes
An Analysis of Xhosa English
Vivian de Klerk

Evaluation and Stance in War News
A Linguistic Analysis of American, British and Italian television news reporting of
the 2003 Iraqi war
Edited by Louann Haarman and Linda Lombardo

Evaluation in Media Discourse
Analysis of a Newspaper Corpus
Monika Bednarek

Historical Corpus Stylistics
Media, Technology and Change
Patrick Studer

Idioms and Collocations
Corpus-based Linguistic and Lexicographic Studies
Edited by Christiane Fellbaum

Meaningful Texts
The Extraction of Semantic Information from Monolingual and Multilingual
  Corpora
Edited by Geoff Barnbrook, Pernilla Danielsson and Michaela Mahlberg

Rethinking Idiomaticity
A Usage-based Approach
Stefanie Wulff

Working with Spanish Corpora
Edited by Giovanni Parodi

Studies in Corpus and Discourse

Corpus Linguistics and The Study of Literature
Stylistics In Jane Austen's Novels
Bettina Starcke

English Collocation Studies
The OSTI Report
John Sinclair, Susan Jones and Robert Daley
Edited by Ramesh Krishnamurthy
With an introduction by Wolfgang Teubert

Text, Discourse, and Corpora. Theory and Analysis
Michael Hoey, Michaela Mahlberg, Michael Stubbs and Wolfgang Teubert
With an introduction by John Sinclair

New Trends in Corpora and Language Learning

Edited by

Ana Frankenberg-Garcia,
Lynne Flowerdew and Guy Aston

B L O O M S B U R Y
LONDON • NEW DELHI • NEW YORK • SYDNEY

Bloomsbury Academic
An imprint of Bloomsbury Publishing Plc

50 Bedford Square	175 Fifth Avenue
London	New York
WC1B 3DP	NY 10010
UK	USA

www.bloomsbury.com

First published by Continuum International Publishing Group 2011
Paperback edition first published 2012

British Library Cataloguing-in-Publication Data
A catalogue record for this book is available from the British Library.

ISBN: HB: 978-1-4411-5996-0
PB: 978-1-4411-8211-1

Library of Congress Cataloging-in-Publication Data
New trends in corpora and language learning / edited by Ana Frankenburg-Garcia,
Lynne Flowerdew and Guy Aston.
p. cm. – (Corpus and discourse)
Includes bibliographical references and index.
ISBN 978-1-4411-8211-1 (pbk.) – ISBN 978-1-4411-5996-0 –
ISBN 978-1-4411-1202-6 (PDF) – ISBN 978-1-4411-4499-7 (ePub)
1. Corpora (Linguistics) 2. Computational linguistics. 3. Discourse analysis.
I. Frankenburg-Garcia, Ana. II. Flowerdew, Lynne. III. Aston, Guy.

P128.C68N49 2013
410.1'88–dc23

2012011030

Typeset by Newgen Imaging Systems, Pvt Ltd, Chennai, India

Contents

List of Figures

List of Tables

Preface

Lou Burnard

Is 'teaching and language corpora' still an area in need of research and investigation or does it now constitute an established set of methods and skills within current pedagogic practice? If the former, should the focus of the research be the establishment of the practices which constitute the latter, or should it rather be in the application of those skills, as a major contribution to fundamental linguistic research within such areas as pragmatics, sociolinguistics, or more generally cultural studies? Are the biennial TaLC conferences representative of an emergent new academic community, with a shared set of assumptions and methods, and a coherent set of pedagogic or research goals, with a significant contribution to make in the practice of language teaching? If so, is this community based primarily on praxis, defined by its methods, or does it share a more fundamental set of priorities and assumptions about the nature of language pedagogy? Such ontological questions bedevil most varieties of specialist conferences, particularly perhaps those which have successfully established a community, in the simple sense of a bunch of practitioners who get along with each other, like to discuss matters of common interest, and (perhaps most significantly in the academic context) are in a position to valorize each others' achievements. There are only two possible evolutionary paths for such communities. Following the initial burst of enthusiasm and excitement ('I am not alone!') common to both, one path leads via boundary-defining manifestos and clarification of common purpose: a well-defined research agenda; the other leads to a loose confederation of methodologically overlapping but intellectually variegated set of practices. In either case, however, the biggest danger is one of stagnation. Academic discourse at all levels thrives on the tension between dogma and challenge; when academic conferences cease to attract new and challenging contributions, and become little more than engines for reinforcing a dominant unquestioned ideology, they cease to be conferences and become something else instead. The reader is invited to decide for him or herself the position TaLC now occupies on which of these trajectories by a careful reading of this rich volume from the eighth Teaching and Language Corpora Conference, organized with exemplary efficiency and congeniality at the Instituto Superior de Línguas e Administração in Lisbon in July 2008. As is customary, the papers in this volume have since been carefully edited and selected, and thus represent a polished and considered expression of what may have been only preliminary in oral presentation. Nevertheless, like other such books, they give an excellent opportunity to pause and take stock of the art amongst those for whom the application of large scale digitally-encoded language resources (as we must now call language corpora) now forms a crucial element in their teaching and research practice. The three parts into which this volume is divided reflect different routes one might take in organising a coherent discourse about this practice. The first group reports a wide range of evaluations about the introduction of language corpora to language learners, necessarily presenting the subject from the point of view of the language teacher, and focussing on the way in corpora are experienced by the language learner. The second is more methodologically focussed, and describes a number of specific techniques and methods which have been used in the same context, while the third demonstrates the important role that corpora of material produced by (rather than for) language learners increasingly play in the field of language pedagogy. As might be expected, there is variation within these three broad attitudes. In section one, Tono reports on a high-impact television series, which turned 'Mr Corpus' into a household name in Japan, and stimulated a major expansion of awareness and enthusiasm concerning corpus-based methods within the language teaching community there. His report demonstrates vividly how such methods can be applied in a way which is accessible to the general public, and the benefits of so doing. In a report on the application of hands-on concordancing within a smaller and more traditional academic context, the teaching of key rhetorical functions to language learners at Oxford University, Charles nevertheless reports a similarly striking degree of enthusiasm for such methods amongst language learners, as do other papers in this section, from Kettemann, working within the Cultural Studies paradigm in Graz, from Kaszubski, working in the English for Academic Purposes field in Poznan, and Kübler, working in the field of language translation in Paris. It seems clear from even the most casual reading of these studies that students in a wide range of learning situations positively enjoy and consequently benefit from direct access to real life data, whether or not this access is partially mediated by the language teacher. It might be of interest to explore possible connexions between this enthusiasm and other aspects of the learning environment appropriate to the new generation of 'digitally-native' language learners – after all, for many of these students, most aspects of their social life are mediated by Google searches and Facebook interactions, both of which have significant points of convergence and contrast with the use of online language corpora. Section two provides state-of-the art reports on some specific tools which have been found useful in the language teaching context. For the most part these demonstrate customized variations on the traditional use of concordance-based search engines, providing accessible interfaces which have been optimised for the language-learning environment. Both Warren and Liu et al., for example, describe tools which automate the identification of appropriate collocations for a given node word, thus going a lot further than a simple spelling corrector. Curado provides an overview of an integrated suite of MT-based utilities and language corpus resources used in the Language for Specific Purposes (LSP) context. This section also contains valuable contributions reminding us that corpora need not be limited in their content to written materials: Coccetta describes some interesting new tools for the annotation and analysis of non-linguistic interaction features such as gesture and gaze; Widmann et al. present a similarly-motivated tool-suite developed for the SACODEYL multilingual multimodal corpora.

Corpus-based methods enable the language learner to gain an insight into both the norms of specific registers of a language and variations from them. The advantages claimed for those methods (not always explicitly) such as exhaustivity, objectivity, and novelty should also, in principle at least, apply when the same methods are turned to the investigation of sets of language data derived from the rather specific register of 'language learner production'. Empirical studies of learner corpora may seem to teachers to have solely diagnostic value; but they are also of immense value to the learner in promoting self-awareness, and in facilitating contrastive study. Contributors to this volume provide a range of perspectives on these uses: Osborne's paper is thoughtful and stimulating on the extent to which the problematic notion of 'fluency' may be assessed automatically; others drill deeper into the variability of the ways that a core linguistic concept such as attitudinal stance may be conveyed by different communities. De Cock, for example, contrasts the use of evaluative adjectives by native speakers and by advanced EFL learners; while Hatzitheodorou and Mattheoudakis contrast the differing rhetorical strategies employed by American university students and Greek students writing in English, speculating about possible explanations for these. Bennett and McKenny report a well conducted study of the

English academic discourse produced by Portuguese-speaking scholars which seems to support the hypothesis that at least one such explanation (interference caused by the transfer of sociopragmatic features from L1 to L2) has considerable validity. Further insights into the challenges faced by those aspiring to proficiency in English academic discourse, and ways of surmounting them, may be expected as a consequence of the wider availability of specialised corpora such as the British Academic Written English Corpus reported by Nesi. BAWE will provide a fertile source for further contrastive studies of the inherent variability to be found even within a corpus of material all produced by ostensibly proficient speakers. In that sense, it serves as a valuable reminder that we are all, in some sense, language learners; that what separates and distinguishes language varieties may be as important for the learner to grasp as what unites them. Empirical studies of well organized language production should encourage us to support and promote diversity rather than to promote or enforce a uniform set of received truths about 'native English' or 'English as a Lingua Franca'.

Notes on Contributors

Guy Aston holds a PhD in English for Speakers of Other Languages from the University of London, UK. He has been using corpora in language and translation teaching and research for 15 years, being closely involved in the British National Corpus project and the Teaching and Language Corpora (TaLC) conferences. His publications in this area include many papers and the edited volumes *Learning with corpora* (Athelstan 2001) and *Corpora and language learners* (Benjamins 2004).

Karen Bennett is a member of the Centre for Comparative Studies, University of Lisbon, Portugal, where she researches in Translation Studies. Her PhD, *English Academic Discourse: its hegemonic status and implications for translation,* was based upon her extensive experience as academic translator and teacher of EAP and Translation (with the Catholic University of Portugal, University of Coimbra, Polytechnic of Leiria and British Council). She has published a number of articles on this subject and others, and is planning soon to publish her first book, entitled *Translating Academic Discourse: Technical, Ethical and Epistemological Issues.*

Lou Burnard is Assistant Director at Oxford University Computing Services, UK. He has worked with digital textual resources since the 1970s, and is closely associated with the development of the Oxford Text Archive, the Text Encoding Initiative, and the British National Corpus. He is currently working with a major French digital research infrastructure, the TGE ADONIS.

Maggie Charles is a Tutor in English for Academic Studies at Oxford University Language Centre, UK, where she specializes in teaching academic writing to graduates. Her research interests include the pedagogical applications of corpus linguistics, the study of stance/evaluation and discipline-specific discourse. Her work has appeared in, among others, *Applied Linguistics, Journal of English for Academic Purposes, English for Specific Purposes* and *System.* Most recently she has co-edited *Academic Writing: At the Interface of Corpus and*

Discourse with Diane Pecorari and Susan Hunston. She has also acted as a consultant on academic writing for the *Oxford Advanced Learner's Dictionary*.

Francesca Coccetta is currently a lecturer in English language and translation at the Universities of Padua and Pavia, Italy. Her research interests include multimodal corpus linguistics and the use of e-learning and ICT techniques in language teaching and learning. She has collaborated with the University of Padua's Language Centre in the creation and annotation of the *Padova Multimedia English Corpus*. Her articles on multimodal corpora have been published in *Hermes* and *ReCALL* and various edited collections. She is currently working on a co-authored book with Anthony Baldry on multimodal and language-only forms of web concordancing.

Alejandro Curado Fuentes teaches EFL/ESL at the University of Extremadura, Cáceres, Spain. His research focuses on academic English, corpus linguistics and Spanish students' use of IT and ESP in technical studies. He has published various articles and book chapters in international volumes on corpus-based lexical analysis and DDL. His current interest includes context-based Machine Translation and oral tools for Moodle-related resources.

Sylvie De Cock is a lecturer in English language and linguistics at the Université catholique de Louvain and at the Facultés universitaires Saint-Louis, Belgium. She is also a member of the Centre for English Corpus Linguistics (Université catholique de Louvain), directed by Sylviane Granger. Her main research interests include corpus linguistics, learner corpora, phraseology, pedagogical lexicography and the study of English for Specific Purposes (Business English). She has been involved in the compilation of the Louvain International Database of Spoken English Interlanguage (LINDSEI) since 1996 and collected and compiled the Louvain Corpus of Native English Conversation.

Lynne Flowerdew holds a PhD in Applied Linguistics from the University of Liverpool, UK. She has published widely in different areas of corpus linguistics in international journals and refereed edited collections. Her most recent authored book is *A Corpus-Based Analysis of the Problem-Solution Pattern*, published by John Benjamins (2008). She is a member of the Editorial Board of *TESOL Quarterly, English for Specific Purposes, Journal of English for Academic Purposes* and *Text Construction*.

Ana Frankenberg-Garcia holds a PhD in Applied Linguistics from Edinburgh University, UK. She is Auxiliary Professor at Instituto Superior de Línguas e Administração, Lisbon, Portugal, and invited Auxiliary Professor at Universidade Nova de Lisboa, Portugal. She was jointly responsible for creating COMPARA, a three-million word parallel corpus of English and Portuguese, available online at *www.linguateca.pt/COMPARA*. Her work on applied uses of corpora has been published in various books and journals, including *International Journal of Lexicography*, *International Journal of Corpus Linguistics*, *Corpora*, and *English Language Teaching Journal*.

Anna-Maria Hatzitheodorou is a Teacher of English for Specific/Academic Purposes at the Centre for Foreign Language Teaching (CFLT), Aristotle University of Thessaloniki, Greece, where she teaches at the Law School. She holds an MA in English from Ohio State University, Columbus, Ohio and a PhD in written discourse analysis (*Comprehension and Production of Written Discourse in a University EFL Context*) from Aristotle University of Thessaloniki. Her main research interests lie in the areas of written discourse analysis, academic discourse and genre, corpora and their applications.

Przemysław Kaszubski, Assistant Professor at the School of English, Adam Mickiewicz University, Poland, is a teacher of academic writing at both general and specific levels. He has been exploring corpora for research and pedagogic purposes for over ten years, recently focusing on the development and testing of customized web-based concordancing tools to assist EAP writing instruction.

Bernhard Kettemann is Professor of English Linguistics at Graz University, Austria, editor of *Arbeiten aus Anglistik und Amerikanistik*, co-editor of *Moderne Sprachen*, president or member of governing boards of VERBAL (the Austrian Association of Applied Linguistics), of VÖN (the Austrian Modern Languages Association), and of AAUTE (the Austrian Association of University Teachers of English). His main research interests include Corpus Linguistics, Critical Discourse Analysis and Cultural Studies.

Kurt Kohn is Professor of Applied English Linguistics at the University of Tübingen, Germany. He is a member of the steering committee of 'Sprachen & Beruf' Düsseldorf and of the advisory board of the *International Journal of Applied Linguistics* (INJAL). His research interests include theoretical and empirical issues of second/foreign language learning and teaching, technology-enhanced language learning and teaching (CALL, multimedia, e-learning), pedagogic corpora, content and language integrated learning (CLIL), English as a Lingua Franca, processes and strategies of translation. Publications include books and articles in these areas. Since the early 1990s, he has been involved in numerous EU-funded projects both as co-ordinator and partner.

Natalie Kübler is a full professor at Université Paris 7, France, where she teaches corpus linguistics and machine translation to translators. She was the Coordinator of the MeLLANGE project between 2004 and 2007, in which a learner translator corpus in several European languages was developed. Her current interests mainly deal with the relationship between corpus linguistics and translation theory and practice, and corpus-based writing aids in English for Specific Purposes for French-speakers.

Anne Li-E Liu received her MA degree in TESOL from Tamkang University, Taiwan. Her MA thesis was a corpus-based lexical semantic investigation in which she examined verb-noun miscollocations produced by Taiwan learners. She recently received her MPhil degree from the Research Centre for English and Applied Linguistics at the University of Cambridge. She is undertaking her PhD studies in the Centre for Research in Applied Linguistics at the University of Nottingham. Her research interests are in L2 lexical acquisition, computational linguistics and lexical semantics.

Marina Mattheoudakis is an assistant professor at the Department of Theoretical and Applied Linguistics, School of English, Aristotle University of Thessaloniki, Greece. She holds an MA in TEFL from the University of Birmingham, UK and a PhD in Lexicology (*Problems Related to Greek-English Lexical Loans*) from Aristotle University of Thessaloniki, Greece. She teaches courses in second language acquisition and methodology of language teaching. She is one of the scientific coordinators of the teacher training courses held in the department. Her main research interests lie in the areas of second language learning and teaching, corpora and their applications.

John McKenny is a lecturer in English Language and Applied Linguistics at the University of Nottingham, Ningbo, China and an associate at the Centre for Research in Applied Linguistics, Ningbo, China. He previously worked as a *Professor Adjunto* at Viseu Polytechnic (Portugal) for twelve years and as Senior Lecturer at Northumbria University for 5 years. His PhD thesis at Leeds University was entitled *A corpus-based investigation of the phraseology in* *various genres of written English with applications to the teaching of English for academic purposes.*

Hilary Nesi joined Coventry University, UK, as Professor in English Language in October 2007, having worked for 20 years in the Centre for English Language Teacher Education at the University of Warwick. She led the AHRB funded project to create the BASE corpus of British Academic Spoken English (2001–2005) and also the ESRC funded project *An Investigation of Genres of Assessed Writing in British Higher Education* (2004–2007), which involved the creation of the BAWE corpus. She remains involved in research relating to the use of English as a medium of instruction in international higher education.

John Osborne is a professor of English Language and Linguistics at the University of Savoie, Chambéry, France. His principal research interests are in linguistics and second language learning, particularly the sources of persistent errors in more advanced learner language, and the components of fluency in spoken production. He is currently involved in a European project for online CEF-based assessment of oral proficiency for intercultural professional communication, and in two corpus-based projects: the Scientext corpus (a corpus and tools to carry out a linguistic study of authorial position and reasoning in scientific texts), in collaboration with the universities of Grenoble and Lorient (France), and the PAROLE corpus of spoken learner language.

Yukio Tono is Professor of Corpus Linguistics in the Graduate School of Global Studies at Tokyo University of Foreign Studies, Japan. He received his PhD from Lancaster University. His research interests include L2 vocabulary acquisition, L2 learner corpora and pedagogical applications of corpora. He co-authored *Corpus-Based Language Studies* (Routledge) with Tony McEnery and Richard Xiao.

Nai-Lung Tsao received his PhD in Computer Science and Information Engineering from Tamkang University, Taiwan. Currently, he holds a postdoctoral position at the Graduate Institute of Learning and Instruction at National Central University. He is also an adjunct assistant professor of the Department of Computer Science and Information Engineering at Tamkang University. His research focuses on Natural Language Processing, Information Retrieval and Data Mining.

Martin Warren teaches and researches in the areas of corpus linguistics, discourse analysis, discourse intonation, intercultural communication, lexicology and pragmatics. He has published a number of journal articles and book chapters, and two books (*Features of Naturalness in Conversation* and *A Corpus-driven Study of Discourse Intonation* (with Winnie Cheng and Chris Greaves)) published by John Benjamins.

David Wible is Distinguished Professor in the Graduate Institute of Learning and Instruction at National Central University in Taiwan. His research interests include Chinese and English comparative syntax, constructions and multiword expressions in second language lexical acquisition, second language reading and writing, and the design of computational tools for second language learning. He is one of the co-founders of the IWiLL online language learning platform.

Johannes Widmann is a junior researcher who is working on his PhD in Applied English Linguistics. He teaches linguistics at the University of Tübingen, Germany, with a focus on teacher education. He has contributed to the Socrates-Minerva SACODEYL project and to the EU LdV EntecNet and CIP projects (see http://www.ael.uni-tuebingen.de/projects/index.html for details). His interests are in computer-aided language learning (CALL), using VLEs such as Moodle to support blended language learning scenarios, and in corpus-based materials production. He has been working as a freelance language teacher for English and French for many years.

Ramon Ziai has a BA in computer linguistics and is an expert in JAVA server-based programming applications. He has a special interest in corpus-based language learning and web-based search tools. With this expertise he has been involved as lead programmer in the EU Minerva project SACODEYL.

List of Abbreviations

ACTFL	American Council on the Teaching of Foreign Languages
AH	Arts and Humanities
AMU	Adam Mickiewicz University
BACS	British and American Studies Foundation Course
BAWE	British Academic Written English Corpus
BLEU	Bilingual Evaluation under Study
BNC	British National Corpus
BYU	Brigham Young University
CALL	Computer-assisted Language Learning
CBMT	Context-Based Machine Translation
CEFR	Common European Framework of Reference
CHAT	Codes for the Human Analysis of Transcripts
CLAWS7	Constituent Likelihood Automatic Word-tagging System
COBUILD	Collins Birmingham University International Language Database
COCA	Corpus of Contemporary American English
COLT	Bergen Corpus of London Teenage Language
CQL	Corpus Query Language
CULT	Corpus Use and Learning to Translate
DDL	data-driven learning
DIALANG3	diagnostic language assessment system
DP	Dynamic Programming
EAP	English for Academic Purposes
EFL	English as a Foreign Language
EGAP	English for General Academic Purposes
ELISA	English Language Interview Corpus as a Second-Language Application
ELT	English language teaching
ELTS	English Language Testing Service
ESAP	English for Specific Academic Purposes
ESP	English for Specific Purposes
ESRC	UK Economic and Social Research Council

GPL   Gnu General Public Licence
GRICLE   Greek International Corpus of Learner English
ICLE   International Corpus of Learner English
IFA   Instytut Filologii Angielskiej
IFA Conc   IFA Concordancer
IMRD   Introduction, Methods, Results, Discussion
IWiLL   Intelligent Web-based Interactive Language Learning
JEFLL   Japanese EFL Learner
JLE   Japanese Learner of English
KWiC   Key Word in Context
L1   first language
L2   second language
LINDSEI   Louvain International Database of Spoken English
               Interlanguage
LL   Log Likelihood
LOCNEC   Louvain Corpus of Native English Conversation
LOCNESS   Louvain Corpus of Native English Essays
LS   Life Sciences
LSP   Language for Specific Purposes / Languages for
               Specialised Purpose
LTA   language teaching and assessment
MAHT   Machine-aided Human Translation
MCA   Multimodal Corpus Authoring System
MeLLANGE   Multilingual eLearning in Language Engineering
MI   mutual information
MICASE   Michigan Corpus of Academic Spoken English
MICUSP   Michigan Corpus of Upper-level Student Papers
MLU   mean length of utterance
MSUs   meaning shift units
MT   machine translation
MWE   multi-word expression
NHK   Nihon Hosou Kyokai
NICT   National Institute of Information and Communications
               Technology
NLP   Natural Language Processing
NNS   non-native speaker
NS   native-speaker
ON   overlapping nouns
Padova MEC   Padova Multimedia English Corpus
PAROLE   Parallèle, Oral, en Langue Etrangère

PELCRA	Polish and English Language Corpora for Research and Applications
PERC Corpus	Professional English Research Consortium Corpus
PICLE	Polish International Corpus of Learner English
POS	part of speech
PS	Physical Sciences
PSA	Present Situation Analysis
RA	research article
SACODEYL	System Aided Compilation and Open Distribution of European Youth Language
SCN	Shogakukan Corpus Network
SMIL	Synchronized Multimedia Integration Language
SPICLE	Spanish International Corpus of Learner English
SST	Standard Speaking Test
SWICLE	Swedish International Corpus of Learner English
TaLC	Teaching and Language Corpora
TEI	Text Encoding Initiative
TeMa Corpus	Textbook Materials Corpus
TOEFL iBT	TOEFL Internet-based Test
TSA	Target Situation Analysis
USAS	UCREL Semantic Analysis System
VN	verb-noun
WBO	WordBanksOnline

Introduction

The word *new* carries multiple meanings. Prototypically, it refers to something that is different from all that existed before in a certain context. At the same time, it subtly asserts that this very feature is intrinsically ephemeral. This book aims to capture this fleeting moment when original latent trends surface and are worth circulating while still fresh. Many novelties were presented during the eighth *Teaching and Language Corpora* (TaLC) conference, held in Lisbon in the very hot summer of 2008. We have strived to include here a subset of notable contributions to three distinct directions which have been evolving steadily in the field:

– corpora *with* language learners: use,
– corpora *for* language learners: tools,
– corpora *by* language learners: learner language.

These macro-areas were originally identified by Stewart et al. (2004), and although they will often overlap, we believe the distinction remains extremely useful in helping us to understand what has been going on in this relatively recent strand of Applied Corpus Linguistics. This introduction explains how each of the three sections captures different aspects of 'new trends' in corpora and language pedagogy.

Corpora with language learners: use

It seems fitting to commence the volume with a section containing contributions which put the spotlight on the learner's role in corpus-based pedagogy. While still far from being part of mainstream language teaching practices, all five authors in this opening section report on favourable reactions to very distinct uses of corpora by different groups of language learners in Japan, England, Austria, Poland and France.

Tono's chapter is innovative not only for its account of popularising corpora through television programmes and computer game applications in

Japan, but also for its reflective style describing his personal journey in what is probably the most extraordinary success story in TaLC. Bernardini (2004) put forward the notion of the 'learner as traveller' in the discovery learning approach associated with data-driven learning (DDL) (see Johns 1991); Tono's chapter can be viewed as a personal narrative of the 'corpus practitioner as traveller', illustrating the manifold directions in which corpus use can take the teacher, researcher and materials designer, and its potential to revolutionize national practices in language learning and language pedagogy.

Charles' chapter reports on students' evaluation of using a corpus of theses written by native speakers for examining key rhetorical functions in EAP. Charles' work is methodologically innovative for its discourse-analytic approach to corpus queries addressing EAP writers' concerns, and for its three-stage set of goals of 'corpus awareness', 'corpus literacy' and 'corpus proficiency', in helping students to achieve corpus competence. The following chapter by Kettemann also proposes a staged approach, carefully moving from a teacher-centred approach using highly processed corpus data to a more student-centred exploratory one. The originality of this chapter lies in its exploitation of corpora drawn from 'new technologies' materials such as blogs, one of the prime artefacts in computer-mediated communication (see King 2009), to teach a content area hitherto uncharted using corpus linguistic techniques, that of Cultural Studies.

The chapter by Kübler reports on using corpora in another specialist content area, that of translator training. While the majority of reports on corpora for translation concern specialised corpora, Kübler's account is of note for highlighting the advantages of general monolingual corpora in this area: 'In formulating the target language text so that it is adapted to its culture, a general monolingual corpus is the student's best friend, as it helps them to find correct collocations, colligations, semantic prosodies and preferences' (p. 76).

The chapter by Kaszubski reporting on IFAConc, an online concordancing environment, could equally have been included in the following section on new tools. However, we decided to include it as the last chapter in this section as it aligns the design of an interactive tool with theories of language learning. This tool's pedagogic and theoretical underpinnings are inspired by Tim Johns' (1991) pioneering work on DDL on the one hand, and Hoey's (2005) lexical priming theory on the other. Also influenced by constructivist learning and Widdowson's (2000) call for authentication and personalisation of corpus data, this interactive tool places the student at the heart of the learning process, encouraging them to use corpora collaboratively as well as to get teacher feedback on their corpus queries.

Corpora for language learners: tools

This section contains five chapters focusing on corpora *for* language learners. In the past corpus tools were only for a small, restricted community of language engineers and linguists, and criticisms were often levelled against those proposed for language learners as they were usually one and the same set as those used by corpus researchers. However, what we see in this section are innovative, learner-centred and classroom-oriented developments of tools specifically designed with language learners and their attendant difficulties in mind.

The first chapter in this section by Liu et al. reports on a novel statistical corpus method to automatically identify and correct learners' miscollocations, by matching these against collocates retrieved from the BNC using the search engine Collocation Explorer. With an eye to providing learners with collocational information as and when needed, Liu et al. say that the next step in their project 'will be to implement our approach as an application in the digital writing environment of IWiLL, an online language learning platform' (p. 118).

Coccetta's chapter examines another recent area of development in TaLC, that of audio-visual corpora, which she enriches with semantic and pragmatic annotation. Transcripts are tagged for functions and notions, which learners can access through a list-driven concordancer, and the program allows access to sound and film clips of the concordance output for a particular notion or function, thus showing learners the synchronisation that exists between paralinguistic features and speech in meaning-making.

The following contribution by Curado Fuentes describes a sophisticated Context-Based Machine Translation (CBMT) system incorporating a variety of resources which can be harnessed to help learners with specialized discourse. Like Kaszubski (see Section I), Curado Fuentes also draws on Hoey's (2005) theory of lexical priming for its delineation of lexico-grammatical information concerning collocations, colligations, semantic associations, textual collocations and textual colligations for retrieval of linguistic information. And like Curado Fuentes, Warren's chapter also places its focus on phraseology with ConcGram, a new application for the teaching and learning of phraseological variation. Warren sees at least three ways this software can contribute to pedagogy: to analyse texts, to raise awareness of Sinclair's (1991) idiom principle by helping learners identify associated words, and to provide insights into the discourse of specialised fields and specific genres.

This section concludes with a chapter by Widmann et al. on SACODEYL, a suite of pedagogically motivated audio-visual corpora of video-recorded interviews with teenagers in several European languages. The focus of the chapter is on the search tools developed to date, which allow access to the corpus through four different search modes (browse, section search, co-occurrence search and word search). This contribution stands out as a rare example of an application of corpora to language learning at the secondary school level.

The tools described in this section are all applied to native-speaker or 'expert' corpora. Liu et al. use the BNC to retrieve collocates, while Warren promotes ConcGram using a specialised corpus of engineering English and a general corpus of English. The CBMT system described by Curado Fuentes comprises not only a large target general language corpus (in Spanish), and a smaller source language corpus of English, but also a bilingual, fully inflected, English-Spanish dictionary. The audio-visual interview corpora utilised by Widmann et al. consist of teenager talk from seven different L1s (English, French, German, Italian, Lithuanian, Romanian and Spanish), and while Coccetta notes that the speakers in her film clips include some non-native and bilingual speakers, it is assumed that these are expert users of the language, and their inclusion would seem to reflect the growing acceptance of English as a Lingua Franca (ELF) corpora for teaching purposes (see Mauranen 2007). In contrast, the chapters in the final section are all concerned with the language of non-native, learner or apprentice corpora of various kinds.

Corpora by language learners: learner language

The last five chapters in the book explore corpora of written and spoken texts produced *by* language learners. These enable us to analyse learner language more systematically than ever before and to identify non-obvious peculiarities about it that are not always easy to pin down. Although it may not always have a direct impact on the way we teach, understanding what makes learner language different can help us become more attuned to it.

Osborne's chapter shows how a corpus of L2 learner speech can contribute to streamlining the assessment of foreign language speaking skills within the Common European Framework of Reference (CEF). It draws on a corpus of spoken productions by learners of English with various L1s performing comparable tasks, collected as part of a European project on the collaborative assessment of oral language proficiency. It examines the degree of convergence between different measures of fluency and the extent to which these are reflected in raters' perceptions of proficiency, and suggests that if fluency is measured as a bundle of features, these can be used to benchmark representative samples illustrating different CEF levels. Osborne's chapter reflects the newly emerging trend of corpora being used to inform language testing and assessment (LTA) at the national and international level (see Barker 2010 for a review of these LTA projects).

The following chapter by De Cock investigates the use of positive and negative evaluative adjectives in native and learner speech, drawing on the Louvain Corpus of Native English Conversation (LOCNEC) and the Louvain International Database of Spoken English Interlanguage (LINDSEI). A novel aspect of De Cock's investigation is that in LOCNEC she uncovers their non-obvious role in evaluative relative clauses introduced by *which*, (*the way that they speak English which is great for me cos I speak no Dutch at all*), noting that 'Evaluative sentential relative clauses would in fact be a particularly good candidate for inclusion in ELT reference materials such as a contextualised discourse-oriented grammar of speech' (p. 207).

Nesi's chapter provides a detailed description of the rationale, design, composition and markup of the British Academic Written English (BAWE) Corpus. While the vast majority of the assignments in this corpus are written by native speakers, in another sense BAWE can be considered a learner corpus (or perhaps more strictly speaking, a corpus of apprentice writing), as these are novice writers who are developing skills to master the specialist genres of their disciplines. BAWE is the only corpus of its kind in the public domain, thus offering new opportunities to investigate student writing which has been judged to conform to departmental requirements, but which differs markedly from expert and near-expert professional academic writing in terms of its communicative intent.

The last two chapters in this section bring a contrastive rhetoric dimension to corpus analysis. Hatzitheodorou and Mattheoudakis examine attitude in corpora of essays written by Greek and American university students. Their findings suggest that the two groups employ different rhetorical conventions to indicate stance, and they propose that the ways in which the Greek students structure their arguments may be influenced by L1 and L2 instruction in argumentation, transfer from L1, and development as writers in the L2. The essays form the Greek International Corpus of Learner English (GRICLE), a subset of the ICLE corpus (see Granger et al. 2002). While stance markers have been investigated in other components of ICLE (i.e. French, Spanish and Swedish subsets), Hatzitheodorou and Mattheoudakis are breaking new ground in investigating this phenomenon in the GRICLE component.

The final chapter of the volume is of note for its comparison of two kinds of expert writing. Bennett and McKenny compare a corpus of English academic prose written by established Portuguese academics with a control corpus of articles published by native-speaker academics in the same or comparable humanities journals. Their findings reveal that in the English texts produced by Portuguese scholars there was significant overuse and a corresponding underuse of certain pragmalinguistic and sociopragmatic features, indicating transfer from their L1. Bennett and McKenny conclude their article by tantalisingly suggesting that corpus evidence may provide a means to counter rigid cultural attitudes: ' . . . corpus studies may have a part to play in raising awareness of hitherto-unperceived cultural differences, thereby encouraging greater acceptance of alternative ways of construing knowledge' (pp. 323–324). This critical pragmatic approach to writing in the academy has recently been gaining increasing currency; see, for example, Mur Dueñas (2009). Lou Burnard's thought-provoking preface to this volume urges the corpus linguistics community 'to pause and take stock' of issues such as these (p. xx).

This series of snapshots of methodological and technological innovations in the use of corpora for language learning and teaching is addressed to researchers in Applied Corpus Linguistics, lecturers with an interest in ongoing research related to language learning and teaching and postgraduate students working towards the development of original studies in the area. We hope they will find solid background and fresh stimuli to further contribute to this fast-developing field, thus paradoxically – albeit gratifyingly – converting these *New Trends in Corpora and Language Learning* into something which will eventually cease to be so new, and thereby engender the next generation of corpus studies applied to teaching and learning.

On a final note, we wish to thank our editors at Continuum, Colleen Coulter and Gurdeep Mattu, for their guidance and support throughout the project, the series editors, Wolfgang Teubert and Michaela Mahlberg, for recommending our book for their series, the external reviewers for their constructive comments on our initial proposal and draft volume and the contributors for their noteworthy submissions. Thanks also go to the organising committee of the eighth TaLC conference who helped make the conference such a success and memorable occasion.

Ana Frankenberg-Garcia
Lynne Flowerdew
Guy Aston

References

Barker, F. (2010), 'How can corpora be used in language testing?', in A. O'Keeffe and M. McCarthy (eds), *The Routledge Handbook of Corpus Linguistics*. London: Routledge, pp. 633–646.

Bernardini, S. (2004), 'Corpora in the classroom: an overview and some reflections on future developments', in J. Sinclair (ed.), *How to Use Corpora in Language Teaching*. Amsterdam and Philadelphia: John Benjamins, pp. 15–36.

Granger, S., Dagneaux, E. and Meunier, F. (2002), *The International Corpus of Learner English/Handbook and CD-Rom*. Louvain-la-Neuve: Presses Universitaires de Louvain.

Hoey, M. (2005), *Lexical Priming: A New Theory of Words and Language*. London: Routledge.

Johns, T. (1991), 'Should you be persuaded: two examples of data-driven learning'. *English Language Research Journal*, 4. Department of English, University of Birmingham, pp. 1–16.

King, B. (2009), 'Building and analysing corpora of computer-mediated communication', in P. Baker (ed.), *Contemporary Corpus Linguistics*. London: Continuum, pp. 301–320.

Mauranen, A. (2007), 'Investigating English as a lingua franca with a spoken corpus', in M.C. Campoy and M.J. Luzón (eds), *Spoken Corpora in Applied Linguistics*. Berlin: Peter Lang, pp. 33–56.

Mur Dueñas, P. (2009), 'Logical markers in L1 (Spanish and English) and L2 (English) Business research articles'. *English Text Construction*, 2, (2): 246–264.

Sinclair, J. McH. (1991), *Corpus, Concordance, Collocation*. Oxford: Oxford University Press.

Stewart, D., Bernardini, S. and Aston, G. (2004), 'Introduction: ten years of TaLC', in G. Aston, S. Bernardini and D. Stewart (eds), *Corpora and Language Learners*. Amsterdam and Philadelphia: John Benjamins, pp. 1–18.

Widdowson, H.G. (2000), 'On the limitations of linguistics applied'. *Applied Linguistics*, 21, (1), 3–25.

Part I

Corpora with language learners: use

Chapter 1

TaLC in action: recent innovations in corpus-based English language teaching in Japan

Yukio Tono

This chapter discusses the effective use of corpora in English language teaching by introducing various areas of corpus-based applications in Japan, including the world's first TV English conversation programme based on corpora. The areas of application are divided into two, following Tudor's (1997) needs analysis framework: the creation of teaching resources and materials based on the analysis of native speaker corpora, viewed as the target for learners and the investigation of L2 learner and textbook corpora, viewed as their present situation. Various case studies show that a corpus-based approach has been very effective in reforming English language teaching in Japan, and can be applied in other countries.

1.1. Introduction

Corpus-based research has become increasingly popular in applied linguistics. Applications in English language teaching have three major areas: (a) indirect use of corpora, (b) direct use of corpora and (c) compilation of corpora for educational purposes (Leech 1997). Indirect use involves the development of corpus-based materials such as educational word lists, dictionaries, grammar books, conversation textbooks, etc. Direct use usually involves using corpora in the classroom, where the typical approach is Data Driven Learning (Johns and King 1991). The creation of educational corpora concerns specialised areas such as textbook corpora, classroom observation corpora, learner corpora and corpora of texts with controlled vocabulary. In this paper, I will share my experience of corpus-based approaches to various areas of English language teaching in Japan, in order to illustrate the considerable potential of 'teaching and language corpora'.

To better situate the use of corpora in English language teaching, I shall adopt the framework of needs analysis proposed by Tudor (1997). Tudor distinguishes between two different kinds of needs analysis: Target Situation Analysis (TSA) and Present Situation Analysis (PSA). TSA deals with the analysis of learners' targets. Without a clear understanding of learners' goals, it is difficult to design a syllabus to achieve them. In the case of language teaching, TSA should be based on the analysis of the core components of the target language, and for this purpose native-speaker (NS) corpora can provide useful information about high-frequency lexis and grammar. PSA, on the other hand, analyses learners' present situation, thus showing the gap between this and the target. In ELT, this means assessing the language proficiency of prospective learners, and in a corpus-based approach, we can employ learner corpora to investigate interlanguage features of their speech and writing.

Within this needs-analysis framework, I have carried out several kinds of research, as illustrated in Figure 1.1. First, I have created a user-friendly interface for accessing mega-corpora which English teachers can use for teaching purposes. Second, I have produced corpus-based teaching materials in English, including TV conversation programmes, conversation books,

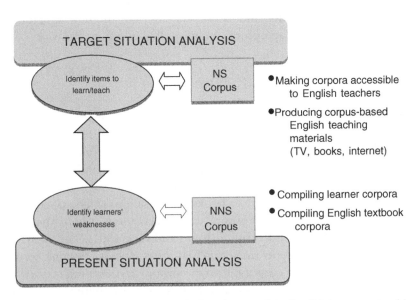

FIGURE 1.1 Needs analysis and corpus-based research in English language teaching

Internet e-learning contents and multimedia applications. Both these areas of research are based on the analysis of native speaker corpora, which is related to TSA, as explained above. Third, I have compiled two educational corpora: a learner corpus and an English textbook corpus. These corpora have been used to analyse the present situation of learners and how their output is affected by textbook input (PSA), and hence to diagnose the gap between the present and the target situations.

In this paper, I outline some of my research activities in these areas. First, the project for creating web-based corpus query services for English teachers will be illustrated. Secondly, I shall describe the development of the first corpus-based TV English conversation programme in Japan, and discuss its impact on English teaching there. Thirdly, I will mention some related educational materials based on corpora. The last part of my paper will be devoted to corpus-based analyses of learner language and textbooks. I will show how learner corpora shed light on the transitional characteristics of interlanguage development, and how textbook corpora reveal deficiencies in English textbooks published in Japan in comparison to those in other major Asian countries. In Japan, a corpus-based approach to ELT has proved very successful, and I will argue that the same approach can be taken in other countries.

1.2. Creating a user-friendly web-based corpus query system

Before 2000, little was known about corpus linguistics among ELT communities in Japan. The only exception was the COBUILD project and its products. I discussed the possibility of a corpus query system with Shogakukan Inc., one of the largest publishers in Japan, whose dictionary division went on to develop a set of Corpus Query Language (CQL) and web-based query tools called SAKURA (see Figure 1.2).

These tools were originally designed for in-house use by lexicographers, but the team was encouraged to build them in such a way that novice corpus users would be able to use them intuitively. At the end two versions of SAKURA were released, an advanced version and a simplified one. The latter was developed into a web-based interface for the Shogakukan Corpus Network (SCN), the first commercial web corpus query service in Japan (http://www.corpora.jp). This provided a unified interface to different corpora such as the British National Corpus (BNC), WordBanksOnline (WBO), the PERC Corpus and the JEFLL Corpus. While web query tools

FIGURE 1.2　Shogakukan Corpus Query System, SAKURA BNC interface

for large corpora are often slow and fail to deal well with simultaneous access, SAKURA can handle a dozen mega-corpora simultaneously, and can be accessed by more than fifty people at the same time from the classroom.

1.3.　Developing a corpus-based TV English programme in Japan

The second major area of corpus applications to ELT was the project to develop the world's first corpus-based English conversation TV programme. The public broadcasting center NHK (Nihon Hosou Kyokai, the Japan Broadcasting Center) is well known for excellent educational broadcasts, which include more than thirty programmes for the major foreign languages, including English, Chinese, German, French, Italian, Korean, Spanish, Russian and Arabic. In 2002, NHK reformed its foreign language broadcasting, and decided to produce a programme which would be screened every day. I suggested that this should consist of dozens of short episodes, each featuring one important English word and its use.

1.3.1. The '100-Go' programme

The basic features of the '100-go' programme were to be as follows:

(a) 10-minute English conversation TV programmes (4 units per week for 25 weeks, approximately 6 months);
(b) 100 units focusing on 100 key words;[1]
(c) Key words to be selected on the basis of frequency data from the BNC spoken component;
(d) Useful corpus data to be presented for each key word;
(e) Fun, exciting and educational;
(f) For all levels, including false beginners.

1.3.2. The making of '100-Go'

To design the syllabus, I extracted the frequency list of lemmas with part-of-speech information from BNC-spoken. This showed that core vocabulary does most of the work: out of 57,457 types in BNC-spoken (c. 10 million words), the most frequent 100 words cover 67% of the corpus tokens. Figure 1.3 shows the breakdown of the selected words, which are mainly

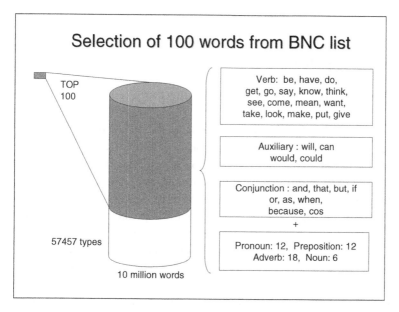

FIGURE 1.3 Selection of 100 words from the BNC-spoken list

major lexical verbs and function words (pronouns, prepositions, adverbs, conjunctions, auxiliaries).

The fact that only 100 words cover almost 70% of the entire spoken data shows that these basic words are used in a variety of ways. Most of the verbs have more than one meaning and take complex complementation patterns. The prepositions, conjunctions and auxiliaries are all polysemous. The adverbial particles are difficult to use when combined with verbs to form phrasal verbs. Thus, even though these words may look familiar, learners often lack sufficient knowledge of their usage.

The programme thus focused on these very core lexical items, featuring mainly verbs, auxiliary verbs, conjunctions and prepositions. For each key word, two kinds of corpus data were prepared: (a) collocation lists for given colligation patterns (e.g. 'verb + noun' or 'verb + prep/part'), and (b) n-grams using the key word. The verb 'give', for example, appeared three times as a key word, in three different constructions: 1. *give* + *sb* (=somebody) + regular noun, 2. *give* + preposition/particle, 3. *give* + deverbal noun. For each construction, lists of collocations were extracted from BNC-spoken to show the most frequent patterns of use. Thus, in the case of '*give* + deverbal noun', learners were taught the following collocation sets: (a) *give (sb) a ring*, (b) *give (sb) information*, (c) *give (sb) a kiss*, (d) *give (sb) some advice* and (e) *give (sb) an answer*. N-gram information was used when it was more suitable as a framework than colligation patterns.

Another original feature was the selection of topic vocabulary sets for each key word. For instance, the collocation pattern 'give (sb) a ring' can be used with temporal expressions as follows:

Give me a ring tomorrow / this evening / at seven o'clock

For each key word a set of ten additional words or phrases was prepared to go with the patterns in the collocation list. In this way, the key word multiplies, and learners will get to know how it is used in context. Figure 1.4 illustrates this design feature diagrammatically.

After selecting all 100 key words with their collocation rankings and accompanying topic vocabulary sets, native speaker writers were asked to write skits to show the use of those collocation patterns in real contexts.

Each unit in the monthly textbook accompanying the series has a six-page format. The first two pages show the key word title and model dialogues in English, with Japanese translations. Page 3 provides the collocation ranking and usage notes for the key word, while page 4 features key sentences in the skits. Finally, pages 5 and 6 provide exercises, including

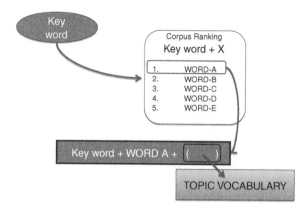

FIGURE 1.4 The concept of '100-Go': one key word will multiply

FIGURE 1.5 'Mr Corpus' introducing corpus ranking

mechanical drills using collocation sets, as well as situation-based, gap-filling oral compositions.

Given the success of the first series (Tono 2003), the TV programme ran for three years (2003–2005) with different varieties of English (US, Australian and UK). Each year there were a good-looking bilingual guy and a beautiful girl as MCs, and a special character called 'Mr Corpus', who introduced the corpus ranking (see Figure 1.5). I, as Dr Corpus, appeared for one minute to summarise the main points surrounding the key words. Tono (2004a) was essentially based on the same key word lists, but with improved collocation rankings and fashionable computer graphics (a 'Ninja' version of Mr Corpus). In Tono (2005a), the key word list was expanded to 200 to incorporate basic nouns and adjectives.

1.3.3. Impact of '100-Go'

More than one million people watched the TV programme each year, and 'Mr Corpus' became popular among children. The first three monthly textbooks sold out, for the first time in the history of NHK's TV English programmes. The production team won the NHK President Award for the best programme and the best textbook of 2003. 'Corpus' became a buzz word, and many teachers became aware of the usefulness of corpus data as teaching and learning resources. Corpus-based English teaching materials gained increasing attention, and began to influence syllabus and materials development. The first TV series reran in 2008, and a brand new series was launched in 2009 (Tono 2009a).

1.4. Developing corpus-based English teaching materials in Japan

1.4.1. Conversation books

A series of books were published in relation to the NHK TV series. Tono (2004b) featured the programme's 100 key words and their collocation data with model sentences and exercises. Tono (2005b, 2006a) covered the second and third series respectively. DVD-book series were published for each edition of the programme (Tono 2004c, 2005c, 2006b). These were exported to other Asian countries and translated into Korean (Tono 2004d) and Chinese (Tono 2005d). Many became bestsellers, attracting attention from English learners as well as teachers.

I also published other types of conversation books. Tono (2005e) focused on 150 key words, where the information from corpora was centred on the phraseology surrounding each key word. Thus in the case of 'give', the phraseology was:

(a) I'm going to/I'll give you . . .
(b) give it to . . .
(c) give up . . .
(d) can you give me . . . ?
(e) let me give you . . .

As can be seen, this list is based on frequent phrase patterns rather than particular colligation patterns.

Tono (2005f, 2007a) focused on the use of nouns as productive vocabulary. Learners often only know a one-to-one relationship between English words and their translation equivalents, and find it difficult to use these words in actual contexts. For example, they know the word *hand* and its translation equivalent (*te* in Japanese), but they often have difficulties in expressing *te no hira* (*the palm of one's hand*), or *te wo ageru* (*put one's hand up*) in English. The books focused on fifty common nouns used in everyday conversation (Tono 2005f) and in business contexts (Tono 2007a). In each unit English collocation lists are presented in 5 x 5 tables (with the key word in the centre and 24 collocations), along with a corresponding table of Japanese translations (see Figure 1.6). Learners can use the Japanese table to test whether they can come up with the corresponding English phrases, and their lexical knowledge becomes more productive as they learn how to express different concepts using the key noun.

1.4.2. Reference materials

Another major area of corpus application in English teaching remains that of developing reference materials, such as dictionaries and vocabulary lists. Tono (2004e) is a semi-bilingual version of the *Cambridge Learner's Dictionary* (2nd edition). It provides translation equivalents for each sense of each word, so that learners can use it as a bridge between bilingual and monolingual dictionaries. It also provides special notes on word usage and common learner errors based on the Cambridge International Corpus and the Cambridge Learner Corpus.

Tono (2005g) is probably the world's first synonym dictionary to be based on corpora. It has 200 thematic entries in Japanese, each of which shows two to four English synonymous translation equivalents. For example, the Japanese thematic entry *sukuu* lists three translation equivalents, *save, rescue* and *relieve*. Each equivalent is illustrated with its five most salient collocation patterns in the BNC, so that these near synonyms can be compared.

save + N	*rescue* + N	*relieve* + N
(1) life	(1) hostage	(1) pressure
(2) planet	(2) economy	(2) pain
(3) queen	(3) country	(3) boredom
(4) child	(4) prisoner	(4) burden
(5) soul	(5) child	(5) poverty

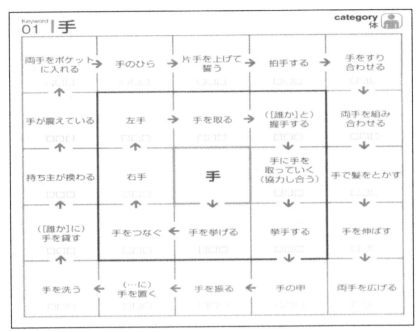

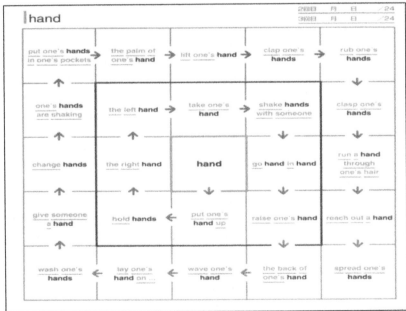

FIGURE 1.6   Japanese vs. English noun collocation table (Tono 2005f)

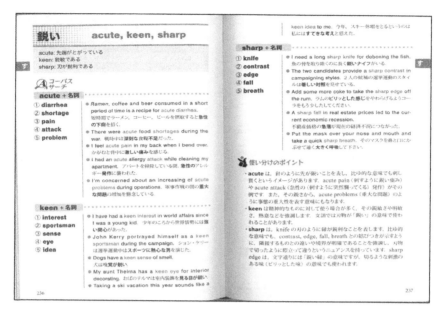

FIGURE 1.7 Sample page for the entry '*surudoi*' – *acute, keen, sharp* (Tono 2005g)

This approach is a direct application of Firth's (1957) notion of 'knowing a word by the company it keeps'. 'Save' is the most general word, covering physical life, concrete persons or objects, as well as a spiritual one ('soul'). 'Rescue' implies saving someone or something in immediate danger, while 'relieve' involves reducing pain or making a problem less difficult. Figure 1.7 shows a sample page of the entry for *surudoi* (*acute, keen, sharp*).

Tono (2008) is a bilingual learner's dictionary targeted at elementary to lower-intermediate level learners of English at secondary school. It has special 'Focus Pages', which are basically corpus-based summary pages of core vocabulary. Figure 1.8 shows the focus page for the word *have*.

Each focus page has various sections:

(a) *Core image*: an image showing the core meaning of the word
(b) *Semantic map*: a list of senses in a dictionary entry
(c) *Structure ranking*: a frequency list of major verb patterns
(d) *Corpus phrases*: major colligation patterns with collocation lists
(e) *Spoken phrases*: phrases taken from spoken corpus data
(f) *Textbook phrases*: phrases taken from a textbook corpus

There are approximately a hundred of these focus pages, each providing corpus-based information on the usage of the word and the most useful

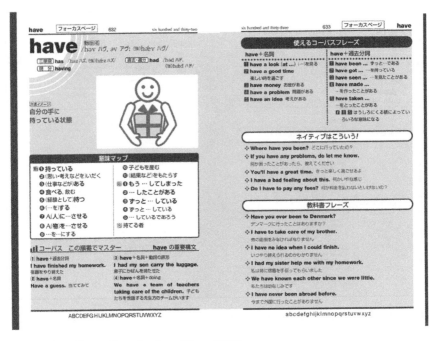

FIGURE 1.8   Focus Page for *have* (Tono 2008)

structures and phrases in which it occurs. Again, this builds on the idea that it
is essential to acquire a working knowledge of the core vocabulary that covers
70% of speech. The dictionary proposes a clear boundary between essential
vocabulary and the rest: 100 core words are featured in the focus pages, an
additional 2,000 words are treated with an emphasis on their use as active
vocabulary, and the next 3,000 words are highlighted typographically but
treated less extensively. Words below the 5,000 word level are given minimal
space, with only translation equivalents and a few illustrative examples. In this
way, Japanese learners of English at the secondary school level should be able
to see which words they should learn to use, which words they should know
the meaning of and which words they can just look up if necessary. Use of the
dictionary is thus closely linked to vocabulary learning strategies.

1.4.3. Computer game applications

Fun and excitement can be incorporated into language learning through
computer game applications. Tono (2009b) is a newly developed iPhone
English vocabulary learning programme (see Figure 1.9), which has become

FIGURE 1.9   English Vocabulary iPhone application

one of the most popular iPhone applications for language learning. It has ten different vocabulary levels, each of which has special training menus with amusing exercises involving reading, listening and writing. People can win belts for certain grades by obtaining high scores in the tournament.

The NHK programme '100-go' was so popular that the plan to develop a Wii application is now underway (Tono, forthcoming), and this may well be the world's first corpus-based language learning game application.

To sum up, corpus-based English teaching materials have been hugely successful in Japan, and this corpus-based approach to developing teaching materials should work equally well in other countries. There are several good reasons. First, people are eager to find the most economical way of learning a foreign language. I do not mean that there is any magical, instant way, but simply that some are more cost-effective. Corpus rankings based on frequencies provide users with very clear guidelines for learning lexical combinations. By focusing on frequent collocation or phrase patterns, learners will be able to acquire the core component of L2 knowledge faster and more effectively than they can with materials without information from corpora. Second, people like to get an objective measure of the importance of items to learn, for which corpora provide evidence. Viewers of my TV programmes responded very positively to the corpus rankings as an efficient way of making their goals concrete and objective. Knowing the importance of the items to learn leads to higher motivation. Finally, corpus data give learning materials greater credibility. In the past, the design of syllabuses and teaching materials depended largely on the materials developers' experience and intuitions. The advent of computer technology and corpus linguistics has made it possible to access large amounts of naturally occurring language data, showing how the language is actually used by native speakers. People are now aware that the use of corpus data makes learning materials more reliable.

In the following section, I move on to describe my second major area of research, based on L2 learner corpora. This will illustrate the present situation of L2 learners in Japan, the second kind of input required for an effective needs analysis (see Figure 1.1 above).

1.5. L2 learner corpus research

1.5.1. Compilation of the NICT JLE Corpus and the JEFLL Corpus

Compiling a learner corpus is a major project. I have been involved in two such projects for Japanese-speaking learners of English. The first, the NICT JLE Corpus, is a collection of transcripts of more than 1,200 subjects' oral proficiency test interviews. The test is the Standard Speaking Test (SST) developed by ALC Press, which is a customised version of the ACTFL Oral Proficiency Interview. Each 15-minute interview has five parts: warm-up, picture description, storytelling, role play and wind-down. Each interview script has an individual proficiency score on nine levels: beginner (level 1) to near-native (level 9). The corpus is available as a book with a CD-ROM (Izumi et al. 2004) and also in electronic format under license.

The other L2 learner corpus, the JEFLL Corpus (Tono 2007b), is a collection of more than 10,000 Japanese secondary school students' English compositions. It contains timed, in-class, free compositions in English on six different topics (argumentative or narrative). Each task was given as part of regular classroom activities, not as homework. Subjects were not allowed to use dictionaries, but if there were any words they could not come up with in English, they were allowed to write them in Japanese. The average length of each essay is rather short (about sixty to seventy words), but with more than 1,000 compositions in each school year category, we could approximate the patterns of use and possibly paths of learning. The JEFLL Corpus is available via the Shogakukan Corpus Network (http://scn02.corpora.jp/~jefll04dev/), where it can be accessed using a web-based query tool in English.

1.5.2. Some findings

The main objectives of these projects are (a) the description of inter-language development in terms of overuse vs. underuse as well as correct use vs. misuse of certain linguistic features, (b) the identification of criterial features which distinguish one proficiency level from another and (c) the development of a list of language features which are learnt particularly slowly, and perhaps call for revision or modification of teaching syllabi or methodologies. Theoretically, we also hope to distinguish those patterns of overuse/underuse/misuse which are specific to the learners' L1, and those which appear common to learners from whatever background. In this way, we could possibly redesign syllabuses, adjusting them to the L2 learning path, and ask people working on action research in the classroom to test the effects of the modifications. This will all lead us to a better understanding of the gap between the target situation and the present situation illustrated in Figure 1.1 above, and how best to fill that gap.

1.5.3. Identification of criterial features

Tono (2000a) investigated the relationship between the subjects' school year and frequencies of part-of-speech (POS) tag sequences in the JEFLL Corpus (sequences of three tags = trigrams). By looking at these sequences, we can observe frequent patterns of use, which helps us understand the process of acquiring syntactic patterns in the target language. This was done by POS tagging the learner data and extracting tag sequences, and then performing a data reduction statistical procedure called Correspondence Analysis over the frequencies of tag sequences across different school-year groups. The results are shown in Figure 1.10.

The analysis shows that the beginning level has a tendency to be more closely associated with verb-related patterns, while noun- and preposition-related trigrams are more closely associated with lower-intermediate and advanced learners respectively. This clearly shows that more advanced students have a tendency to use more complex noun phrases and prepositional phrases. We also observed constant underuse of auxiliaries and articles. In the early stages of acquisition, learners tend to use short sentence units, consisting mainly of verbs and arguments (e.g. subjects or objects, etc.) with minimum modifiers. At more advanced levels, on the other hand, learners start to expand arguments by adding adjectival or adverbial modifiers. This is one of the first studies in learner corpus research to investigate the syntactic features characterising different stages of acquisition.

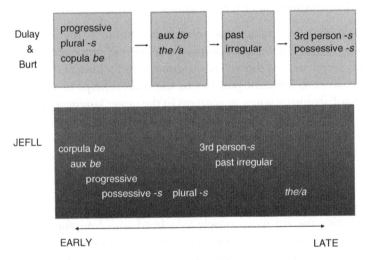

Correspondence Analysis (Year x POS trigrams)

JEFLL

Prep-related
UNI

V-related   SH2
JH2
JH3

Dimension 1

N-related

JH1

UNI   Prep-related

JH1   N-related

Dimension 2

JH2   SH2

JH3   V-related

• Beginning:
→ Verb-centred

• Lower-intermediate:
→ Expansion of NP

• Advanced:
→ Expansion of PP

• Constant underuse of
AUX & ART

▫   Trigram types

◻   School Year

FIGURE 1.10   Analysis of POS tag sequences across school years (Tono 2000a)

Dulay & Burt

| progressive plural -s copula be | → | aux be the /a | → | past irregular | → | 3rd person -s possessive -s |

JEFLL

corpula be
aux be
progressive
possessive -s   plural -s

3rd person-s
past irregular

the/a

EARLY   LATE

FIGURE 1.11   Dulay and Burt's (1972, 1974) morpheme-order study replicated using learner corpora (Tono 2000b)

1.5.4. Error frequencies across proficiency

A second area of studies has been the analysis of error frequencies across proficiency levels. Tono (2000b) was one of the first learner-corpus-based studies of acquisition order for grammatical items (see Figure 1.11).

This replicated the English grammatical morpheme studies by Dulay and Burt (1972, 1974), and showed that while there were many similarities in the order of acquisition, Japanese learners also showed distinctive tendencies. In the so-called universal order of acquisition, the article system is supposed to be acquired in the middle of the acquisition order, while the possessive *–s* is acquired very late. But the article system was the last to be acquired by the Japanese learners, while the possessive marker was acquired relatively early. The article system is difficult for the Japanese, because there is no article system in our language. On the other hand, the possessive *–s* seems relatively easy because the Japanese genitive marker *-no* behaves in a very similar way. These findings are consistent with previous empirical studies on Japanese EFL learners (cf. Shirahata 1988).

1.5.5. Automatic error identification

In order to analyse learner errors, the entire JEFLL Corpus was examined by a native speaker and corrected for errors. Tono and Mochizuki (2009) used Dynamic Programming (DP), a sequence alignment method of finding corresponding patterns in text, in order to identify the similarities and differences between the original essays and the corrected ones. Automatic extraction of omission, addition and misformation errors (see James 1998) was performed and the output further processed by Correspondence Analysis. Figures 1.12 and 1.13 show the results for omission/addition errors in relation to school year.[2]

Omission errors are the type that learners make when they omit words or morphemes in a position where they are obligatory. As Figure 1.12 shows, lower-level learners (J1, J2) tend to omit verbs, conjunctions and personal pronouns, whereas learners at higher levels tend to omit determiners, prepositions and adverbs. There is a strong tendency for elementary level learners (J-level) to omit core sentence elements, like verbs or pronouns used as subjects or objects. Conjunctions work as phrase/clause connectors, and elementary level learners have difficulties handling these as well. Intermediate learners (H-level), on the other hand, have overcome these fundamental omission errors, but make new types of errors involving more complex noun/verb phrase structures. Thus they tend to omit prepositions when modifying noun phrases, and adverbs when modifying verbs and adjectives.

Figure 1.13 shows patterns of addition errors. Noun addition errors are common at the very beginning stage of learning (see Circle C, closely

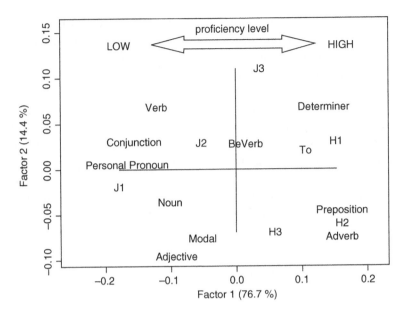

FIGURE 1.12 Correspondence Analysis – omission errors by part of speech vs. school year

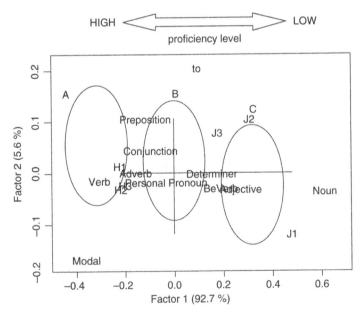

FIGURE 1.13 Correspondence Analysis – addition errors by part of speech vs. school year

associated with J1 level), but soon the number decreases dramatically. This is partly due to the fact that sentences by novice learners are often a series of nouns without verbs and function words. Once this stage is over, they acquire the basic SV+X pattern of English. Another significant tendency is shown in Circle A. Intermediate learners tend to make addition errors for prepositions, conjunctions, verbs and adverbs. This may seem to contradict the findings for omission errors, but actually both types are frequent. Intermediate-level learners risk using more complex sentence structures, making extensive use of modifiers and sentence connectors, leading to more addition as well as omission errors.

Learner corpus analysis has not yet been integrated into the mainstream of syllabus construction and materials design, despite some fragmentary references in usage notes in learner dictionaries (e.g. *Cambridge Advanced Learner's Dictionary, Longman Dictionary of Contemporary English*). Identifying criterial features of L2 developmental stages will surely help towards a more learner-centred, acquisition-conscious materials design.

1.6. English textbook corpora across Asian countries

My last major area of research has involved compiling textbook corpora in order to assess the quality and quantity of L2 input for Japanese learners of English. This too is a part of what Tudor (1997) calls Present Situation Analysis. I have compiled corpora of English textbooks in Japan, Korea, Taiwan and China in order to make comparisons across different Asian countries where English is taught as a foreign language.

Figure 1.14 shows the overall text size of the junior high school English textbooks in the four countries. Compared to Korea and Taiwan, English textbooks published in Japan are 3 to 4.5 times smaller in terms of total amount of text. Textbooks in China are four to six times larger. This means that the amount of exposure to English provided by the textbooks used in Japan is relatively limited.

Table 1.1 shows the coverage of vocabulary in senior high school English textbooks in the four countries for the top 10,000 words in the entire BNC.

The first column shows the vocabulary level (1,000 to 10,000 based on the BNC frequencies). The second column indicates the number of these types found in the textbooks across the four countries. Out of the top 1,000 words in the BNC, for instance, 972 types were found across the textbooks in the four countries, 89.81% of those 972 words were found in Korean textbooks, and so on. The coverage of the 5,000–10,000 level words is

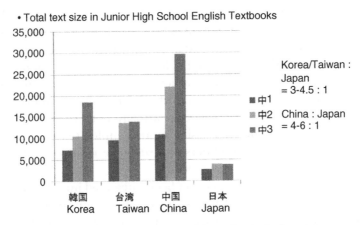

FIGURE 1.14   Text size in Junior High English textbooks in four Asian countries

Table 1.1   Textbook coverage of the BNC top 10,000 words

BNC frequency ranks	Words found	Korea	Japan	China	Taiwan
1–1000	972	89.81%	77.98%	84.16%	96.71%
1001–2000	863	63.73%	45.54%	52.72%	87.02%
2001–3000	656	43.14%	24.70%	32.01%	76.98%
3001–4000	454	37.67%	16.96%	23.57%	68.94%
4001–5000	342	35.96%	19.30%	14.91%	69.30%
5001–6000	250	30.40%	14.40%	18.40%	66.80%
6001–7000	150	33.33%	8.00%	16.00%	63.33%
7001–8000	129	28.68%	10.08%	9.30%	69.77%
8001–9000	93	30.11%	10.75%	10.75%	70.97%
9001–10000	70	27.14%	12.86%	15.71%	62.86%

around 30% in Korean textbooks, and 15% in Chinese textbooks respectively. Textbooks in Taiwan, on the other hand, tend to use very high-
level vocabulary in the texts, indicated in the higher coverage rates of the

vocabulary levels 5,000–10,000. This suggests that English textbooks in Taiwan use native-like authentic texts as they are, while Korea and China provide more vocabulary control. China especially seems to have a sensible policy of providing a large amount of easy-to-read text in order to promote better reading skills.

Compared to these three countries, high school English textbooks in Japan have serious problems. First, coverage of the 1,000 word level vocabulary is less than 80%, which is low compared with the other three countries. This is probably due to the fact that the size of the textbooks is so much smaller. The same can be said about the coverage of the 2,000 word level. With little exposure to these basic lexical items, Japanese learners at high school are forced to read more difficult English texts without having had the chance to read simpler ones. This is the exact opposite of the way Chinese textbooks expose learners to the language.

In May 2008 I made a report on my comparative study of textbooks to the Education Reform Round Table set up under the auspices of ex-Prime Minister Yasuo Fukuda. The committee subsequently recommended a drastic reform of English education in Japan. This was a case where corpus data caused a change in national language policy.

1.7. Conclusions

In this paper, I have shared some of my research activities and practice in Japan. Corpus-based approaches to language teaching have made a significant difference in redesigning language policy, language syllabuses and modes and methods of learning. Japan is one of the most technology-aware nations in the world, which could be one of the reasons why people are attracted by the idea of using computational analysis to improve language education. This same approach, however, may be applicable to other countries, and some of the methodologies and materials developed can be shared among researchers and practitioners. I hope that my research and experience – based on data of attested language use – may also contribute to a better practice and pedagogy in foreign language teaching and learning elsewhere.

Notes

[1] This notion of 'key word' is different from what Scott (2004) calls a key word. Here it simply means a core lexical item or word feature in a unit.

² The accuracy rate for misformation errors was relatively low in this experiment, and clearly in need of further refinement. Consequently data for this class of errors is not given here.

References

Dulay, H.C. and Burt, K.M. (1972), 'Goofing: an indicator of children's second language learning strategies', *Language Learning*, 22, (2), 235–252.

Dulay, H.C. and Burt, K.M. (1974), 'Natural sequences in child second language acquisition', *Language Learning*, 24, (1), 37–53.

Firth, J.R. (1957), 'A synopsis of linguistic theory 1930–1955', in *Studies in Linguistic Analysis* (Special Volume of the Philological Society). Oxford: Blackwell, pp. 1–32.

Izumi, E., Uchiyama, K. and Isahara, H. (eds.) (2004), *Nihonjin 1200-nin no Eigo Speaking Corpus*. (An Oral Corpus of 1200 Japanese Learners of English). Tokyo: ALC Press.

James, C. (1998), *Errors in Language Learning and Use: Exploring Error Analysis*. London: Longman.

Johns, T. and King, P. (eds.) (1991), *Classroom Concordancing. English Language Research Journal*, 4. Birmingham: University of Birmingham.

Leech, G. (1997), 'Teaching and language corpora: a convergence', in A. Wichmann, S. Fliegelstone, T. McEnery and G. Knowles (eds.), *Teaching and Language Corpora*. London: Longman, pp. 1–22.

Scott, M. (2004), *WordSmith Tools 4*. Oxford: Oxford University Press.

Shirahata, T. (1988), 'The learning order of English grammatical morphemes by Japanese high school students', *The JACET Bulletin*, 19, 83–102.

Tono, Y. (2000a), 'A corpus-based analysis of interlanguage development: analysing part-of-speech tag sequences of EFL learner corpora', in B. Lewandowska-Tomaszczyk and J. Melia (eds.), *PALC '99: Practical Applications in Language Corpora*. Frankfurt am Main: Peter Lang, pp. 323–340.

Tono, Y. (2000b), 'A computer learner corpus-based analysis of the acquisition order of English grammatical morphemes', in L. Burnard and T. McEnery (eds), *Rethinking Language Pedagogy from a Corpus Perspective: Papers from the Third International Conference on Teaching and Language Corpora*. Frankfurt am Main: Peter Lang, pp. 123–132.

Tono, Y. (2003), *100-go de Start! Eikaiwa*. (Let's start English with 100 Words! USA Edition), 6 vols. Tokyo: NHK Publishing.

Tono, Y. (2004a), *100-go de Start! Eikaiwa*. (Let's start English with 100 Words! Australia Edition), 6 vols. Tokyo: NHK Publishing.

Tono, Y. (2004b), *Corpus Renshucho*. (*Corpus Drill Books*). Tokyo: NHK Publishing.

Tono, Y. (2004c), *100-go de Start! Eikaiwa: DVD-book*. (Let's start English with 100 Words! USA Edition: DVD-book). Tokyo: NHK Publishing.

Tono, Y. (2004d), 우선순위 100 단어로 터뜨리는 영어회화. Seoul: Darakwon.

Tono, Y. (2004e), (ed.) *Cambridge Learner's Dictionary: Semi-bilingual Version*. Tokyo: Cambridge University Press and Shogakukan Inc.

Tono, Y. (2005a), *100-go de Start! Eikaiwa*. (Let's start English with 100 Words! UK Edition), 6 vols. Tokyo: NHK Publishing.

Tono, Y. (2005b), *Super Corpus Renshucho. (Super Corpus Drill Books)*. Tokyo: NHK Publishing.

Tono, Y. (2005c), *100-go de Start! Eikaiwa: DVD-book.* (Let's start English with 100 Words! Australia Edition: DVD-book). Tokyo: NHK Publishing.

Tono, Y. (2005d), 關鍵100生活英會話. Taipei: Kai Hsin Publishing.

Tono, Y. (2005e), *Mimi kara Oboeru Corpus Gensen 150-go.* (Learn 150 Words by Listening: a Corpus-based Approach). Tokyo: Takarajimasha.

Tono, Y. (2005f), *Eikaiwa Corpus Drill: Nichijo Kaiwa Hen.* (English Conversation Corpus Drills: Daily Conversation). Tokyo: ALC Press.

Tono (2005g), (ed.) *Shogakukan Corpus-Based Dictionary of English Synonyms.* Tokyo: Shogakukan Inc.

Tono, Y. (2006a), *Corpus Renshucho Plus.* (Corpus Drill Books Plus). Tokyo: NHK Publishing.

Tono, Y. (2006b), *100-go de Start! Eikaiwa: DVD-book.* (Let's start English with 100 Words! UK Edition: DVD-book). Tokyo: NHK Publishing.

Tono, Y. (2007a), *Eikaiwa Corpus Drill: Business Hen.* (English Conversation Corpus Drills: Business English). Tokyo: ALC Press.

Tono, Y. (2007b), *Nipponjin Chukousei 10,000-nin no Eigo Corpus.* (A Corpus of English Compositions by 10,000 Japanese Secondary School Students). Tokyo: Shogakukan Inc.

Tono, Y. (2008), (ed.) *Sanseido's ACE CROWN English-Japanese Dictionary.* Tokyo: Sanseido.

Tono, Y. (2009a), *Corpus 100! De Eikaiwa.* (English Conversation with Corpus 100), 6 vols. Tokyo: NHK Publishing.

Tono, Y. (2009b), *Tono Yukio no Eitango Dojo.* (The English Vocabulary Boot Camp by Yukio Tono). Tokyo: Tokyo Shoseki.

Tono, Y. (forthcoming), *100-go de Start! Eikaiwa.* NINTENDO Wii version. (Let's start English with 100 Words!). Kyoto: NINTENDO.

Tono, Y. and Mochizuki, H. (2009), 'Toward automatic error identification in learner corpora: a DP matching approach', Paper presented at Corpus Linguistics conference 2009, University of Liverpool, UK, 22 July 2009.

Tudor, I. (1997), *Learner-Centredness as Language Education.* Cambridge: Cambridge University Press.

Chapter 2

Using hands-on concordancing to teach rhetorical functions: evaluation and implications for EAP writing classes

Maggie Charles

This study proposes a pedagogic approach which combines discourse analysis with corpus investigation and reports on students' feedback on the materials. Forty-nine international graduates evaluated the corpus work on a five-point scale. Results show that attitudes were generally very favourable: percentages agreeing with positive statements about the tasks ranged from 62% to 96%. The study examines the practical implications of using hands-on concordancing in large mixed-discipline EAP writing classes and concludes by proposing a three-stage set of goals for such classes on a cline of increasing corpus competence, from basic corpus awareness through corpus literacy to advanced corpus proficiency.

2.1. Introduction

Although discourse analysis and corpus investigation have been seen as opposing approaches (Swales 2002), there have been significant recent advances in integrating the two, especially with regard to research on academic writing. Conrad (2002), Partington (2004) and Baker (2006) have all stressed the need for a combined approach, while Lynne Flowerdew (1998, 2002, 2005) has worked extensively on the use of corpus methods in discourse analysis, arguing that this can enhance pedagogical applications. Further illustration of this point is provided by her recent corpus analyses of the problem-solution pattern in professional and student report writing (Flowerdew, 2008). Two other recent volumes illustrate this trend in EAP research. In Biber, Connor and Upton (2007), corpus and discourse approaches are applied to the genre analysis of biochemistry and biology research articles, while the (2009) volume edited by Charles, Pecorari and Hunston focuses specifically on research in academic writing, seeing it in terms of a cline from top-down (more discourse-analytic) to bottom-up (more corpus-based) approaches.

However when we turn to research on specific pedagogical applications of corpora, there is still a tendency to focus on lexicogrammatical rather than discoursal awareness raising. The problem here is that the use of a corpus to investigate a series of individual lexicogrammatical patterns does not necessarily constitute a systematic and pedagogically valid set of course materials. Moreover, while it is certainly true that advanced EAP students need lexicogrammatical 'fine-tuning' (Lee and Swales 2006), they also have higher level discourse concerns. I would argue that if corpus consultation is to be incorporated routinely into the class teaching of academic writing, it must also help students to address these discourse issues. There is a need, then, for applications which integrate corpus and discourse approaches in the classroom. Charles (2007) describes an initial attempt to combine discourse and corpus work in the EAP writing class, but could not provide an assessment of the approach due to lack of data. The first aim of the present paper, then, is to examine whether the use of hands-on concordancing can be of value in raising students' awareness and understanding of discourse features.

Studies of concordancing have been reported in various EAP classroom contexts, but there is concern that its use has not so far been widely taken up (e.g. Boulton 2010; Thompson 2006). One contributory factor may be that the experimental groups are likely to differ from mainstream EAP classes in certain key respects. For example, a number of studies deal with single discipline groups (Bondi 2001; Gavioli 2005; Hafner and Candlin 2007; Weber 2001), a teaching situation which may very well not pertain in many EAP courses. This homogeneity has the advantage of allowing the use of tailor-made corpora and means that classes have specific shared goals to address through corpus consultation. However, the type of corpus work reported in these situations may not be readily transferable to mixed-discipline classes.

There are also several studies of groups whose discipline concerns language itself, including language majors (Chambers 2005, 2007; Kennedy and Miceli 2001) and students of translation or interpretation (Bernardini 2002; Frankenberg-Garcia 2005a). Such students are likely to be interested in the investigation and analysis of language *per se* and so may well find corpus work easier, or at least more engaging, than EAP students, who are predominantly non-linguists. Teaching mixed-discipline non-linguist groups, then, raises distinct issues with regard to the type of corpus work that is feasible and useful. The prime motivation of students in such classes is instrumental: they need to improve their academic writing for degree purposes and the time available is strictly limited. It is essential, therefore, that students perceive each session to be of immediate benefit to their writing, and the class must be managed to ensure that all members achieve specific learning goals.

Two studies that report on the use of corpora with mixed-discipline groups are those by Yoon and Hirvela (2004) and Lee and Swales (2006). These propose rather different roles for corpus work in the writing class. In the Yoon and Hirvela study, corpus use functioned as a supplement to language work. Two groups were investigated, intermediate and advanced, both of which had four initial corpus training sessions. Thereafter the intermediate students spent about 20 minutes on corpus activities in each class, while the advanced group were left to consult the corpus on their own. Responses indicated a less favourable attitude to corpus work in the advanced than in the intermediate group, which the authors attribute to the lack of teacher support and class-based practice. By contrast, Lee and Swales made corpus work the focus of their course, which trained a small group of six advanced-level students in corpus techniques over a period of thirteen weeks. The course culminated in participants building their own corpora and presenting individual corpus-based projects. Given this intensive input, the students became skilled and enthusiastic corpus users, but, as the authors note, the success of the approach may depend on working intensively with limited numbers of highly motivated students. The results of the above studies indicate that even advanced-level students need considerable guidance and in-class practice in order to benefit fully from corpus work, but the level of resourcing and commitment seen in the Lee and Swales study is unlikely to be available in many EAP situations. A second aim of this study, then, is to investigate whether hands-on concordancing can be used to benefit mixed-discipline classes operating under less ideal conditions, with relatively large groups and fewer class hours.

This study proposes an approach which combines corpus investigation with discourse analysis in order to address both the lexicogrammatical and discourse concerns of the students. In contrast to other approaches, corpus consultation is used here in order to study rhetoric. Thus lexicogrammatical patterns are examined systematically, as realisations of the specific rhetorical function studied. Corpus work is neither the main focus of the course, as in Lee and Swales, nor is it peripheral to the class work as in Yoon and Hirvela. Rather it is one of two equally important elements of class activity: both discourse and corpus tasks are designed to contribute to the overall aim of enhancing rhetorical awareness and competence.

2.2. Background to the study

2.2.1. The course

The course described here was offered as part of Oxford University Language Centre's programme of open-access academic writing classes for graduates. It expands and takes forward the pilot version presented in Charles (2007). Five parallel groups, each with around sixteen participants, attended one weekly two-hour session on 'Investigating Rhetorical Functions' for six weeks. The materials begin with discourse-based tasks to raise students' awareness of a given function and continue with hands-on concordancing, which uses the corpora to focus on specific lexicogrammatical options for performing that function. The rhetorical functions are: Situating your research in the field; Defending your research against criticism; Portraying your professional competence; Making and modifying claims; Criticising others' research; Making and countering arguments. The corpora consist of successful theses written by native-speakers (approximately 190,000 words in politics and 300,000 words in materials science) and were examined using the concordancer of WordSmith Tools (Scott 2004).

2.2.2. The participants

The participants were international graduates or researchers. Forty-nine students completed both an initial questionnaire adapted from Yoon and Hirvela (2004), which provided information on their backgrounds and attitudes towards computer use, and a final evaluation, which asked participants to rate sixteen statements about the corpus work on a five-point scale from *strongly disagree* to *strongly agree*. Roughly 55% were doctoral students, 41% Masters students and 4% postdoctoral researchers. Thirty-three different research fields were represented: about 33% natural sciences, 45% social sciences and 22% humanities. Twenty-one different native languages were spoken, the most frequent being Chinese (35%). All but one student liked using computers and most did so several times per day. Forty-seven percent had used a corpus before, which reflects the fact that use of the British National Corpus had been introduced in earlier courses. The majority of those students reported consulting a corpus once per week or less. Attendance was not necessarily regular: only 47% attended all six corpus sessions, another factor which may be characteristic of mainstream academic writing classes and which militates against the successful introduction of unfamiliar techniques like hands-on concordancing.

It is clear that these classes were very heterogeneous, particularly in discipline, native language and experience in corpus use, and such diversity may well be characteristic of many academic writing classes. Thus, the Oxford classes provide a useful test case for two research questions. 1. Can corpus work help raise students' awareness and understanding of discourse features? 2. Can hands-on concordancing be used to benefit this type of academic writing class, characterised by heterogeneity, large size, irregular attendance and limited class time?

2.3. An example of classroom procedure: Criticising the work of other researchers

One difficulty often mentioned by students is that of making an acceptable criticism of other researchers' work. They are frequently urged to 'be critical', but given little specific guidance on how to achieve this. It seemed likely, therefore, that a combination of discourse and corpus work would enable students to discover some of the rhetorical and lexicogrammatical patterns associated with this function.

The discourse session begins by focusing on two extracts from successful theses (Extracts A and B). Students are asked to underline the linguistic features that construct the criticism and, in pairs, to compare and contrast the extracts, commenting on their acceptability and persuasive effect. Extract A makes an overt attack rather than a reasoned argument. Extract B instead includes a positive evaluation of other researchers' views and a concession before giving the writer's criticism, signalled in each case by *but*. The purpose of this task is not just to illustrate how criticisms can be made, but to help students reflect on their own attitudes to criticising others' work and the norms of their discipline in this regard.

Extract A

Statements such as a bone collagen $\delta^{13}C$ value of $-18.07‰$ implies a dietary content of 16% C_4 plants (White & Schwarcz 1994) have been made *and accepted* as possible conclusions. The assumptions on which this statement is based is that all C_3 and C_4 plants can be assigned fixed single $\delta^{13}C$ values . . . This is a **gross oversimplification and disregards all the known data** on the wide variation in plant isotopic values . . .

Extract B

There exists **an important strand of thought** concerning state socialization that limits the scope of investigation to processes affecting individuals *within* states (see Luard: 59–60; Ikenberry and Kupchan 1990: 289–290). **But** states are **not merely** aggregates of individuals. States are corporate actors, possessed of centralized administrative organs. **It is true that** state policy is made by individuals, **but** these individuals are subject to pressure from domestic interests . . .

In the concordancing part of the class, the students focus on two-part rhetorical patterns similar to those identified in Extract B, in which the writer acknowledges the work of another researcher before criticising it. They are asked to perform corpus searches on *but, however* and *though* with *(19** in the context. As the corpora were compiled in the 1990s, this retrieves citations which occur within the context of a contrasting statement signalled by the conjunction. In each concordance, this provides students with several examples of the rhetorical pattern studied. Thus in the materials science corpus, the concordance for *but* in the context of *(19** retrieves 19 lines, of which about half show evidence of this pattern. Part of this concordance appears below:

1. . . . Venables and Maher (1996). Their work **successfully** imaged ion-implanted p+n-junctions, **but did not report** the observation of any contrast in similar n+p-junctions.
2. Humphreys (1993) and Gater (1994) studied the grain boundaries of MA6000 **but failed** to find any evidence of carbides.
3. The early parameterisation of Chadi (1979c) described the band structure **rather well**, and had the **correct** separation of Es and Ep, **but** gave **poor** elastic constants.
4. A similar insensitivity of SE-imaging was reported, **but not explained**, by Venables and Maher (1996).
5. Norenberg, Bowler and Briggs (1997) also **found** an increase in the amount of c(4x4) with Ga exposure, **but** were **unable** to measure the Ga coverage in Auger.

Focusing questions are given to help students notice features of the rhetorical function studied, thereby providing some pedagogical mediation of the concordance data (Flowerdew 2009). Students are asked to identify which lines construct criticisms and how they are signalled (e.g. *but*, negation, negative evaluation). They are also asked to note any features which soften the effect of the criticisms (e.g. factive verbs, positive evaluation). The aim of the task is to draw students' attention to a way of mitigating the effect of criticism by first indicating what the other researcher **has** achieved before drawing attention to limitations or flaws. In pairs, students discuss their findings and the class ends with a whole-group report-back session. Paper versions of the concordances are provided so that students have a record of the data, and homework is to write a short criticism of others' work in their own field.

The other rhetorical functions are dealt with in a similar way. Each session focuses on a single function, with initial discourse work leading on to subsequent corpus consultation.

2.4. Results of the students' evaluations

The results of the students' evaluations appear in Table 2.1 below.

Table 2.1   Results of the students' evaluation questionnaire

Statement about the corpus work	Strongly disagree	Somewhat disagree	Neither agree nor disagree	Somewhat agree	Strongly agree
1. In general, working with the concordances helped me to learn about the rhetorical functions.	0%	4%	6%	55%	35%
2. Working with the concordances helped me to understand how the rhetorical functions are used.	0%	2%	12%	49%	37%
3. Working with the concordances helped me to learn how the rhetorical functions are expressed.	0%	4%	2%	57%	36%

4.	Working with the concordances helped me to learn the grammar of the rhetorical functions.	0%	0%	15%	52%	33%
5.	Working with the concordances helped me to learn the vocabulary of the rhetorical functions.	0%	8%	6%	47%	39%
6.	Working with the concordances was a useful supplement to working with the texts.	0%	4%	10%	40%	46%
7.	Working with the concordances was interesting.	6%	6%	14%	35%	39%
8.	Working with the concordances helped me to use the rhetorical functions in my own writing.	0%	4%	22%	49%	24%
9.	Working with the concordances helped me to learn other useful aspects of academic writing, apart from the rhetorical functions.	0%	2%	35%	39%	24%
10.	Working with the concordances made me more aware of the rhetorical functions in my reading.	0%	6%	6%	46%	42%
11.	It was easy to perform the searches using the WordSmith Concordance program.	0%	18%	20%	35%	27%
12.	Analysing the concordance lines was difficult because of the language.	9%	54%	28%	4%	4%

(Continued)

Table 2.1 (Cont'd)

	Statement about the corpus work	Strongly disagree	Somewhat disagree	Neither agree nor disagree	Somewhat agree	Strongly agree
13.	Analysing the concordance lines took too much time because there was a lot of data.	20%	22%	22%	24%	10%
14.	I intend to use a corpus (e.g. the British National Corpus) for help with my English in the future.	0%	6%	10%	29%	54%
15.	I would like to use corpora in an English course in the future.	2%	6%	14%	37%	41%
16.	I would recommend other international students to use a corpus for help with their English.	0%	4%	0%	41%	55%

The results of the final questionnaire show that attitudes towards the corpus work were generally very favourable, although it was rather disappointing that the numbers of those who *strongly* supported corpus work were somewhat low, with an average of 38%. Nonetheless, taking an average of those who *somewhat agree* or *strongly agree* with the positive statements about corpus work gives the figure of 82%, showing that students considered working with concordances to be useful and worthwhile. In providing the following brief overview, I now combine the categories '*somewhat*' and '*strongly*' and refer to 'agree' or 'disagree'. Ninety percent or over agreed that concordances helped them learn about rhetorical functions and how they are expressed and would recommend other international students to use a corpus for help with their English. Between 80% and 90% agreed that working with the concordances was a useful supplement to working with the texts and intend to use a corpus in the future; it also helped them to understand how rhetorical functions are used, to learn the grammar and vocabulary associated with them and to become more aware of them in their reading. Between 70% and 80% agreed that working with concordances was interesting, that it helped them to use rhetorical functions in their own writing and that they would like to use corpora in a future English class. In answer to the research questions, then, these students considered that concordancing could help them learn features of discourse, and the positive feedback suggests that this type of corpus work can be beneficial even in large heterogeneous groups.

Lower percentages were recorded for agreeing that working with concordances helped students learn other aspects of academic writing (63%) and that it was easy to perform the searches (62%). There was also relatively low disagreement with the negative statements that analysing the concordance lines was difficult because of the language (63%) and that it took too much time because there was a lot of data (42%). I now discuss in more detail the students' evaluations of the four statements which evoked a less favourable response, as these raise wider issues relevant to incorporating concordancing into mainstream academic writing courses.

2.5. Discussion

2.5.1. 'Working with the concordances helped me to learn other useful aspects of academic writing, apart from the rhetorical functions'

The relatively low percentage of those who agreed with this statement (63%) was somewhat surprising as it has been claimed that corpus work has beneficial effects that extend beyond the immediate task performed (Aston 2001; Johns 1991). There are several possible reasons for this result. First, it may simply be that the students had not considered this possibility, an explanation supported by the relatively high figure for those who neither agree nor disagree (35%). It is also possible that the positive effects of corpus work may be more long term and general (Boulton and Tyne 2008). It may be unrealistic, then, to expect students to notice such benefits after only six sessions.

A further possibility, however, is that students are so focused on the assigned task that they do not notice other useful features of the concordance lines. This raises the issue of the extent to which corpus work should be planned into a course or incidental to it. The 'incidentalism' of much corpus work has been criticised, among others by Swales (2002) and Lee and Swales (2006), while other researchers, most notably Bernardini (2000), have viewed what they term 'serendipitous' learning as a positive advantage. I have argued elsewhere (Charles 2007) that the use of controlled searches at the early stages of corpus work has the advantage of providing a clear, shared focus for the class, making it possible for the teacher to check learning and for students to gain a sense of achievement by completing set tasks. Clearly, however, each group of learners has different pedagogic needs, and care must be taken not to inhibit students from pursuing 'triggered queries' (Flowerdew 2009), that is, individual lines of enquiry arising from the data.

2.5.2. 'Analysing the concordance lines was difficult because of the language'

Another issue of concern is the language of the concordances. Nine percent agreed with the statement above, and only sixty-three percent disagreed, indicating a somewhat negative evaluation of the language. Difficulties with the language of concordances have been pointed out by others (Aston 1997; Kennedy and Miceli 2001), but usually in the context of work with large corpora, or with intermediate level students. Here, however, the corpora were small and the students at advanced level. Language problems, then, may be due to the content of the corpora. Although about half these students were already used to reading short extracts from both corpora, they may have found it too challenging to be confronted with several examples of specialist language in an area not their own.

This raises the important issue of what corpus to use. In terms of genre, the corpora used here consist of theses rather than research articles, that is, student rather than expert texts. I would argue that a thesis corpus is particularly appropriate for use with graduates, as it provides exemplars of the texts that the students have to write. In mixed groups of Masters and doctoral students it cannot be assumed that the research article is a target genre for all. Furthermore, as there are important differences between genres even within the same discipline (Hyland 2008; Koutsantoni 2006), it may not always be appropriate to consult a research article corpus when the goal is to write a thesis.

Perhaps even more important is the decision as to disciplinary content. Disciplinary characteristics are vital to the construction of appropriate academic texts (see Hyland 2000) and there is also considerable variation within disciplines (Thompson 2005). However, an individual class is likely to contain students from a number of different fields. Moreover, the disciplinary composition of classes will probably vary each year and many students have fields of enquiry which are interdisciplinary. Thus it would be impractical to provide a corpus appropriate to each student. Lee and

Swales' (2006) solution to this problem is to have students create their own tailor-made corpora and this seems a good way forward. However, as noted above, it may well be difficult with larger groups and shorter courses.

The approach taken here was to use pre-compiled corpora in two contrasting disciplines likely to be relevant to many of the students. Clearly, it would be desirable to expand the disciplines represented, particularly to include humanities theses. However, it is not claimed that these corpora match students' fields exactly; rather it is argued that they provide an indication of some of the lexicogrammatical options available for expressing the rhetorical function studied. When working with such corpora, it is important to emphasise that the results should always be compared with what students observe in their own discipline. In fact, one advantage of using such corpora is precisely that it discourages students from viewing the corpus results as providing the single 'right' answer; instead they are predisposed to exercise caution and check findings against their own disciplinary knowledge. What students learn from their concordancing is the more general skill of noticing and interpreting linguistic features and this can be profitably applied in their own fields.

2.5.3. 'Analysing the concordance lines took too much time because there was a lot of data'

The next issue concerns the amount of data consulted, which caused difficulty for some students: 34% of participants agreed with the statement above, while only 42% disagreed. This problem has also been noted before, though usually because of the number of individual concordance lines (Frankenberg-Garcia 2005b; Gavioli 2005). Here, the numbers of lines were limited (typically around 10–20), but a greater amount of context was examined. When studying rhetorical functions, it is important that students examine enough context to ensure that they can observe the patterns, without being overwhelmed by the quantity of data.

However, concordances do have an important role to play in investigating context (Charles 2007). In particular I would argue that, far from being mere instances of 'decontextualised' language (Widdowson 2000), concordance lines enable students to understand the importance of context better than paper-based materials in certain respects. First, when working with relevant specialised corpora, EAP students will be familiar with the general social and communicative context of the source texts (Flowerdew 2008). More significantly, however, when a student reads a concordance line, it is clear that they are looking at a fragment of text, and this incompleteness acts as a stimulus to expand lines and/or access the original file, two ways of examining the wider linguistic context which are not available with paper-based extracts. Thus concordances are valuable not just for studying relatively short lexicogrammatical patterns, but also for working with extended contexts and investigating discourse level features such as rhetorical functions.

2.5.4. 'It was easy to perform the searches using the WordSmith Concordance program'

Only 62% of respondents agreed that performing the searches was easy, while 18% somewhat disagreed, giving one of the lowest positive evaluations in the feedback. Class attendance did not seem to be a factor, as even the students with full attendance returned very similar percentages to those given above. I would suggest that there are two main reasons. First, the necessity of ensuring a limited number of concordance lines leads to more complicated searches, involving, for example, context items or wild cards. For a beginner in corpus work, this undoubtedly presents a challenge. Secondly, if the main focus of the class is on learning the rhetorical function, it is more difficult to present the corpus tasks in a systematic and graded sequence, with the result that students may be overloaded with new technical information at the beginning of the course, and there may be little sense of progression in concordancing skills. These disadvantages may thus derive from the decision to subordinate the learning of corpus techniques to the study of discourse functions. While some further adjustments in the difficulty and sequencing of the corpus tasks can certainly be made, it is probably unavoidable that some students will still experience difficulties.

Given the four problematic issues discussed above, we must ask whether the benefits of the approach outweigh the costs. In addition to the considerable resource and training needs pointed out by others (e.g. Thompson 2006), I would highlight some practical issues of class management. On the negative side, corpus work takes a considerable amount of class time, not all of which may be profitably spent. Most obviously, there may be problems with the hardware or software that cause delays in performing searches, with the result that little actual analysis of the concordance lines takes place. For teachers without readily available technical support, time spent sorting out computing problems is time taken from the pedagogical focus of the class; it can sometimes seem as though one is teaching computing rather than academic writing.

Second, performing searches and interpreting concordance lines are new techniques. Even using controlled searches and focusing questions, students find them difficult and require considerable practice. For example, they may need help to see how individual concordance lines fit the pattern studied or how they themselves can make use of the data. For the teacher of a large class, it is difficult to keep track of the progress of all the students and ensure useful outcomes for everyone. Irregular attendance also means that training on technical aspects may have to be repeated, which further reduces the time available for task-related guidance. Such practical class management problems undoubtedly reduce the appeal of using corpora for many teachers who work in mainstream EAP classes.

Even under such circumstances, however, it is still possible to incorporate hands-on concordancing into courses and, as the feedback in this study shows, this can be a positive experience for many students. On the benefit side, as Johns pointed out from the inception of DDL (1991), corpus consultation tends to promote learning based on discovery and induction, which is highly motivating for many, though admittedly not all, students. Moreover, concordancing fosters an evidence-based rather than intuition-based approach, which seems to be particularly attractive to research students. Working with concordance lines provides access to a wealth of examples and promotes detailed attention to language, encouraging students to notice the linguistic features that characterise the searched item, and leading to the discovery and understanding of distinctions in forms of expression. In revealing this patterning of language, then, corpus work facilitates the learning of both lexicogrammar and discourse features.

2.6. Conclusions

I have argued that teaching large groups of mixed-discipline students poses specific problems when incorporating corpus work into academic writing classes. In the course reported here, the use of just two generically appropriate corpora, of controlled searches and of focusing questions posed by the teacher, sought to address students' need to achieve specific goals with limited inputs of time and resources. I have also suggested that advanced students of academic writing need to learn not only local lexicogrammatical patterns, but also higher level discourse features. The materials described here attempted to achieve this by integrating concordancing very closely into work on rhetorical functions. As shown by their positive responses, students considered that they did learn discourse features through the concordance work, engaging with the corpora to bridge the gap between their rhetorical concerns and their lexicogrammatical knowledge. The use of corpus consultation in conjunction with discourse work thus seems to provide a systematic approach that is both feasible and pedagogically valid.

2.7. Three goals on a cline of corpus competence

More generally, I would suggest that a three-stage set of goals could be proposed for mainstream EAP classes. The first (and in my view indispensable) stage is 'corpus awareness'. At this stage, students would know what a corpus is, have an idea of the sort of information it can provide and know how to access one of the freely available corpora. They would have used a concordance, perhaps on paper, but may not have performed any searches themselves. Indeed, as argued by Boulton (2010), 'taking the computer out of the equation' may be a positive advantage here. The introductory 'corpus awareness' stage demands minimal investment of class time by teacher and student. Its limited aim recognises that students may lack the time or motivation to take corpus work further at that point, but provides an option which they can pursue independently in the future. In this regard it is worth noting that a survey of 38 UK higher education institutions by Jarvis (2004) reported that the percentage of institutions using concordancing on at least one EFL course was only 19%. While the situation may well have improved since then, it is still likely that many students pass through EAP courses without ever becoming aware of the existence of corpora as a learning resource.

The second stage would be 'corpus literacy' and, given appropriate training and technical facilities, I think this is an achievable goal for many, and perhaps most mainstream EAP students. At this stage, students can perform simple searches, have a basic understanding of how to interpret concordance data, and are able to use a corpus to answer relatively straightforward queries of their own. This goal demands a considerable investment of class time and the benefits are correspondingly greater. The final stage of 'corpus proficiency' would probably be achieved by only a minority of highly motivated students. It would imply that students are able to build their own corpora, to formulate more advanced searches and to interpret complex results accurately. This stage demands a greater investment of students' own time, as they grapple with learning new skills to an accomplished level. Of course, there is no rigid division between the stages, but distinguishing these three goals on a cline of competence may help to clarify some of the issues involved in deciding what level of commitment to corpus work is appropriate in a given EAP teaching situation.

References

Aston, G. (1997), 'Enriching the learning environment: corpora in ELT', in A. Wichman, S. Fligelstone, T. McEnery and G. Knowles (eds), *Teaching and Language Corpora*. London: Addison Wesley Longman, pp. 51–64.

Aston, G. (2001), 'Learning with corpora: an overview', in G. Aston (ed.), *Learning with Corpora*. Bologna: CLUEB, pp. 7–45.

Baker, P. (2006), *Using Corpora in Discourse Analysis*. London: Continuum.

Bernardini, S. (2000), 'Systematising serendipity: proposals for concordancing large corpora with language learners', in L. Burnard and T. McEnery (eds), *Rethinking Language Pedagogy from a Corpus Perspective*. Frankfurt: Peter Lang, pp. 225–234.

Bernardini, S. (2002), 'Exploring new directions for discovery learning', in B. Kettemann and G. Marko (eds), *Teaching and Learning by Doing Corpus Analysis*. Amsterdam and New York: Rodopi, pp. 165–182.

Biber, D., Connor, U. and Upton, T. (eds) (2007), *Discourse on the Move*. Amsterdam and Philadelphia: John Benjamins.

Bondi, M. (2001), 'Small corpora and language variation', in M. Ghadessy, A. Henry and R. Roseberry (eds), *Small Corpus Studies and ELT*. Amsterdam and Philadelphia: John Benjamins, pp. 135–174.

Boulton, A. (2010), 'Data-driven learning: Taking the computer out of the equation'. *Language Learning*, 60, (3), 534–572.

Boulton, A., and Tyne, H. (2008), 'Learning with corpora: changing learning practices'. Paper presented at the 4th Inter-Varietal Applied Corpus Studies Conference (IVACS), University of Limerick, Ireland, 14 June 2008.

Chambers, A. (2005), 'Integrating corpus consultation in language studies'. *Language Learning and Technology*, 9, (2), 111–125.

Chambers, A. (2007), 'Language learning as discourse analysis: implications for the LSP learning environment'. *ASp, La Revue du GERAS*, 51/52, 35–51.

Charles, M. (2007), 'Reconciling top-down and bottom-up approaches to graduate writing: using a corpus to teach rhetorical functions'. *Journal of English for Academic Purposes*, 6, (4), 289–302.

Charles, M., Pecorari, D. and Hunston, S. (eds) (2009), *Academic Writing: At the Interface of Corpus and Discourse*. London: Continuum.

Conrad, S. (2002), 'Corpus linguistic approaches for discourse analysis'. *Annual Review of Applied Linguistics*, 22, 75–95.

Flowerdew, J. (ed.) (2002), *Academic Discourse*. London: Longman.

Flowerdew, L. (1998), 'Corpus linguistic techniques applied to textlinguistics'. *System*, 26, (4), 541–552.

Flowerdew, L. (2002), 'Corpus-based analyses in EAP', in J. Flowerdew (ed.), pp. 95–114.

42 Maggie Charles

Flowerdew, L. (2005), 'An integration of corpus-based and genre-based approaches to text analysis in EAP/ESP: countering criticisms against corpus-based methodologies'. *English for Specific Purposes*, 24, (3), 321–332.

Flowerdew, L. (2008), *Corpus-based Analyses of the Problem-Solution Pattern*. Amsterdam and Philadelphia: John Benjamins.

Flowerdew, L. (2009), 'Applying corpus linguistics to pedagogy: a critical evaluation'. *International Journal of Corpus Linguistics*, 14, (3), 393–417.

Frankenberg-Garcia, A. (2005a), 'A peek into what today's language learners as researchers actually do'. *International Journal of Lexicography*, 18, (3), 335–355.

Frankenberg-Garcia, A. (2005b), 'Pedagogical uses of monolingual and parallel concordances'. *ELT Journal*, 59, (3), 189–198.

Gavioli, L. (2005), *Exploring Corpora for ESP Learning*. Amsterdam and Philadelphia: John Benjamins.

Hafner, C. and Candlin, C. (2007), 'Corpus tools as an affordance to learning in professional legal education'. *Journal of English for Academic Purposes*, 6, (4), 303–318.

Hyland, K. (2000), *Disciplinary Discourses: Social Interactions in Academic Writing*. Harlow: Longman.

Hyland, K. (2008), 'As can be seen: lexical bundles and disciplinary variation'. *English for Specific Purposes*, 27, (1), 4–21.

Jarvis, H. (2004), 'Investigating the classroom applications of computers on EFL courses at Higher Education Institutions in UK'. *Journal of English for Academic Purposes*, 3, (2), 111–137.

Johns, T. (1991), 'Should you be persuaded: two samples of data-driven learning materials', in T. Johns and P. King (eds), *Classroom Concordancing. English Language Research Journal*, 4. Birmingham: University of Birmingham., pp. 1–16.

Kennedy, C., and Miceli, T. (2001), 'An evaluation of intermediate students' approaches to corpus investigation'. *Language Learning and Technology*, 5, (3), 77–90.

Koutsantoni, D. (2006), 'Rhetorical strategies in engineering research articles and research theses: advanced academic literacy and relations of power'. *Journal of English for Academic Purposes*, 5, (1), 19–36.

Lee, D. and Swales, J. (2006), 'A corpus-based EAP course for NNS doctoral students: moving from available specialised corpora to self-compiled corpora'. *English for Specific Purposes*, 25, (1), 56–75.

Partington, A. (2004), 'Corpora and discourse, a most congruous beast', in A. Partington, J. Morley and L. Haarman (eds), *Corpora and Discourse*. Bern: Peter Lang, pp. 11–20.

Scott, M. (2004), *WordSmith Tools 4*. Oxford: Oxford University Press.

Swales, J. (2002), 'Integrated and fragmented worlds: EAP materials and corpus linguistics', in J. Flowerdew (ed.), pp. 150–164.

Thompson, P. (2005), 'Points of focus and position: intertextual reference in PhD theses'. *Journal of English for Academic Purposes*, 4, (4), 307–323.

Thompson, P. (2006), 'Assessing the contribution of corpora to EAP practice', in Z. Kantaridou, I. Papadopoulou, and I. Mahili (eds), *Motivation in Learning Language for Specific and Academic Purposes*. Macedonia: University of Macedonia. [Online]. http://www.reading.ac.uk/internal/appling/thompson_macedonia.pdf (accessed May 1, 2009).

Weber, J.-J. (2001), 'A concordance- and genre-informed approach to ESP essay writing'. *ELT Journal,* 55, (1), 14–20.

Widdowson, H. (2000), 'On the limitations of linguistics applied'. *Applied Linguistics,* 21, (1), 3–25.

Yoon, H., and Hirvela, A. (2004), 'ESL student attitudes towards corpus use in L2 writing'. *Journal of Second Language Writing,* 13, (4), 257–283.

Chapter 3

Tracing the Emo side of life. Using a corpus of an alternative youth culture discourse to teach Cultural Studies

Bernhard Kettemann

This chapter presents an experimental investigation of the utility of corpora and corpus analysis, both as a method of investigation and as a data source, for the teaching and learning of Cultural Studies. The data presented to students included a list of the most frequent content words, a semantically categorised list of verbs following the pronoun *I*, a keyword list comparison between the Emo corpus and the Bergen Corpus of London Teenage Language (COLT) and concordances of *alone, lonely* and *on my own*. A questionnaire was used to evaluate students' reactions to these materials.

3.1. Introduction

Corpus analysis, both as a method of investigation and a source of data, has something to offer to the teaching and learning of Cultural Studies. Various studies have demonstrated potential benefits, albeit from very different angles; among others, Eppler et al. (2000), Kettemann and Marko (in press, 2011), Minugh (2007). And it is not difficult to find aspects relevant to the teaching of culture in many other applications of corpus analysis, especially from those engaging in corpus-based discourse analysis (see Baker 2006 for an overview). But despite these efforts, no firm connection has been established between corpus analysis and Cultural Studies, which is reflected in the fact that none of the recent TaLC conference proceedings (Burnard and McEnery 2000; Kettemann and Marko 2002; Aston et al. 2004; Hidalgo et al. 2007) include references to the field. Mukherjee's (2002) introduction to applications of corpus linguistics in the (English) classroom contains a section in which the connections between culture, teaching/learning and corpora are discussed, but it focuses on the intercultural dimension of foreign language competence rather than on Cultural Studies in its own right. The present chapter explores the potential use of corpus analysis in Cultural Studies.

3.2. Teaching Cultural Studies

The past two decades have seen the rise of Cultural Studies not only as a subject in its own right, but also as a major component of philological disciplines. This development has gone hand in hand with a pedagogical reconceptualisation of these disciplines. The focus is no longer on the top-down transfer of knowledge from teacher to student, but has shifted towards awareness-based competencies. This requires pedagogical procedures which no longer rely on a strict separation of teacher and student roles, but reduce teachers' authority as a reservoir of explicit knowledge and strengthen students' confidence in their ability to find their own paths of understanding. This can be described as a shift from traditional teaching to exploratory learning. The main differences are captured in Figure 3.1.

On the level of culture, this means moving away from factual knowledge of historical, geographic, political, economic and social details of different countries towards a sociocultural awareness which enables students to become sociocultural mediators and disseminators – roles that are likely to be at the core of what they will be doing professionally in the future. It seems plausible to assume that Cultural Studies, as a field focusing on ideologies and narratives and their impact on a society's interpretation of the world, is better able to meet such needs than traditional 'facts and figures' courses, which usually present decontextualised snippets of information.

Traditional teaching		Exploratory learning
teacher-centred	→	student-centred
deduction	→	induction
instruction	→	association[1]
knowledge	→	awareness

FIGURE 3.1 From traditional teaching to exploratory learning

3.3. The role of corpus analysis in the teaching of Cultural Studies

Cultural Studies, however, poses serious pedagogical challenges due to the abstractness of the ideas presented, which at first sight may seem even further removed from students' life worlds than the old facts and figures.[2] Cultural Studies emphasises language as the means by which ideologies and narratives are disseminated across a society, and examining language in use means trying to understand how we make sense of the world and ourselves. Corpus analysis and its products – word lists, cluster lists, keyword lists, concordances, collocations – and data derived from these, e.g. on semantic domains and semantic prosodies, provide valuable tools to raise students' awareness, enabling them to explore cultural meanings and eventually to 'teach' cultural competence themselves – whether as teachers or in other functions.

The use of corpora in a Cultural Studies course can be seen as involving two steps:

Step I: Teacher input
Students work with corpus material and data specially prepared by the teacher.

Step II: Student-centred exploratory research
Students work with corpora provided by the teacher and later with their own corpora in an exploratory, data-driven fashion.

In this study I concentrate on the first step in this awareness-raising approach, focusing on teacher-prepared data derived from a corpus of English texts written by Emos.

Emo is the label applied to an alternative youth culture characterised by introversion and withdrawal from an outside (adult) world perceived as unsympathetic, misunderstanding and demanding, with a concomitant emphasis on negative and depressive moods and suicidal ideas. Externally, Emos show a preference for dark colours in clothes, hairstyle and make-up and for androgynous styles (Kelley and Leslie 2007). Emo discourse seems an appropriate topic for Cultural Studies because it offers a starting point for discussing cultural concepts such as lifestyles, identities and values and the opposition mainstream vs. alternative. I also assume that students can be motivated to deal with this topic, as most of them will have had some connections to Emos and their ideas.

3.4. The corpus

The corpus used was compiled by Kerstin Florian during a seminar for third and fourth year students of English entitled 'The language of alternative lifestyles', held in the winter term 2007/2008. It consisted of a hetero-geneous set of texts written and made publicly available by young people identifying as Emos, including articles, blog entries, forum threads, poems and song lyrics. Overall it contained 50 prose texts and 400 poetic ones,[3] where prose and poetry each accounted for approximately 50% of the total number of words. The corpus is very 'quick-and-dirty' in Tribble's sense (1997), that is, informally produced for an immediate purpose, without elaborate deliberations concerning its composition.[4] But it can be argued that its heterogeneity mirrors the chaotic textual universe in which young people shape and enact their Emo identities.

Considering its heterogeneity, Florian's corpus was a small one, (141,614 word tokens). But since my focus was more on the motivational potential of corpus data than on the methodologically sound production of analytic results, I decided to stick with it. For the analysis, Wordsmith Tools 4.0 was used (Scott 2004).

3.5. The study

The study reported here was carried out in June 2008 at the English Department of Karl-Franzens University in Graz. It used questionnaires to find out about students' interpretations of data from the Emo corpus. The students were taking a 'British and American Cultural Studies Foundation Course'. This is a first-year course in the English and American Studies programme, and normally constitutes students' first contact with Cultural Studies.

About forty students attended the course. For this study, they were pre-sented with four sets of data and with interpretatory questions concerning the construction of an Emo identity and an Emo perspective on life. These four sets of data were subjected to declining degrees of preprocessing, from highly processed to raw. They thus represented four stages in progress from a teacher-centred towards a student-centred approach – bearing in mind that the distinction between traditional teaching and corpus-based explor-atory learning is a scalar rather than an absolute one. This use of different stages aimed to show whether students could learn to interpret data cultur-ally within a short time span, and whether they were able to move towards exploratory learning once they had been pointed in this direction.

3.5.1. Method

Students were asked to complete a questionnaire based on the four data sets (see Appendix). The questionnaire had to be handed in within a week. To limit effects to those of the corpus data, no other information had been provided about Emos. The final section of the questionnaire asked about their general evaluations of the project, especially focusing on the role of language. As I was focusing on the teacher-centred phase of the learning procedure, all corpus data was provided by me, and students did not work with the corpus for themselves.

Stage 1: Verbs following first person I

The first data set provided qualitatively and quantitatively processed data concerning verbs with the first person singular pronoun *I* as their subject, insofar as what Emos say they are doing is pivotal in their construction of their own identities. The search was limited to the word immediately following *I*. In the qualitative processing, the verbs found were categorised semantically into twelve different categories (see below, in bold); in the quantitative processing, the corpus frequency of the verbs pertaining to each category was provided (see below, in brackets). Verbs which could not be easily assigned to any of these categories were excluded from the analysis.

Existence and change (of attributes and identity): live (11); get (become) (9); become (4); exist (3); change (2); go Emo (2); grow (2); disappear; turn (become).

Communicative processes: say (48); write (37); tell (22); ask (16); scream (9); swear (6); bet (5); call (5); agree (4); pray (4); promise (4); beg (2); blame (2); explain (2); lie (not to tell the truth) (2); plead (2); recommend (2); talk (2); admit; answer; apologise; convince; defend; disagree; mutter; preach; read; refuse; scribble; stutter; text; voice.

Social processes: meet (8); help (2); break up; celebrate; date; go out; join.

Style: wear (26); look (appear visually) (9); dress (8); dye (4); pierce (2); put on (2); braid; clip; color; put hair in a ponytail; sport.

Cognition: think (127); know (122); guess (30); remember (19); mean (13); wonder (10); realise (9); believe (6); get (understand) (6); dream (5); pick (4); plan (4); decide (3); doubt (3); learn (3); look back (metaphorically) (3); suppose (3); choose (2); expect (2); figure (2); reminisce (2); understand (2); consider; forget; recognise.

Emotion: want (109); feel (105); love (102); need (92); hate (71); like (54); wish (44); hope (29); care (14); miss (10); bottle up (5); dig (5); fall in love (4); fear (4); break (down) (3); fall for (3); adore (2); long for (2); bother; cherish; crave; dare; deal ('cope'); dislike; dread; heart; look forward; pity; prefer; revel; suffer; take ('bear'); take it to the heart; trust.

Perception: see (75); look ('gaze') (19); hear (17); watch (5); stare (4); listen (3); taste (3); gaze (2); glare; notice; peer.

Physiology: cry (42); die (18); bleed (6); wake (up) (5); fall asleep (4); sleep (4); laugh (3); awake (2); eat (2); collapse; drain; draw a breath; drink; drown; faint; pass away; starve; swallow; take a breath; take medication; weep.

Physical contact: cut (27); hold (14); tear (7); push (4); smash (4); stab (4); grab (3); press (3); rip (3); turn (3); beat (2); break sth. (2); give a kiss (2); hit (2); kick (2); kiss (2); pull sth. out (2); clench; clutch; embrace; grasp; grip; hug; press sb. close; pull; scratch; slash; slice; snap; snatch; squeeze; strike; touch; unwind; wipe; wrap.

Movement and static position: go (18); walk (10); fall (9); come (7); move (4); run (3); crawl (2); get (somewhere) (2); skate (2); approach; bow; creep; glide; hop on; march; slide, lie (horizontal bodily position) (17); sit (10); lean (4); stand (3); kneel.

Possession: have (main verb) (139); get (receive) (42); give (20); take (12); lose (11); keep (4); belong; buy; gain; steal.

Phases: start (18); stop (9); end (3); keep (on) doing (3); launch (3); begin (2); give up (2); stay (2); finish; go on; keep up; resign.

The part of the student questionnaire related to this data set (see Appendix, questions 1.1–1.4) focused on general conclusions concerning Emo identity, especially in comparison to other youth culture identities. Students were asked to indicate – as in the ensuing tasks – whether there was any item that surprised them and which they would like to pursue further, e.g. by looking at concrete examples.

Stage 2: Keyword comparison between two teenage corpora

The second data set presented a keyword comparison between the Emo corpus and the Bergen Corpus of London Teenage Language (COLT), a 500,000-word component of the BNC collected in 1993 (http://torvald. aksis.uib.no/colt). In the definition of WordSmith Tools (Scott 2006),

Table 3.1   The fifty most significant
keywords of the Emo corpus as
compared to COLT

1.	*Emo*	26.	*feel*
2.	*am*	27.	*eyes*
3.	*my*	28.	*punk*
4.	*hair*	29.	*lol*
5.	*its*	30.	*cause*
6.	*love*	31.	*cry*
7.	*current*	32.	*sorrow*
8.	*heart*	33.	*angel*
9.	*location*	34.	*Emos*
10.	*life*	35.	*clothing*
11.	*pain*	36.	*music*
12.	*help*	37.	*eyeliner*
13.	*broken*	38.	*die*
14.	*mood*	39.	*happy*
15.	*gallery*	40.	*poem*
16.	*me*	41.	*black*
17.	*tears*	42.	*mom*
18.	*poll*	43.	*soul*
19.	*never*	44.	*style*
20.	*need*	45.	*losers*
21.	*alone*	46.	*depressed*
22.	*cut*	47.	*wrote*
23.	*top*	48.	*cerebellum*
24.	*blood*	49.	*smile*
25.	*scene*	50.	*death*

keywords are those that occur significantly (p < 0.000001) more often in one corpus than in another. COLT seemed an ideal comparative corpus to identify the essential features of Emos, even though differences such as mode (i.e., written vs. spoken) may have affected the results. The students were provided with the top fifty keywords occurring relatively more frequently in the Emo corpus, which highlight many aspects which seem peculiar to the Emo perspective on the world (see Table 3.1).

The questions presented to the students relating to this data set were similar to those for the first task (see Appendix, questions 2.1 and 2.2).

Stage 3: List of content words

In the third task, the top fifty content words in the Emo corpus listed in Table 3.2 were presented to the students. This was produced with

Table 3.2 Top fifty content words in the Emo corpus

hair	530	*music*	212
love	472	*location*	211
life/live	416	*tell*	211
think	400	*thing*	204
make/makes/made	382	*time*	204
need	355	*leave/left*	199
say/said	339	*cut*	192
know	338	*way*	192
good	331	*find/found*	181
help	294	*cry/crying*	179
go/going	280	*hate*	177
joined	275	*mood*	170
heart	268	*alone*	162
people	263	*day*	155
friend/s	261	*world/s*	154
dead/death/die	256	*eyes*	153
want	247	*let*	147
see	242	*right*	135
really	239	*gallery*	134
top	235	*guy*	134
current	234	*try*	134
feel	234	*take*	133
pain	222	*new*	131
black	220	*blood*	130
look	218	*girl*	130

Wordsmith's Wordlist tool, with the help of a stop list of function words. Different word forms pertaining to the same lemma were grouped together.

The questions presented to the students relating to this data were practically the same as the ones in the second task (see Appendix, questions 3.1–3.3), with a slightly stronger focus on the difference between thematically motivated lexemes and ones whose inclusion could be explained with reference to the nature of the corpus (e.g. the structure of blog or forum entries).

Stage 4: Concordances of alone, lonely, on my own

The fourth data set presented to the students consisted of concordances of *alone, lonely* and *on my own* (concordance 1). They represent three different ways of expressing the concept of loneliness, which is supposedly the dominant emotional condition of Emos. The concordance lines were not sorted in any particular content-related way.

Concordance 1. *alone, lonely, on my own*

etimes I do feel rlly depressed cuz im so **lonely** and I just dont feel many ppl unde

and felt like trying it. I cannot survive **alone**, it feels like I lost everything I'

the broken hearts, for the people who are **lonely** and lost, the ones who run out of

ybe living isn't for everyone." Ever felt **alone**, unwanted, deserted, unloved, close

The world is silent, should forever feel **alone** - NO! Cause you are gone and I will

sh which will be my last I cannot survive **alone**, it feels like I lost everything I'

2007 11:41 pm Post subject: ur so not **alone** . i get called emo ...mostly cause

7:35 pm Post subject: Well,i'M really **aloNe** in faCt i don haVe any close friend

t friend that pays attention to me too im **alone** ....alot well im here if u wanna ta

ted suicide and now i'm left cursed to be **alone** if there is a god he truly hates me

have about a zillion piercings in my face **alone** rite now...lol?•??my <3 whispers fo

d listenin to her...i started doin things **on my own**....the only thing she didn't ag

i dont feel that im ready to take that on **on my own** rite now... just respect them a

... so im just waiting to do that till im **on my own**... and i dont feel that im rea

l. I hate it , i wish they would leave me **alone**. Im at high school now , ive lost t

Trust me, it comes in handy on those cold **lonely** nights. Back to top Deathonabun Us

ted suicide and now i'm left cursed to be **alone** if there is a god he truly hates me

mom more gentle wid u or is ur dad ..talk **alone** id one of them n if it goes well ta

ackdoor? 4. do you leave your boyfriends **alone** when they are trying to ignore you?

I look back up and realize I'm once again **alone**. The lamp post slowly flickers on a

er801.html About Me: I miss walking under **lonely** lamp posts, looking down at me as

wreck i cant stop shaking i sit at lunch **alone** listening to my ipod they ignore me

ck to say you're sorry Why'd you leave me **alone~**? And now my mama's depressing smil

, From pre-k to present, It's all sad and **lonely**, And I'm still a peasant. My life

art, dont attack loving you makes me hack **alone** now, and black A lonley sleep (plz

ow? you left me here to feel like a queer **alone** i hate being together isnt my fate

remember Make me cry and wish I wasn't so **alone** Make me wish it wasn't my fault I c

my smile and hope its good enough.... <3 **ALONE** Empty room and empty heart But why

resort ive tried hiding smiling and being **alone** it just leaves time for thoughts to

own Live with no regrets, you may end up **alone**… what am i?? 12-17-2007 1:47 pm Wha

own Take a chance in life, you may end up **alone** I can still smell his Axe, feel his

where in the dark, my thoughts are flying **alone**. Now is my turn, to realise what is

old and unloved Hated and pained Hurt and **alone** Nothing is gained Helpless and sad

e And without an answer he thought he was **alone** He walked the many stairs Up to the

the dice I waited and sat in the darkness **alone** It happened you left now I'm chill

3:54 pm i'm sat here waiting, in my room **alone**. i'm gripping and clenching, onto m

k alone so0o0 alone 12-30-2007 3:09 pm So **alone** in my bed Alone listening to nightl

rs are show up Here I am Sitting here all **alone** Waiting for something I lay down h

```
l me what you guys think!!! Current Mood: lonely (2 broken hearted losers | you'll
thought of your goodbye. How you leave me alone. Crying till the mildew comes. Drea
 love of my life and my best friend I sit alone in the dark, I look at the view of
knew now you would be fine. Now I feel so alone, I cant face the people at home, I
h for them I'm just a mistake I wish I we alone with no one here just me, myself, a
te my life theres no doubt about that, my lonely shame; for that I'll always have I
           3 pm - my emo poem HIDDEN FEELINGS On my own feeling lonely, Tension buildin
 never need) x_vampire_kid_x 10:30 pm I'm lonely and depressed I'm broken and I'm b
r need) x_vampire_kid_x 10:18 pm Standing alone on a beach Cold wind bites my skin
took your life away, You thought you were alone But bady i was by your side NOW IM
opes and dreams you came to me so sad and lonely you told what he did to you I bega
 it was great but now we dont date for im alone and she is gone but the memories th
It doesn't make me happy It makes me feel alone I'm not good enough for anyone And
ld heart still searching for something My lonely soul is lost in the darkness Try t
I can find my true love? Sitting here all alone Watching the stars Hoping for the s
cribed in her scars She's now broken Left alone in the dark Never to be found As sh
```

The questions presented to the students with regard to this data dealt with the conceptions of loneliness revealed by the concordances, also touching upon peculiar linguistic features, e.g. deviant orthography (see Appendix, questions 4.1–4.8).

3.6. Results and discussion

With the end of the summer term approaching, I eventually only received 10 completed questionnaires; a rate of return of approximately 25% – insufficient to warrant clear conclusions concerning the relevance of corpus-based approaches to the teaching and learning of Cultural Studies. I will nevertheless try to identify some interesting tendencies in the responses received.

3.6.1. Motivation and involvement

Some comments in students' answers to the questionnaire, as well as their responses in the evaluative section, indicate a high degree of motivation and involvement. This is apparent from the many digressions to be found (as digressions mark instances where students do more than required, they are interpreted as signs of motivation and involvement). They seemed to take every opportunity to show their knowledge and familiarity with youth culture and subculture, as can be seen in this meta-comment:[5]

> I liked task 4 best, because I faded away from the actual topic most there ;-)

Sometimes, students went well beyond the scope of the questions:

> I think people often try to find the happiness by doing business. I still wonder, if that is the only way to the 'easy' life? And is easy life the way to happiness? I think when you can do your job with a huge enjoy, that is the way to a happy life. You can find the balance of life in that way.

A certain degree of emotionalisation can also be noticed in many responses, particularly in the evaluations of Emos or other groups:

> I don't know whether Emos think that destiny is especially cruel to them, or if they think that their peers should just spend more time thinking about their tragic existence.

> I know about several different youth cultures although I am hoping that some of them will disappear immediately.

It might be objected that digressions and evaluations go counter to a scientifically distanced approach to the study of culture. While this is true when it comes to the systematic analysis of cultural phenomena, the fact remains that an approach like the one proposed seems able to trigger some kind of energy, manifested in these digressions and evaluations. And it is exactly such energy that is required to go further in the study of culture.

The problem here, of course, is whether motivation and involvement are a result of the approach, or due to the nature of the topic. Current youth culture seems to be something that students are interested in, but which is often treated as irrelevant by their not-so-young professors.

> I think youth culture and subculture should generally be discussed within Cultural Studies.

3.6.2. Inductive and deductive student-centredness

One of the great assets of the approach seems to be the shift towards students' life worlds. This, however, does not seem to lead to exclusively inductive learning. The answers rather suggest a mixture of inductive and deductive interpretations.

In inductive learning, students take the data and draw their own new conclusions from them. That they engaged in this kind of learning can be seen from the ways they answered the questions posed in the questionnaire.

> What is also interesting is the fact, that the words 'am', 'my', 'me', which all refer to the Self, are used much more frequent than in other teenager language. The reason could be, that Emos are introverted persons who focus on their own emotion and reflect on their own existence more than other teenagers do.

They also emphasised this dimension in their evaluations:

> I did learn something about this Emo culture, mostly because I really had to think about it because I had to come up with my own ideas.

> Maybe such an approach could be integrated in BACS [British and American Studies Foundation Course], because it's interesting to find out something about a culture and culture in general on your own and with real examples.

> [...] it is always easier to learn something if you have an example or if you have to do something on your own.

This means they preferred such an approach – even just as an alternative – to the rather complex ideas and theoretical frameworks presented in the coursebook, Hall's *Representation: Cultural Representations and Signifying Practices* (1997). They particularly appreciated the first-hand accounts, and they valued the chance to come up with their own ideas.

In deductive learning, students take the data and examine whether it is compatible with preconceptions and prior knowledge. Where this happened is difficult to tell because of the language-oriented focus of the questions. But that it plays a role is obvious from the digressions cited above (which point to extensive background knowledge).

If students can manage to combine inductive with deductive approaches, they can definitely profit with regard to their Cultural Studies competencies. Deduction can further promote students' motivation. After all, they can count on their own expertise, which in the area of youth culture is probably greater than their teacher's. In some cases, however, giving priority to their own experience may make them misinterpret or neglect the real data. Students are aware of this:

> I hope that my previous impression of what constitutes an Emo doesn't influence the evaluation of the results.

> Once again, the problem is whether we should attribute positive effects to the methodological approach or to the subject matter.

3.6.3. Awareness of the connection between language and culture

Both the questionnaire answers and the comments in the evaluation section reveal an increased awareness of the connection between language and culture. This is probably a result of the practical and authentic nature of the data, and the form of its presentation, which highlights the role of language in the construction of identities.

The participants in the study may have even gone too far in this direction, jumping to conclusions too quickly. They tended to take the linguistic data at face value and assign immediate cultural significance to all the items presented. If, for instance, a word ranked high in a keyword list or a content word list, this was automatically interpreted as a sign of its importance in the construction of the Emo identity.

> I would describe Emos as very emotional because according to this table they use a lot of words that belong into the emotional class.

Interpretations that go beyond such immediate cultural mappings are lacking. Consequently, semantic domains that do not readily match students' views of Emos create confusion. In the following example, the student saw *angel* merely as a religious term, rather than as a potential term of endearment or nickname (here, of course, students could have checked concordances had they worked with the corpus themselves).

> One element that does not fit into the list is the word angel, because there are no other words that correspond to religious belief.

This may, however, also be due to the form of the presentation. Students had to complete a fairly long questionnaire, which they probably wanted to do in one go rather than spread over several sessions. They might have proceeded differently if the approach described here had been spread over the entire course, rather than treated as a one-off event.

3.6.4. Semantic domain approach

Recognising patterns, whether in language or in culture, requires classifying phenomena and thus seeing them as belonging to different areas of experience, i.e. semantic domains. While we draw upon such domains all the time, a scientific approach to the study of culture means using a consistent and plausible set of such meaning-based classes. The first task in the questionnaire provided such a set, and I was interested to see whether students would be stimulated to come up with their own categories in the other tasks. The responses showed that this was indeed the case:

Category A: love, heart, life, pain, help, broken, mood, tears, need, alone, cut, top, blood, feel, cry, sorrow, angel, die, happy, black, soul, losers, depressed, smile, death

Category B: hair, eyes, clothing, music, eyeliner, style [. . .]

Category A deals again with Emos' emotions, whether positive or negative. This category also includes terms usually associated with emotions.

Category B represents the 'mainstream' aspects of Emo, the few superficial characteristics that are now successfully sold by mass media (clothing and music industry).

These examples show that it was the approach that was central, rather than just the set of categories. However, applying semantic domains to the analysis of concordances proved more difficult, probably because the students did not know exactly what to categorise.

3.7. Conclusion

Ten questionnaires can hardly be considered a basis for confident conclusions. Nonetheless, this small-scale study suggests that a corpus-based exploratory approach, if only to complement other forms of teaching, may be a valuable addition to a course on Cultural Studies.

Having said this, there are still a host of problems that need to be addressed. First, there is the question of topic. Even if choosing a subject matter closer to students' worlds seems a valid alternative to the 'trodden paths' of traditional Cultural Studies, it may be objected that Emo culture is not peculiar to the Anglophone world, which is supposed to be the main focus of English and American Studies. (This, of course, also applies to other philologies and their respective 'target' cultures.) Second, the choice of texts and text-types to include in a corpus for students to work with will always be a challenge, though I am positive that it can, with due care, be accomplished. Third, we must decide how corpus work should be pedagogically integrated into the structure of the course. Possibly the best solution would be to have students explore the corpus on their own outside class, with assignments to be done and handed in by the end of term. Guidance and support must be offered, whether by the teacher or by a special tutor. Programmes involving compulsory courses in corpus analysis would of course be welcome, because the intensive phase of introducing corpus analysis and its tools could then be 'outsourced'.

There is still a lot of work to be done. But I hope to integrate a corpus analytic strand into my Cultural Studies course – even if just for a testing phase – in the near future. And I am optimistic that my students will benefit from it.

Notes

[1] In the sense of following one's own associative thinking, rather than pre-patterned thinking based on instruction.
[2] There is currently a conservative backlash in Cultural Studies, and 'facts and figures' courses are making their comeback in some institutions – not least my own.
[3] It is impossible to clearly distinguish between these genres, since blogs and articles contain an interactive element with comments being added, and threads in forums usually start with some lengthy statement. This also applies to the distinction between song lyrics and poems.
[4] We are probably more justified in using this corpus in teaching/learning than in research, even though it was initially compiled for research purposes.
[5] All quotes from student responses are verbatim, and include mistakes.

References

Aston, G., Bernardini, S. and Stewart, D. (eds) (2004), *Corpora and Language Learners*. Amsterdam and Philadelphia: John Benjamins.
Baker, P. (2006), *Using Corpora in Discourse Analysis*. London: Continuum.

Burnard, L. and McEnery, T. (eds) (2000), *Rethinking Language Pedagogy from a Corpus Perspective*. Frankfurt am Main: Peter Lang.

Eppler, E., Crawshaw, R. and Clapham, C. (2000), 'The Interculture Project corpus: data classification, access and the development of intercultural competence', in L. Burnard and T. McEnery (eds), pp. 155–164.

Hall, S. (ed.) (1997), *Representation: Cultural Representations and Signifying Practices*. London: Sage.

Hidalgo, E., Quereda, L. and Santana, J. (eds) (2007), *Corpora in the Foreign Language Classroom*. Amsterdam and New York: Rodopi.

Kelley, T. and Leslie, S. (2007), *Everybody Hurts – an essential guide to Emo culture*. New York: HarperCollins.

Kettemann, B. and Marko, G. (eds) (2002), *Teaching and Learning by Doing Corpus Analysis*. Amsterdam and New York: Rodopi.

Kettemann, B. and Marko, G. (in press, 2011), 'Data-driving critical discourse analysis. Learning about language and ideology by autonomously exploring a corpus of creationist literature.' In N. Kübler, (ed.) *Language Corpora, Teaching, and Resources: From Theory to Practice*. Bern: Peter Lang.

Minugh, D. (2007), 'George Bush and the Last Crusade or the fight for truth, justice and the American way', in E. Hidalgo et al. (eds), pp. 191–205.

Mukherjee, J. (2002), *Korpuslinguistik und Englischunterricht. Eine Einführung*. Frankfurt am Main: Peter Lang.

Scott, M. (2004), *WordSmith Tools 4*. Oxford: Oxford University Press.

Scott, M. (2006), *The Bergen Corpus of London Teenage Language* (n.d.). University of Bergen. [Online]. *http://torvald.aksis.uib.no/colt/* (accessed May 28, 2008).

Tribble, C. (1997), 'Improvising corpora for ELT: quick-and-dirty ways of developing corpora for language teaching', in B. Lewandowska-Tomaszczyk and P.J. Melia (eds.), *PALC '97 Practical Applications in Language Corpora*. Łodz: Łodz University Press, pp. 106–117.

Appendix: The questionnaire

Stage 1: Verbs following first person *I*

Question 1.1: Based on the results in the table, how would you describe Emos? What is important / central / decisive / . . . for them?

Question 1.2: Which youth cultures other than Emos do you know? In how far is Emo identity similar or different to other youth cultures?

Question 1.3: If you compare the class 'physical contact' to the class 'emotion', do you see any connection between these two? Are there some elements in one class that contradict elements in the other class?

Question 1.4: Is there anything in the list that surprises you? Which elements do not quite fit into the list (please explain why)? Which elements did you expect, but did not find in the list?

Stage 2: Keyword comparison between two teenage corpora

Question 2.1: Based on the results in the table (Table 3.1 in text), how would you describe Emos? In how far do your conclusions differ from those in question 1.1?

Question 2.2: Is there anything in the list that surprises you? Which elements do not quite fit into the list (please explain why)? Which elements did you expect, but did not find in the list?

Stage 3: List of content words

Question 3.1: Which content words in the table (Table 3.2) are closely connected to Emo lifestyle or can be argued to constitute this lifestyle?

Question 3.2: In contrast to question 3.1, which content words are not concerned with the lifestyle itself but are rather hints for the type of texts in the corpus? Which words refer to the medium (or the media) where Emos published the texts?

Question 3.3: Can you relate the way Emos communicate (i.e., which medium they use to communicate) with Emo lifestyle? In how far do your answers to questions 1 and 2 fit into this?

Stage 4: Concordances of *alone, lonely, on my own*

Question 4.1: Which words in the text excerpts above are not standard English? Explain what makes these words peculiar.

Question 4.2: In how far can you relate the peculiar syle (cf. your answer to question 4.1) to Emo's state of mind?

Question 4.3: Which elements do you find that indicate the age of the Emos who wrote the texts of the corpus?

Question 4.4: Which elements do you find that indicate the gender of the Emos who wrote the texts of the corpus?

Question 4.5: Based on your answers to questions 4.3 and 4.4, which element ('age' or 'gender') seems to be more important in the Emo corpus? Explain why this could be the case.

Question 4.6: Based on concordance 1, how would you describe Emo's relation to society?

Question 4.7: Based on concordance 1, how would you describe Emo's relation to like-minded, peers and/or people of the same age?

Question 4.8: Who are the Emo's addressees of antipathy in concordance 1 (i.e., who/what don't they like or who/what can they not relate to)? Who are the Emo's addressees of sympathy (i.e., who/what do they like or who/what can they relate to)?

Evaluation

Question 1. Which of the tasks (1–4) was easiest for you? Which did you like best? Why?

Question 2. Did you notice a change in how you answered the questions from Task 1 to Task 4? What kind of change?

Question 3. Did you learn anything about a culture or culture in general that was not touched upon in the course? If you did, did the form of presentation (i.e. the more practical approach using language data and the autonomy you have to come up with your own interpretations and conclusions) play a role in this?

Question 4. Do you think such an approach should be integrated into the British and American Cultural Studies Foundation Course or into any other Cultural Studies course? How and why?

Chapter 4

Working with corpora for translation teaching in a French-speaking setting

Natalie Kübler

Corpus use in translation teaching has established itself for some time now. Several types of corpora have been taken into account in this field, such as parallel (also called translation) corpora, comparable corpora, monolingual corpora, disposable corpora, specialised vs. 'general' corpora etc. Depending on the translation type – literary or pragmatic translation – corpus use can offer a variety of approaches to help learners with the act of translating. This chapter focuses on using corpora in teaching pragmatic translation in France.

4.1. Introduction

Studies on corpus use for translation, translation teaching and translation studies started during the nineties. Baker (1999) investigated translators' behaviour by studying parallel corpora in order to assess the distance between the language of translation (what she called translationese) and the language of native speaker texts. Around the same time, Aston (1999) outlined the uses of corpora in translation and translation teaching, and the first Corpus Use and Learning to Translate (CULT) conferences took place (first Bernardini and Zanettin 2000; then Zanettin et al. 2003; then Beeby et al. 2009). Much work has since been put into creating and enhancing corpora and corpus tools in order to study translation, and to showing how appropriate corpora can help translators find the information they need to translate.

Despite this interest in academic circles, professional translators are still not very keen on using corpora for translation. A survey carried out in 2005 by the European project MeLLANGE[1] (also reported in Bernardini 2006),

Table 4.1 Results from the MeLLANGE questionnaire

1. Do you collect domain specific texts?		6. What do you use to search the corpora you use?	
No	59.5%		
Yes	40.5%	Search facility in word processor	65.9%
		Concordancer	19.0%
		Other search tools (specify: Trados, Concordance in translation memory)	14.4%
		UNIX utilities	0.7%
2. How do you collect them?		7. If you do not use corpora, why?	
In electronic form	69.4%	Never heard about them	41.9%
On paper	30.6%		
3. How do you use them?		8. Would you be interested in a service which quickly provided domain- and language- specific corpora tailored to your needs?	
Search them with software	53.1%		
Read them	46.9%		
		Yes	78.6%
		No	21.4%
4. Do you use corpora in your translation practice?		9. Would you be interested in a tool for extracting terminology from a domain-specific corpus?	
No	60.2%		
Yes	39.8%		
		Yes	77.9%
		No	22.1%
5. If yes, do you use:		10. Would you be interested in learning more about the potential that corpora offer?	
Corpora of the target language?	26.1%		
Corpora of the source language?	23.1%		
Parallel corpora?	19.7%	Yes	82.4%
Domain specific corpora?	15.3%	No	17.6%
Comparable corpora?	13.6%		
General language corpora?	2.3%		

obtained 623 completed questionnaires, the majority returned by UK professional translators, but also by professionals in France, Italy and Germany. This survey showed that of the 40.5% who collected domain-specific-texts, most (69.4%) saved these in electronic form and used computer software (mainly word processing packages), to explore them. In contrast, 41.9% said they had never heard of corpora, even if they would be interested in learning more about them (see Table 4.1).

Why do so many professional translators not use corpora? First, not all training syllabuses include corpus use as a skill to be taught. And where it is included, students also learn to use other tools, such as translation memories and Google, which may seem easier to approach. Second, corpus resources are not equally available in all languages and domains, and although query tools have improved considerably over the last decade, they still require specific competences and may not seem user-friendly. Third, corpus skills are never mentioned in job advertisements on the translation market (Bowker 2004). Fourth, the impact of cultural studies seems to have reduced interest in linguistics in the translation community. All of these factors may negatively influence attitudes towards the use of corpora, not just of professional and trainee translators, but also of translator trainers. There is still limited use of corpora in pedagogic settings. As Frankenberg-Garcia (2010) notes as far as language teaching is concerned, insufficient attention is paid to training teachers to use corpora. This is true of translation teaching as well.

So how can we render the use of corpora more attractive? A great deal of work is being put into providing better tools for term extraction and corpus querying. We will concentrate here on the teaching situation, and ways in which trainee translators can be taught how to obtain relevant information from corpora.

Beeby et al. (2009) propose that the conjunction of corpora and translation in teaching can be seen from two perspectives:

- *Learning to use **corpora** to translate,* i.e. using corpora as tools and corpus linguistics as a method to find linguistic information useful in the translation process;
- *Learning to **translate** using corpora,* i.e. studying the process of translating using corpora, as in Castagnoli et al. (in press, 2011), who show how using a learner translator corpus in the classroom can lead to raising students' understanding of different translation strategies.

This paper illustrates how different types of corpora can be used from the first of these perspectives.

4.2. The activity of translation

We are concerned here with pragmatic specialised translation. Pragmatic translation, defined by Newmark (1988: 133) as a practice taking into account the *reader's or the readership's reception of the translation*, is the type of translation in which corpus use is at its best. A pragmatic *translator* should know that the source text may not be perfect, and that the most important thing to take into account is its communicative intent (Froeliger 2004).

This means that the translator must take the real world into account, and have a global general knowledge of the source and target cultures. Specialised translation will be viewed as the translation of texts written in languages for specific purposes (LSPs), not just as conventionally defined, such as science, medicine, or law, but also in the broader senses of general academic language or general business language. Pragmatically translating LSPs requires not only knowledge of the source and target cultures in general, but also knowledge of very specific areas. Even a very well-educated translator may not know the terminology, phraseology, or even grammar of a particular specialist domain. So what is the solution? Calling on the specialists for help? Becoming specialised in a specific domain? Experts often disagree about interpretations in their field, and for a translator to become specialised can be a frustrating experience, as they will never be as specialised as the true specialists. Using corpora can help the translator to acquire specialised knowledge in a subject area, to discover a specific domain and to find linguistic information which enables them to convey the intent of the source text.

The issues of intent, genre and register are central to the translation task, but common linguistic difficulties should not be put aside, or cultural gaps. Students must be trained to think 'bilingually', which means being able to understand the source text (meaning and intent) in the context of a specialised domain, and to formulate what they have understood in the target language. This means finding out about terminology, phraseology and more delicate questions such as semantic prosody. Training future translators means raising their linguistic awareness, both in the source and target language. They must be taught to avoid literal translations, distortions of meaning, use of the wrong register and so on. These are all areas where corpora can help, as one of the tools available in the translation process. As Bernardini (2006) notes, translation is in many ways an ideal field for corpus applications.

This paper focuses on specialised translation, trying to show in what ways corpus use is ideal in this case. Examples from practical situations in the translation classroom will show some advantages and drawbacks of corpus use for the translation process.

4.3. Corpus types and corpus tools

Depending on the type of task to be performed, different types of corpora may be called for. However, not all may be equally available. What seems the ideal tool for the translator is a parallel corpus, in which source texts are aligned with their translations in the target language. An appropriate parallel corpus can provide the terminology and phraseology necessary for the translation, as well as examples of alternative translation strategies. However, parallel corpora do not exist for many language pairs and domains, and to compile one requires specific competences and is very time-consuming. Comparable corpora, i.e. collections of texts dealing with the same subject in the source language and the target language, can help overcome problems of 'artificiality' in parallel corpora (Kübler 2003: 41) and can largely make up for the lack of them (Frankenberg-Garcia 2009). These are much easier to compile, even if the task of extracting bilingual terminology and phraseology from them is more complex.

Varantola (2003) calls small comparable corpora compiled from the Web *disposable corpora*. They may never be reused, but are nonetheless well-suited for a specific task. Such corpora are collections of texts in a specific subject area, which may belong to different genres. For example, a specialised corpus in physics can consist of papers from specialised journals, textbook materials and popular science articles. These can be backed up by reference monolingual corpora, such as the BNC for British English, the COCA for American English, or Kosmas for German, to provide information about more general linguistic features.

While all these types of corpora can be used in the translation classroom (and also by translation professionals), their limited availability represents one of the reasons why professional translators use them so little. English is well served as far as reference corpora are concerned. But French does not have a reference corpus like the BNC. The Frantext corpus, which contains 4000 texts from the end of the 16th century up to the 21st in arts, literature, sciences and technologies, is hardly a reference corpus for contemporary French. While currently being completed with more contemporary texts, it is not a balanced corpus, even if it contains 210 million running words, and at most may be useful to literary translators. Some newspaper-based tools are available: thus Glossanet[2] allows users to create and query their own online specialised corpora from French and Belgian newspapers; concordances are sent to the user by e-mail. *Les voisins de le Monde*[3] allows users to search ten years of *Le Monde* and find collocates for arguments which are governed by verbs, nouns, or adjectives, or predicates (i.e. different POS which govern argument collocates) as well as the distributional neighbours of arguments and predicates (i.e. arguments or predicates which share the same collocates).

When working in specialised translation with French as a target language, parallel or comparable specialised corpora are also necessary. All information concerning LSPs, such as terminology and different text types, has to be found in specialised corpora. However, it is not always easy to build a comparable French/English corpus in a specialised domain, as French documents belonging to the same genres as the English ones may be rare. For instance, scientific research articles are rarely written or translated into French, as most French scientists publish directly in English. Textbook materials and popular science articles in French are easier to find. So working with comparable corpora in these areas raises issues of how comparable the corpora really are. In technical domains, comparable French texts may be easier to find, but they are not always devoid of mistakes. There may also be confidentiality issues, such as proprietary information of a company. This is especially a problem for terminology and specialised phraseology.

Zanettin (2002) reported the advantages of compiling do-it-yourself corpora to translate specific documents. His hope that corpora would 'find their place in the translator workstation together with other corpus resources and computer-assisted tools' (2002: 8) does not yet seem to have been fulfilled, however. Bernardini (2006) called for work in three different areas: the role of corpus work for awareness-raising, the construction of translator-oriented (e-)learning material and the fact that corpus construction and corpus searching tools should be more user-friendly. But Aston and Kübler (2010) note that the situation has still not changed much. So part of translator education for corpus use must still deal with corpus creation and corpus query tools. Various tools can be used in the classroom, which are equally applicable in professional situations, such as *Wordsmith*[4], *AntConc*[5], *ParaConc*[6], *Xaira*[7]. Let us see how these issues can be faced in the classroom.

4.4. Translation tasks and basic exercises

Corpora can play different roles at different stages of the translation process: (a) during the documentation phase, in which translators look for initial information on content, terminology and phraseology in the source and target language; (b) during the translation phase, in which translators look for solutions to specific terminology and phraseology problems; (c) during the revision phase, in which they investigate other alternative strategies. Each of these phases can be seen as involving a series of tasks. For instance, the first phase requires:

- identifying the genre and register of the document to be translated;
- collecting a corpus;
- exploring the domain and understanding difficult or unknown concepts;
- acquiring useful information on linguistic points, particularly terminology and phraseology, in both source and target languages.

To perform these tasks, the translator or learner translator must have already acquired a number of concepts in linguistics, and have attained a certain level of linguistic awareness. This is one reason why corpus linguistics should form part of translator training curricula, as a precondition to using corpora in the translation process. Students must first understand what a corpus is, what types of corpora exist and what is in them. Frankenberg-Garcia (2010) proposes tasks to raise student awareness of these issues, such as understanding different corpora, formulating corpus queries and interpreting corpus output. These can all be adapted for translator training, and need not necessarily be linked to translation tasks as such.

4.4.1. Translation tasks

The two tasks which are described below have been carried out by French-speaking students at the University Paris Diderot in the frame of a Master's in specialised translation for several years. Therefore all the examples mentioned here come from real-life classroom situations. Students had access to the following corpora and tools:

- a one-million word corpus of *Le Monde*[8] (which represents one year) and a home-made concordancer using Perl regular expressions;
- the *Les Voisins de Le Monde* web interface to the ten-million-word *Le Monde* corpus;
- the English/French *Europarl*[9] corpus (Koehn 2005) with *ParaConc*;
- a series of English/French and DIY comparable corpora in Earth Science[8] and in digital camera technology, which have been compiled by students over the years, and queried either with the home-made online concordancer or with *AntConc*.

Task 1: Group translation of a research article in an imposed specific domain: Earth Science

First-year master's students are assigned specialised research articles in two or three sub-domains of Earth Science, such as volcanoes, the birth and evolution of mountains, plate tectonics, hydrology, ice, climatology and mud volcanoes. Each sub-domain and each article are assigned to a group of students. The articles are then divided into sections of about one thousand words, and each student is assigned one section. The aim of the project is to achieve a complete translation of the articles, with a consistent terminology for the sub-domain. The pedagogic objective is to lead students to discover the use of corpora in the process of translating a specialised text in a group translation context.

The task is divided into a series of subtasks, some of which also relate to other courses. These are:

– defining the genre;
– collecting a corpus;
– exploring the domain and understanding difficult or unknown concepts;
– acquiring bilingual information on domain-specific terminology and phraseology, and on the phraseology of scientific argumentation;
– conveying information appropriately in the target (native) language;
– working together to agree on terminology and phraseology;
– revising the translation.

Task 2: Individual translation of a specialised text in any domain

This is a year-long individual project, achieved by second-year master's students, and that deals with a larger text, usually about 5000 words. It must be in a specialised domain, but may be of any genre. The translation process is again divided into a series of sub-tasks.

4.4.2. Identifying genre and register

Understanding genre is vital to the translation process, because the same genre can present very different linguistic features according to the language. For example, the genre of user manuals uses a much more formal register in French than in English. In English, giving instructions is done using the second person (*you*), whereas French tends to use the infinitive or a third person form:

Example 1: extracts from a comparable EN/FR corpus on digital cameras

EN

You *must put these file back after the firmware update has been completed.*
Make *sure you put time aside to learn it properly.*
The SSFDCs are keyed, so **you** *can't insert them backwards.*
You *can adjust the brightness of the LCD at any time by holding down the DISP button.*

FR

Les utilisateurs expérimentés **peuvent** *contrôler et ajuster la sensibilité de l'appareil.*
*Nikon Capture permet d'***ajuster** *la taille de sortie.*
Mettre *le cordon série sur l ordinateur et* **brancher** *la fiche sur l appareil photo.*

As the translator's first task is to define the genre of the text to be translated, emphasis is placed on raising students' awareness of what genre is and
how to distinguish different genres. The main questions to be asked are:

– What is the speaker's purpose and topic?
– Who is the intended audience?

In answering these questions, the student should relate them to linguistic
and rhetorical features. Is it a didactic text, in which definitions and explanations are given? If it is a scientific article, then there will probably be few
definitions and explanations, as the author will take it for granted that the
reader already knows a lot about the subject. If it is a manual for a washing
machine, then the reader will not be presumed to know anything technical
about the field, and the translation should be kept as clear and simple as
possible. Genre and domain are also important from a terminological point
of view: a highly specialised scientific text will require a lot of research on
terminology, while an article in a newspaper may require less such work,
but more on other points, such as general and cultural knowledge. Once
the genre of the text has been determined, the internal characteristics of
the text can be studied. Simple exercises with corpora can give students
insights into these characteristics and lead them to understand more about
internal linguistic characteristics, which are associated with the genre, such
as the difference in addressing the reader in French and English user
manuals, or the use of *nous* for the author in French scientific articles,
where English tends to use the passive.

Take the word *hypothesis*, which is supposed to occur quite often in scientific articles. Even before collecting a comparable corpus for the specific domain, a general corpus can provide important information. The examples below come from the BYU BNC and the BYU COCA[10]. Asking students to search for the collocates of *hypothesis* in the fiction and the academic subcorpora of BNC and COCA very easily led them to see differences between the two genres. There are far more significant collocates for *hypothesis* in the academic subcorpus than in the fiction one (100 against 24 in COCA, 100 against 12 in BNC). In the fiction subcorpus of COCA, only one of these collocates is not a grammatical word, namely *test*. In the academic subcorpus, almost 50% of the top 24 significant collocates are non-grammatical words, as shown in Table 4.2.

Table 4.2 The 24 collocates of *hypothesis* in the fiction subcorpus of COCA, and the top 24 collocates in the academic subcorpus

	COCA fiction subcorpus 78,752,154 tokens		COCA academic subcorpus 79,292,295 tokens
	WORD		
1	N'T	1	SUPPORTED
2	YOUR	2	SUPPORT
3	YOU	3	THIS
4	HE	4	TESTING
5	MY	5	(
6	?	6	RESEARCH
7	I	7	NULL
8	"	8	FOLLOWING
9	IT	9	OUR
10	'S	10	FOR
11	A	11	HYPOTHESIS
12	AS	12	BE
13	WAS	13	THESE
14	,	14	SUPPORTS
15	IS	15	WITH
16	.	16	MAY
17	TEST	17	)
18	AND	18	PREDICTS
19	OF	19	IN
20	THAT	20	;
21	TO	21	WHEN
22	THE	22	FROM
23	:	23	:
24	IN	24	THE

The collocates for *hypothesis* in the two subcorpora show a number of differences in register. The academic subcorpus has no pronouns among the top collocates, whereas four pronouns are near the top of the list for the fiction corpus. The degree of formality also seems lower in fiction, attested by the presence of contracted forms. These simple results can then lead to a discussion of other linguistic differences.

4.4.3. Compiling a comparable specialised corpus

DIY corpora represent a useful documentation resource in specialised translation. Over the years, our students have compiled comparable corpora in a number of specialised domains (Kübler 2003), using the keywords found in the research article on which they are working. As mentioned above, for some domains, especially scientific ones, this poses problems insofar as there are very few research articles written in French. (A parallel corpus is also impossible, because research articles are almost never translated into French).[11] In such cases students are guided to look for PhDs,[12] didactic texts, and websites on popular science.

Students are made aware that their corpora may not be fully comparable, and that this can present drawbacks, particularly as far as terminology is concerned. Young French researchers in hard sciences read scientific literature in English but write their PhDs in French. Even though there has been a French scientific terminology for a long time, most new concepts are coined in English and then translated into French almost literally. As PhDs are not produced for publication, this terminology may not be fully reliable. Some didactic texts can be found on university websites, but most of the French texts that staff use in their university teaching are very difficult to get hold of. There is, on the other hand, plenty of popular science in French available on the web, but again this may not be a reliable source of terminology.

4.4.4. Learning more about the domain

In understanding the source text, not only are language problems at stake, but also cultural ones. In texts that deal with specialised subjects it is necessary to get acquainted with the domain. An expert in the domain can help the translator understand it, but it is not always possible to have an expert at hand, and here corpora can play an important role (see, for example, Maia 2003). In the Earth Science translation task described above, students are required to write definitions for a series of terms before they start to translate, in order to improve their understanding of the domain. They are then encouraged to search for definitions in their corpora, using linguistic markers to find these (Pearson 1998). In the examples below, the markers *is a* and *i.e.* in English, and *est un(e)* and *c'est-à-dire* in French, were used to find term definitions.

Example 2: results of corpus searches for definitions, using linguistic markers

is a
*Gelifluction **is a** thaw-related solifluction (Matsuoka, 2001) that is controlled by elasto-plastic soil deformation.*

est un
*Un bassin avant arc **est un** bassin océanique situé entre la subduction et la terre, au contraire d'une fosse océanique qui est le bassin provoqué par la subduction elle-même.*

i.e.
*an extrusive (**i.e.** mud-volcanic) rather than an intrusive (**i.e.** diapiric) mechanism builds up the mud domes . . .*

c'est-à-dire
*Les roches sédimentaires, **c'est-à-dire** ces roches qui proviennent de la transformation de sédiments comme les sables et les boues . . .*

4.4.5. Terminology and phraseology

The use of corpora to find term equivalents has been abundantly described in the literature (e.g. Bowker and Pearson 2002; Kübler 2003; L'Homme 2004; Maia 2003). While much current research is focused on the automatic retrieval of term equivalents (see Zweigenbaum et al. 2008, for example), there are as yet no available tools for this. So translators must learn how to query comparable corpora to locate term equivalents. This methodology is nowadays well-documented and can also be applied to look for phraseological equivalents. Showing students that one of the prepositional collocates for *hypothesis* is *with* led to an exercise aimed at raising their awareness of the different definitions of a collocation (two words with or without a grammatical relationship, which co-occur in a statistically significant manner), and of the existence of phraseological units that appear more often in academic than in fictional texts. Example 3 shows concordances from the BNC academic and fiction subcorpora. A simple gap-filling exercise, in which students have to fill in the blanks using the words in boldface, shows that there are a number of phraseological units associated with *hypothesis* (*help with, compatible with,* etc.), and that the *hypothesis + with* collocation reported by the tool does not necessarily imply a syntactic relationship between node and collocate, since, in the third-to-last example from the BNC academic subcorpus, *with* occurs in a different sentence from *hypothesis.*

Example 3: phraseological units associated with *hypothesis*

BNC academic subcorpus
*only that can NAEP not **help with** research hypothesis formation or,*
*evidence which was **inconsistent with** the working hypothesis*
*fasten onto those that **agree with** his hypothesis and overlook those*
*behaviour which is **inconsistent with** the hypothesis of budget.*
*This is **compatible with** the hypothesis* that prenatal nutrition affects
*Our results support this hypothesis. **Reactions with** carcinoembryonic*
*formation in these patients is also **consistent with** this hypothesis*
*proposed hypothesis that Mozart suffered **with** Tourette's syndrome.*

BNC fiction subcorpus
*it dishonesty; comparing facts **with** a **hypothesis**. However, even if*

The next step consists in finding equivalents for these phraseological units, using in this case the corpus in Earth Science. Looking for *hypothèse(s)* preceded by *avec* (as a translation of *with*) gives the following results, which provide insights as to French phraseological equivalents:

Example 4: *avec . . . hypothèse* in a hydrology corpus

*compatible **avec cette hypothèse** Chapitre III. Etude géochimique*
*en corrélation **avec cette hypothèse**. Ils permettent de mettre en*
*toluène est compatible **avec cette hypothèse**. Les thiols à courte*
***avec les Mammifères. Cette hypothèse** essaye d'expliquer*
*est en accord **avec une hypothèse** de réajustement tectonique du*
*en accord **avec cette hypothèse**. sur ce volcan est également en*
*accord **avec cette hypothèse** qui, si elle s'avère applicable*
*a été réalisée **avec une hypothèse** de calcul plus réaliste que*

Where equivalents are not found in specialised corpora, general corpora can often provide answers for specialised translations. The following example relates to the translation of *aggressively* in a computer science article entitled 'Index poisoning attacks in peer-to-peer file-sharing systems'. In his comment on translation problems, the student, who had not been able to compile an English/French comparable corpus in this domain because of the lack of research articles in French, noted that *aggressively* was used in two different contexts in the source text:

Example 5: extracts of *aggressively* in two different contexts in a computer science article

*the 'copyright industry' (including the music, film, television, gaming and book publishing industries) is **aggressively** attempting to curtail the unauthorised distribution of content in P2P file sharing systems*
*Attackers have discovered this vulnerability and are now **aggressively** index poisoning popular file-sharing systems.*

His translation hypothesis was to use *agressivement*. However, during the revision phase, this was felt to sound incorrect in French, so it was checked against *Le Monde*.

Example 6: *agressivement* in *Le Monde*

*Mussolini a rompu avec la ligne **agressivement** antibourgeoise des premiers faisceaux,*
*au milieu de cette foule **agressivement** banalisée, on trouve quelques*
*par la recherche d un son cru, **agressivement** dépouillé, son travail de producteur*
*à l'énoncé ce qu'il pourrait avoir d **agressivement** masochiste. N'empêche: même*

In this newspaper corpus, *agressivement* seems to modify adjectives rather than verbs. As its contexts differ substantially from those of *aggressively* in the source text, there is no support for *agressivement* being an appropriate translation. Looking for *aggressively* in the *Europarl* parallel corpus, the interesting equivalent *de manière offensive* was noted, which comes from the domain of war. *Offensif* collocates with *missile, armée, guerre, stratégie* and appears in many metaphors. *Les voisins de Le Monde* gave the following results:

Example 7: neighbours of *agressivement* in *Les voisins de le Monde*

*conforme autoritaire xénophobe **virulent** radical irresponsable brutal inacceptable spontané opposer neutre efficace cibler intelligent muscler inadmissible arbitraire* *contraire généreux provocateur souple violent concerter semblable volontariste préventif juger unilatéral pervers provocant dangereux digne contradictoire inhabituel consensuel énergique défensif civiliser confus ferme similaire scandaleux courageux mesurer prudent identique répressif archaïque transparent paradoxal habile maladroit cohérent suicidaire* **offensif** *discriminatoire polémique destructeur menaçant injuste pragmatique délibérer rationnel coordonner guerrier nuancer inhumain indigne répréhensible conciliant revendicatif*

Among these neighbours, two have a very close meaning to *agressif*, namely *offensif* (already noticed in the *Europarl* corpus) and *virulent*. Looking for their collocates in *Les Voisins de le Monde* showed that the first is used in war metaphors, the second in other metaphors in the discourse. This finally led to the following French translations of the source text sentences containing *aggressively*:

Example 8a: text extract of *avec virulence*

*L'industrie du copyright (qui regroupe l'industrie du film et celle du jeu vidéo, les télévisions ainsi que les maisons d'édition musicales et littéraires) **les attaque avec virulence**.*

Example 8b: text extract of *de manière offensive*

*Les attaquants ont découvert cette faille et **s'en prennent de manière offensive** aux indexs des réseaux P2P les plus populaires afin de les empoisonner.*

The expression *avec virulence* can only be used with speech verbs, whereas *de manière offensive* is found with verbs describing a physical or virtual attack, but not those referring to discourse.

In formulating the target language text so that it is adapted to its culture, a general monolingual corpus is the student's best friend, as it helps them to find correct collocations, colligations, semantic preferences and prosodies.

4.4.6. Discovering the importance of semantic prosody in the translation process

Specialised texts in scientific domains are usually thought to have very limited semantic prosodies. It is commonly held that connotations, be they positive or negative, should be banned from scientific articles, which should be purely factual. Semantic prosody is however an important feature of scientific writing, which is linked to evaluation. Students often do not realise the importance of semantic prosody in their own language, and this leads them to awkward translations. Stubbs (2001) describes the English verb *cause* as having a negative semantic prosody: the things that are caused are generally undesirable. This is also the case of the French *causer*. In the ten-million-word *Le Monde* corpus, nearly all of the objects of forms of *causer* have negative connotations:

Example 9: direct objects of the verb *causer* in French

dommage irréversible dégât irréparable dommage irréparable dégats tracas important dégât frayeur dégât matériel dégât tort ravage dommage désagrément préjudice traumatisme gêne émoi perturbation déception ennui embarras lésion remous trouble embouteillage désastre nuisance chagrin souffrance malheur déboire souci blessure perte infection trou choc désordre décès mort pollution plaie sorbonne destruction inondation scandale douleur émotion mal ruine incendie fracture acci- dent cancer pénurie université surprise chute inquiétude disparition bruit maladie catastrophe préoccupation maximum danger malaise peur retard commune drame problème difficulté tension victime effet risque crise million

In scientific English, on the other hand, *to cause* does not always have a negative semantic prosody. This is probably the reason why more and more cases of *causer* in scientific French have unconnotated objects, which at times seems awkward:

Example 10: *causer* followed by unconnotated objects

migration de joints de grains,? **causant** *une évolution progressive (*better: *générant) partie distale peut?* **causer** *la superposition de différents régimes (*better: *provoquant)*
surface du sédiment. Le flux? **causé** *par l'action des marées a été (*better: *engendré)*

Pinpointing the differences between the general and the specialised cor- pus helps students become aware of the problem, and avoid using *causer* as the translation equivalent of those English verbs of causation that do not have a negative semantic prosody.

4.5. Conclusions

I hope to have shown how available and do-it-yourself corpora can be used in specialised translation training for all phases of the translation process. The examples illustrate the need to raise students' awareness in using corpora, rather than merely looking for translation equivalents. A complete translator education cannot avoid linguistic concepts. This can be done simultaneously with discussion of how to find translation equivalents, which is made much easier by using corpora. If corpus use is to become more popular among professional translators, it is essential not only to provide them with appropriate user-friendly, integrated tools, but also to teach them the rudiments of corpus linguistics as part of their training. In the future it should be an obligatory part of all translation schools' curricula. Choosing very recent scientific articles in which students have almost no prior knowledge helps them grasp very quickly how useful corpora are and how important linguistic analysis is. This choice allows translation students to appropriate the tools and methods corpora and corpus linguistics provide. They can then apply those to any domain and genre of text.

Notes

[1] *MeLLANGE Corpora and e-Learning Questionnaire. Results Summary* (Internal Report, 20.06.05). The report is available at http://mellange.eila.univ-paris-diderot.fr.

[2] Glossanet is available at http://cental.fltr.ucl.ac.be/projects/glossanet/.

[3] *Les Voisins de le Monde* is available at http://www.irit.fr:8080/voisinsdelemonde/.

[4] See Scott (2004) for details of *WordSmith Tools*.

[5] *AntConc3.2.1* is freely available at http://www.antlab.sci.waseda.ac.jp/software.html.

[6] *ParaConc* is available online at http://www.paraconc.com/.

[7] *Xaira 1.25* is freely available at http://sourceforge.net/projects/xaira.

[8] The specialised Earth Science corpora and the small *Le Monde* corpus are available at http://wall.eila.univ-paris-diderot.fr.

[9] The *Europarl* (European Parliament) parallel corpus is freely available at http://www.statmt.org/europarl.

[10] The BYU, devised by Mark Davies, is an interface for the BNC and COCA, freely available at http://corpus.byu.edu/.

[11] Some students also have to compile comparable corpora for Spanish, where they are confronted with similar issues.

[12] In France it is compulsory to write PhDs in French, and they are increasingly available on the Web.

References

Aston, G. (1999), 'Corpus use and learning to translate'. *Textus*, 12, 289–313.

Aston, G. and Kübler, N. (2010), 'Corpora in translator training', in M. McCarthy and A. O'Keeffe (eds) *Routledge Handbook of Corpus Linguistics*. London: Routledge, pp. 501–515.

Baker, M. (1999), 'The role of corpora in investigating the linguistic behaviour of professional translators'. *International Journal of Corpus Linguistics*, 4, (2), 281–298.

Beeby, A., Rodríguez, P. & Sánchez-Gijón, P. (eds) (2009), *Corpus Use and Learning to Translate (CULT): An Introduction*. Amsterdam and Philadelphia: John Benjamins.

Bernardini, S. (2006), 'Corpora for translator education and translation practice: achievements and challenges'. *Proceedings of the L4Trans Workshop at LREC 2006*. [Online] http://www.sdjt.si/bib/lrec06/, pp. 17–22. (accessed November 4, 2009).

Bernardini, S. and Zanettin, F. (eds) (2000), *I corpora nella didattica della traduzione/ Corpus Use and Learning to Translate*. Bologna: Cooperativa Libraria Universitaria Editrice.

Bowker, L. (2004), *Computer-aided Translation Technology*. Ottawa: University of Ottawa Press.

Bowker, L. and Pearson, J. (2002), *Working with Specialised Language: a Guide to Using Corpora*. London: Routledge.

Castagnoli, S., Ciobanu, D., Kunz, K., Volanschi, A. and Kübler, N. (in press, 2011), 'Designing a learner translator corpus for training purposes', in N. Kübler (ed). *Language Corpora, Teaching, and Resources: From Theory to Practice*. Bern: Peter Lang.

Frankenberg-Garcia, A. (2009), 'Compiling and using a parallel corpus for research in translation'. *International Journal of Translation*, XXI, (1), 57–71.

Frankenberg-Garcia, A. (2010), 'Raising teachers' awareness of corpora', *Language Teaching*, doi: 10.1017/S0261444810000480, published online by Cambridge University Press.

Froeliger, N. (2004), 'Felix culpa: congruence et neutralité dans la traduction des textes de réalité'. *Méta, journal des traducteurs*, 49, (2), 236–246.

Koehn, P. (2005), '*Europarl*: a parallel corpus for statistical machine translation'. Paper presented at the *10th Machine Translation Summit Conference*. Phuket, Thailand, 12–16 September 2005.

Kübler, N. (2003), 'Corpora and LSP translation', in F. Zanettin, S. Bernardini and D. Stewart (eds), pp. 25–42.

L'Homme, M.C. (2004), *La Terminologie: Principes et Techniques*. Montréal: Les Presses de l'Université de Montréal.

Maia, B. (2003), 'Training translators in terminology and information retrieval using comparable and parallel corpora', in F. Zanettin, S. Bernardini and D. Stewart (eds), pp. 43–54.

Newmark, P. (1988), 'Pragmatic translation and literalism', *TTR: Traduction, Terminologie, Rédaction*, 1/2: 133–145.

Pearson, J. (1998), *Terms in Context*. Amsterdam and Philadelpha: John Benjamins.

Scott, M. (2004), *WordSmith Tools 4.0*. Oxford: Oxford University Press.

Stubbs, M. (2001), *Words and Phrases. Corpus Studies of Lexical Semantics*. Oxford: Blackwell.

Varantola, K. (2003), 'Translators and disposable corpora', in F. Zanettin, S. Bernardini and D. Stewart (eds), pp. 55–70.

Zanettin F. (2002), 'DIY corpora: the www and the translator', in B. Maia, J. Haller and M. Ulrych (eds) *Training the Language Services Provider for the New Millennium*. Porto: Faculdade de Letras, Universidade do Porto, pp. 239–248.

Zanettin, F., Bernardini, S. and Stewart, D. (eds) (2003), *Corpora in Translator Education*. Manchester: St. Jerome.

Zweigenbaum, P., Gaussier, E. and Fung, P. (eds) (2008), *Proceedings of the LREC 2008 Workshop on Comparable Corpora*. Marrakech, Morocco, 31 May 2008.

Chapter 5

IFAConc – a pedagogic tool for online concordancing with EFL / EAP learners

Przemysław Kaszubski

IFAConc (http://ifa.amu.edu.pl/~ifaconc) is a prototype of an online concordancing environment helping students of the School of English (Instytut Filologii Angielskiej, IFA) at the Adam Mickiewicz University (AMU), Poznań, to explore, gather, annotate, discuss and share facts of usage pertaining to their language needs as academic writers. This chapter introduces the tool and its philosophy of concordancing as a 'top-down' experience, and discusses some early attempts at systematic in-course application.

5.1. Introduction

Concordancing remains largely a bottom-up, word-based activity, whereas, as recently underlined by Coxhead (2008) and Hyland and Tse (2007), a wordlist perspective is rather unhelpful in EAP teaching, as it subordinates meaning and variation in use. What deserve more attention are patterns of co-textual co-selection, which tend to discriminate between genres and domains and thus capture the fundamental interface between General and Specific Academic Purposes.

Direct exploration of corpora with and by learners remains a largely unresolved territory, however, with DDL practitioners recently pointing out the unfulfilled promise of the 'cut-out-the-middleman' approach (e.g. Aston 2004). Despite its potential for raising language awareness and stimulating effective vocabulary learning (e.g. Horst and Cobb 2001), DDL's systematic application and testing has often been marred by technical and practical limitations. One of the most difficult to surmount is time. For one thing, the number of patterns that merit exploitation is potentially vast, putting pressure on material preselection and operational efficiency. Secondly, successful concordance reading and analysis require pre-training, which does not work instantaneously. Finally, even if trained, users may occasionally face tasks that take a prohibitively long time to complete (Kaszubski 2006a). Indeed, many users are put off by the prospect of having to conduct what they perceive to be needlessly complex investigations in order to attain the language insights that interest them (Horst and Cobb 2001).

There arises a strong need to develop tools and solutions that can meet these challenges and aid the practical application of pedagogic concordancing, in both teaching and self-study modes, and facilitate their wider implementation and methodological testing. A good pedagogic concordancer will, in my view, be a tool capable of combining the stimulation of long-term language awareness and metalinguistic knowledge with the making and accumulation of instantly rewarding linguistic insights (many of which are attainable only by looking at corpus data). Accordingly, my long-term goal has been to create a DDL tool that will integrate readily with the content and methodology of my EAP writing classes, be usable both by me and my students, and be reasonably powerful, relevant, friendly, motivating, customisable and freely available. In Kaszubski (2006b), I identified several features of a pedagogic concordancer which, I argued, would suit the needs of EAP writing instruction. Among these features were online access, easy adjustment of vital search parameters (e.g. selection and deselection of corpora), the presence of a guided or 'default route' to facilitate the intake of necessary technical and linguistic knowledge, and compatibility with constructivist trends in CALL. The IFA Concordancer (IFAConc) project (http://ifa.amu.edu. pl/~ifaconc) is an attempt to create and test an environment meeting these requirements. While far from complete, it has proved adaptable for regular in-course application, as I illustrate in the last part of this paper. It should be emphasised that IFAConc is in continuous use while this chapter is being written, and that its features, interfaces, corpus resources and models of application are still evolving.

5.2. IFAConc: an overview

Over the two years of its use, IFAConc has changed from a corpus search engine supporting hyperlinkability into a mini-portal for making, recording, monitoring, guiding and communicating language discoveries for, with and by EAP learners. Three different interfaces have emerged, serving two categories of user – Student and Teacher/Admin:

- the Corpora Search interface – the core module enabling searches over a range of corpora (centrally administered, but also, if the user so wishes, personal text collections);
- History – a searchable record of past work, annotated and optionally tagged at will, containing personal searches as well as 'Shared' entries added by the Teacher/Admin for students to explore, learn from, etc.; the Teacher/Admin's History also serves as a panel for monitoring and guiding users' activities;
- Resources – a special site containing tutorials and recommended content and tasks, with annotated hyperlinks to specific Corpora searches and/or History searches.

In the sections below I discuss the inspirations, roughly divided into pedagogic and theoretical, that have shaped these interfaces and their functions so far.

5.2.1. Pedagogic inspirations

The IFAConc platform attempts to advance several practical solutions and proposals involving concordancing that have appeared in the literature and to adapt them to the needs of academic learner writers.

EGAP-ESAP corpus comparisons: corpora search

As mentioned, the world of EAP is divided over the issue of specialisation, with some practitioners arguing for the primacy of certain generically academic (as opposed to non-academic) features of language and text, while others emphasise the immediate need to immerse in the discourse of concrete, living disciplines (Hyland 2006: 9–15). EAP is traditionally conceptualised as a type of ESP, and Aston (1998) perhaps first demonstrated how accessing properly stratified collections of texts, less and more specific, enables teachers and students to discern and mutually relate general and specialised aspects of language use. Taking advantage of this position, the IFAConc Corpora Search module enables users to probe and compare general vs. specific layers of usage by offering a range of corpora that sample academic, quasi-academic and 'pre-academic' (general) domains, as relevant to the syllabus and disciplinary organisation of the Poznań School of English.[1] A single search interface (see Figure 5.1) – accepting some group-level tweaking – is offered to both EGAP-level students

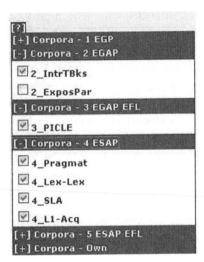

Figure 5.1 The IFAConc corpora selection interface (IntrTBks = introductory textbooks; ExposPar = expository paragraphs from writing textbooks; for PICLE, see Note 1)

(1st- and 2nd-year undergraduates) and ESAP-level students (3rd-year undergraduates, 1st-year graduate students). The benefit is that: (1) EGAP students are given a chance to become acculturated to the linguistic aspects of disciplinary diversity; (2) ESAP students, in turn, can study possibly specialist disciplinary patterns also in the context of the general academic and 'pre-academic' domains.

IFAConc also makes it possible to share particular corpora with specific user groups. The spectrum of text types available for comparison can be broadened by adding personal corpora.

Each corpus is structured as a simple XML file, as specified in Resources tutorials (see Figure 5.2). For enhanced compatibility, sentence and paragraph breaks must be tagged. Thanks to the efforts of MA students, most ESAP corpora have also been marked up with other important textual features: footnotes, section headings, extended quotations, etc. These, as well as POS tagging, are supported by the so-called Enriched corpus search mode,[2] discussed later in this paper.

The potential of diverse cross-corpus comparisons, while not yet fully exploited and optimised, is one of IFAConc's assets, encouraging individualised paths towards communicative and pragmatic competence.

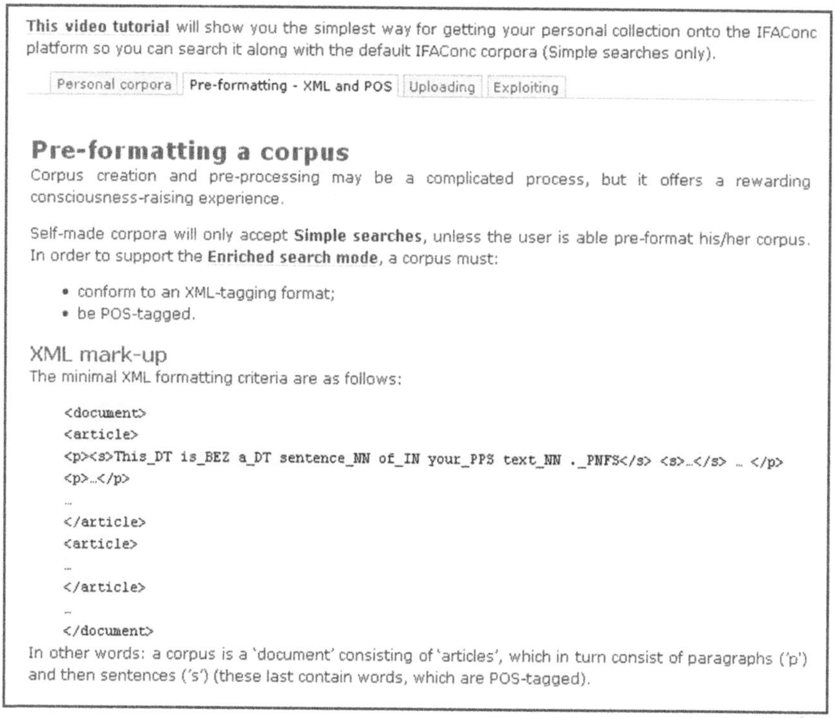

This **video tutorial** will show you the simplest way for getting your personal collection onto the IFAConc platform so you can search it along with the default IFAConc corpora (Simple searches only).

| Personal corpora | **Pre-formatting - XML and POS** | Uploading | Exploiting |

Pre-formatting a corpus

Corpus creation and pre-processing may be a complicated process, but it offers a rewarding consciousness-raising experience.

Self-made corpora will only accept **Simple searches**, unless the user is able pre-format his/her corpus. In order to support the **Enriched search mode**, a corpus must:

- conform to an XML-tagging format;
- be POS-tagged.

XML mark-up

The minimal XML formatting criteria are as follows:

```
<document>
<article>
<p><s>This_DT is_BEZ a_DT sentence_NN of_IN your_PP$ text_NN ._PNFS</s> <s>..</s> ... </p>
<p>..</p>

...

</article>
<article>

..

</article>

..

</document>
```

In other words: a corpus is a 'document' consisting of 'articles', which in turn consist of paragraphs ('p') and then sentences ('s') (these last contain words, which are POS-tagged).

FIGURE 5.2   Basic XML structure of IFAConc corpora files explained on a Resources page

Beyond the Kibbitzers: History and resources

Tim Johns' pioneering work is well known. Particularly vital for the teaching and learning of academic writing via the DDL method are his Kibbitzer pages (Johns 2000), which document discoveries made during one-to-one consultations with international EAP students. Although they offer a great source of contextualised knowledge, the weak point of the concordances provided is that they are static and therefore unable to engage students directly in active exploration. IFAConc, being a web-based search tool, overcomes this limitation by allowing the illustration of commentaries with web links that reproduce not only a pertinent concordance but also an interface to manipulate it. One way of achieving this is through so-called Shared History entries (see Figure 5.3).

History, the second of IFAConc's interfaces, provides users with access to all their past searches, as well as to annotated, recommended Shared

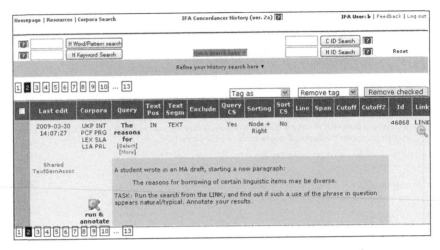

FIGURE 5.3   An example of a 'Shared' entry containing an ESAP task

entries. Figure 5.3 gives a student's view of a simple Shared entry featuring:

- in the first row, a summary of the major parameters of the search (the corpora, the query pattern, etc.);
- hyperlinks for generating/restoring the relevant concordance;
- annotation containing (in this case) a student example prompt and a task instruction.

In order to perform the task, a student must click on the LINK (or on the 'run and annotate' icon), which opens the Corpora Search window with all the standard controls and parameters for re-sorting, adjusting, etc., as required (see Figure 5.4).

The Teacher/Admin's History view comprises an additional annotation field, where notes, answer keys etc. can be kept (see Figure 5.5).

At the moment of writing, there are over 200 clickable Shared History entries (and close to 1,000 more candidates for this status). These are assigned to different categories (marked either with keywords in the Administrator's annotation panel or with special experimental tags). While the full taxonomy is still being developed, some stable categories are:

- 'Finding': entries that contain ready-made insights for students to read about and see concordance illustrations of;
- 'Task': entries that prompt students to run a corpora search, make directed observations and record them in annotations;

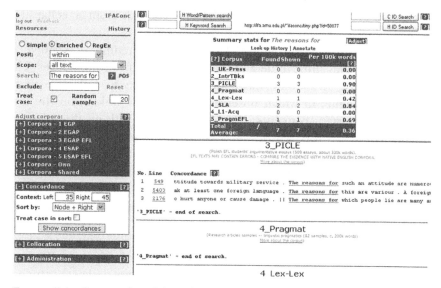

FIGURE 5.4   Corpora Search interface showing the concordance, its basic statistics and the search navigation and query controls

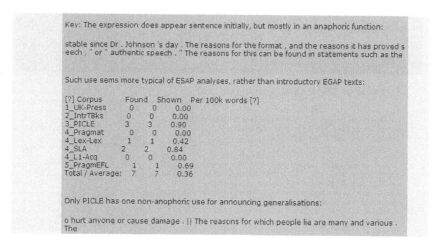

FIGURE 5.5   Teacher/Admin annotation for the History entry shown in Figure 5.3

- 'Help' / 'Tutorial': entries that document cases which often cause difficulty to users, examples of erroneous search patterns and bugs etc;
- Personalised filters, e.g. 'My annotated' etc.;
- EGAP, ESAP, EFL etc.: labels specifying the registers concerned in the annotated entry (level of specialisation-generality; quantitative or qualitative disparity between native and non-native corpus evidence, etc.)

Several of the categories are searchable on-click from a collapsible 'Quick Search Links' panel (see Figure 5.3 above).

Despite its many advantages, History was sometimes described as 'messy', and thus unfit to be a 'default route' for an ordinary user. The third interface, Resources, was conceived in order to provide a more orderly catalogue, in which observations would be linked, on the one hand, to important concepts in the EAP syllabus and, on the other, to (categorised) History entries and/or corpora searches. The special Textbook section of Resources is still sketchy and not yet in regular use, but efforts are being made to systematise it and equip its descriptions with information derived from cited sources and publications, in order to encourage empirical verification of these on the IFAConc platform. Figure 5.6 shows a trial page.

It is hoped that once the Resources Textbook is filled with appropriate content, and as the Shared History database grows in size, the IFAConc site will match in quality, and surpass in terms of scope and active student participation, Johns' original Kibbitzer platform.

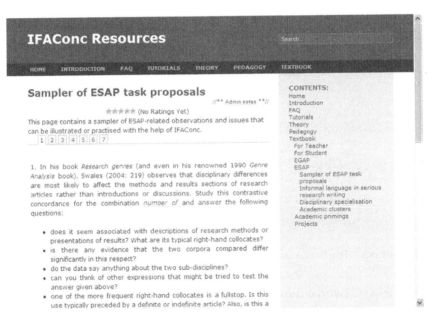

FIGURE 5.6 A Resources Textbook page citing a source and prompting searches on the IFAConc platform

Concordancing and learner writers

Tom Cobb's work has been highly influential in: (1) showing how concordances can beat dictionaries as sources of reference; (2) pointing out that, while difficult to use, concordances enforce deeper-level processing promoting learning; and (3) demonstrating that precast web-links to specific KWiC displays can be applied as corrective feedback for learner writers (Gaskell and Cobb 2004). From a student-researcher's point of view, however, the concordance links used in Cobb's studies are again rather static in nature, and focused mainly on simpler patterns and on generic discourse. They may thus not appear challenging or diversified enough to an academic learner writer.

IFAConc, as already shown, enables comparisons of different registers, stimulating observations that go beyond general grammaticality judgements. It also features a search syntax (inspired by the online *Cobuild Sampler*) offering a wide range of linguistic look-ups (see Figure 5.7).

Semantic information, highly desirable in 'top-down' searching, is not available; however, it is possible to look for grouped patterns with the help of the pipeline separator ('|'), which may provide a substitute for meaning-oriented

---

Quick help on search patterns

(Click + to insert example into your Search)

More Help for IFA users

Simple and Enriched search:

create - specific word-form +
create@ - all the forms of one headword ('lemma') +
like! - word family +
like to - continuous phrase +
in+3of - discontinuous collocation +
what _ _ important - collocation frame +
decide@|choose@ - alternatives (e.g. two lemmas) +
of+3type@|of+3kind@ - complex alternatives +

Enriched search only:

care/NN - word of a class (e.g. *care* as noun) +
VBZ - word-class / part-of-speech (POS) +
VB* - part-of-speech (POS) wildcard +
JJ*+3NN* - discontinuous gram. combination ('colligation') +
in _ NN of - lexicogrammatical frame +

FIGURE 5.7 IFAConc Corpora Search options (Help pop-up window)

■	Last edit	Corpora	Query	Text Pos	Text Segm	Exclude	Query CS	Sorting	Sort CS	Line	Span	Cutoff	Cutoff2	Id	Link
	2009-05-03 15:50:49	POP UKP INT PCF PRG LEX SLA L1A	**WP+6look@ like|WRB+6look@ like** [Select] [More]	IN	TEXT		No	Node + Left	No					48934	LINK 🔍
	Collocat Feedback Shared 🗟 **run & annotate**		Some students would write or say things like: ... how it looked like. TASK: Run this search to determine if such use is typical of native user English. Annotate your result for future reference.												

FIGURE 5.8   A Shared History entry documenting a search for alternatives

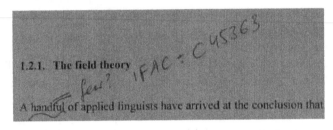

FIGURE 5.9   IFAConc Corpora Search ID pointer used as feedback

inquiries. For example, searches such as that in Figure 5.8 can prompt (especially weaker) learners to compare synonyms or other alternatives (e.g. error vs. non-error options).

Also implemented for some XML-tagged corpora are text – positionally anchored searches inspired by lexical priming theory (Hoey 2005).

It should be reiterated that both Corpora searches and History searches make unique web addresses, and that both can be used as feedback prompts to guide the learner towards concordance-based evidence. As all searches carry unique ID numbers, these can be used when corrections are entered by hand rather than entered electronically (see Figure 5.9).

Entering the concordance search number 45363 into an appropriate C-ID form (available from any IFAConc interface) reveals that *a handful* is associated with near-negation, as in *but a handful, only a handful* or *more than a handful.*

5.2.2. Theoretical inspirations

The second group of influences that IFAConc seeks to implement are some recent insights and frameworks from linguistics, applied linguistics and CALL.

Lexical priming theory

Given its pedagogic orientation and the above-average linguistic awareness of our students, IFAConc comes with a recommended, corpus-friendly theory in mind. Perhaps the most complete and inclusive proposal today is that of Hoey (2005), who speaks of 'primings', or associative loadings, which words (or other linguistic units) take on from their repeated contexts and to which users become naturally exposed. According to Hoey, lexical primings include both local and textual associations: collocation, colligation, semantic association, pragmatic association, textual collocation, textual colligation and textual semantic association. Closer discussion of these concepts is beyond the scope of this paper; also, application of the whole theory is beyond IFAConc's current technological reach. Due to the small sizes of the corpora, a certain amount of reinterpretation is necessary (see Figure 5.10). Briefly, it is believed that IFAConc can help identify likely priming candidates for users interested in performing in the domains and genres represented in the corpora under study. Quantitative and qualitative comparisons between the various collections can help separate primings that are specialised rather than general in nature, or typical of learner language vs. native speaker language, etc. The recording of such findings is the essence of IFAConc use; decisions as to their learning and adoption into production may be left for students and teachers to negotiate.

Primings, patterns and their variability are also mentioned in the guidelines accompanying each pop-up annotation window (see Figure 5.11).

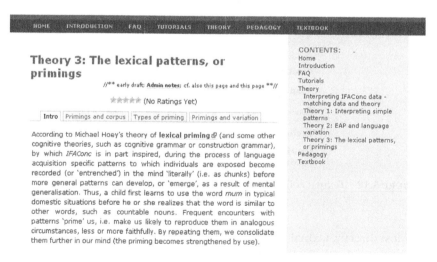

FIGURE 5.10   IFAConc Resources – Introduction to lexical priming

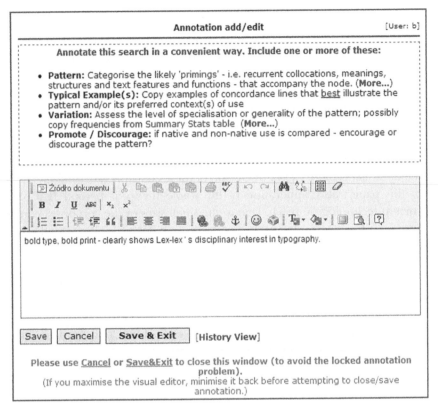

FIGURE 5.11   Annotation window with annotation guidelines

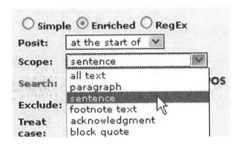

FIGURE 5.12   Textual colligation search in IFAConc

Most directly, textual colligation (the tendency for words and patterns to associate with certain textual positions), has been built into the 'Enriched' Corpora Search interface (see Figure 5.12):

```
                                    2_IntrTBks
                    (UK academic textbooks and introductory books (excerpts, c. 98,000)
                                    More about the corpus)

No.   Line  Concordance [?]
 1    595   onging to his hereditary factors . That is , each body cell contains two sets of chromo
 2    485   lity " as a political battle-cry . That is , I shall argue that when understood as a di
 3    627   ord-player , not a tape recorder . That is , if you introduce into a cell a protein mol
 4    31    red than on the previous evening . That is , in addition to the tendency to feel tired
 5    283   here is often some other problem . That is , it is sometimes found that when there is a
 6    246   mblers are not hugely successful . That is , they do not become millionaires and then s
 7    246   hey produce intermittent rewards . That is , when success occurs occasionally , not eve
 8    96    r the middle of our waking hours . That is not to say that sleep or being awake are the
 9    527   istinct value in freedom as such ? That is the challenge to traditional liberal belief
10    505   e of rational inquiry and action . That is why talk of presumptions in abstract philoso
'2_IntrTBks' - end of search.


                                    3_PICLE
                (Polish EFL students' argumentative essays (509 essays, about 330k words).
        EFL TEXTS MAY CONTAIN ERRORS - COMPARE THE EVIDENCE WITH NATIVE ENGLISH CORPORA.
                                    More about the corpus)

No.   Line  Concordance [?]
 1    121   ntirely for some reason or other . That is also why there is still a growing number of
 2    411   y to spend on animal experiments . That is only a short-term aim . The longer-term aim
 3    1797  can rely on themselves entirely . That is true and nobody is going to deny that women
 4    1708  things we are not able to do . || That is why , every sane man sees himself or herself
 5    169   can not deprive ourselves of it . That is why , many of us are interested in art , the
 6    844   eds much more someone to rely on . That is why a little girl looks for a friend to play
 7    1937  ing is with the computer monitor . That is why people who work with computers in office
 8    2267  er they get impatient or nervous . That is why smacking infants could even lead to more
 9    1028  market economy to Polish reality . That is why the stock exchange was established or Va
10    2330  rve good purposes as well as bed . That is why we do not tell our parents about failed
'3_PICLE' - end of search.
```

FIGURE 5.13   Native vs. non-native sentence openings beginning with *That is*

Used together with other search options, textual positioning offers an opportunity to identify patterns which are often metadiscoursal in nature and prone to characterise students' texts. A search with ID 28765 shows that when beginning a sentence with the combination *that is*, Polish users produce the resultative linking expression *That is why* in 50% of cases, while the more typical option among native English academics is the restating expression *That is*, followed by a comma (see Figure 5.13).

Authentication and personalisation of corpus data

Hunston (2002) has warned of the danger of corpus data becoming decontextualised; in order for excerpts of others' texts to be 'meaningful', the concordance user therefore needs to recontextualise and 'authenticate' them (Widdowson 2000). This may not be hard when teachers and specialists are around, but is nevertheless essential for optimising acquisition. In a similar vein, Gavioli (2005) shows the distinction and transition between 'samples' of data and (typical) 'examples' of use. In her earlier study with Aston (Gavioli and Aston 2001), the need to creatively adapt and adjust evidence from corpora to one's own productive needs is also pointed out.

One solution to the question of authentication may be the provision of rich, locally authenticated corpus annotations (e.g. Braun 2006). The IFAConc approach may adopt this method (future projects are planned for XML tagging of new information layers in corpora); however, given that corpus tagging is labour-intensive, other solutions have been sought:

- providing sample corpora of familiar (i.e. 'homely', Johns 1997) genres and registers, which offer more readily recontextualised input (e.g. EFL sub-parts of the EGAP and ESAP registers, i.e. students' essays and MA theses);
- allowing customised collections for comparison against the standard corpora – to encourage 'self-concordancing' (Coniam 2004) and a more personal response to concordance results;
- providing Shared History annotations and Resources pages containing contextualising commentaries;
- providing search annotation facilities which, whether used personally or collaboratively, stimulate interactive authentication (see below).

Constructivist learning

Constructivism has been variously defined in the educational literature (Cobb 2006). Two points that are vital for the IFAConc project are: (1) that knowledge, also linguistic knowledge, is constructed, rather than acquired or transferred as a whole, via participation in suitable activities, e.g. specially designed ('scaffolded') forms of expert tasks; (2) that collaborative efforts are conducive to knowledge construction ('social constructivism'). Indeed, as Tim Johns famously noted, students are often able to make more revealing observations than their teachers (Johns 1991: 5). Many IFA students' level of proficiency is high enough for them to make interesting contributions, whether based on the typical problems or errors illustrated in the Shared History or originating from independent searches, as in the annotation exchange on the word *cloud* exemplified in Figure 5.14.

At the moment, IFAConc's History and Search co-annotation offer a controlled form of constructivist scaffolding designed mainly for guidance and support. The solution has proved especially useful at early training stages and with less experienced users, although it is demanding on the teacher's time, and restrictive of student-student communication. One step being implemented is the addition of an open commenting system in selected Shared entries, to allow users to collaborate with each other as well as with the Teacher/Admin.

You've probably meant these:

The other approach towards hedges regards that the only association of them with obscurity and dimness may cloud other important function of hedging (Salager-Meyer 1993) .

but a priori assumptions based on the historical phonologist 's theoretical orientation can likewise cloud the judgement when the lack of any agreed method of representing the sounds of English at the time means that so much

I have to admit that it's a very inteesting finding.

Here this word used as a verb appears as completly different in the use and meaning.

The first example to me seems to be close in the meaning *bring*,

whereas the second one is rather closest to *blur*.

PmK: We are talking about the same pattern here cloud + {abstract noun, e.g. function, judgment} ; therefore, the meanings will not be so very different. See *obscurity* and *dimness* in the vicinity of *cloud*? I think you will easily see now which ONE meaning joins the two examples. AND if you look at the one example of *cloud* as noun , that meaning is also not much different.

Certainlly, now it is glimmering. The meaning is much different in them.

I didn't expect that this word will appear so diversive.

PmK: Not sure what you mean by "diversive" . If <u>this</u> , then my intention was somewhat opposite - to point out one major broad meaning similar to obscure or hide with which academics seem to tend to use this word.

Well, now I think I understand.

Indeed the cloud may obscure the view.

The cloud obscured the view from the top of the mountain.

PmK: In general descriptive langauge, yes. Let us remember that in this entry we have been dealing with uses such as *clouded issue* etc.

FIGURE 5.14   Excerpt from a student-teacher interaction about the word *cloud* in academic texts

Full success of a (social) constructivist venture depends partly on a community spirit, which can be stimulated via Internet technologies. IFAConc has been used and publicised through the School's e-learning platform (Moodle), as well as other technologies: a blog, a wiki and an RSS channel. These are not yet fully exploited avenues, but their use is likely to grow in future. The project is open to students' feedback and comments on the Resources site; students have also been involved in the compiling, preprocessing, tagging and pretesting of corpora.

5.3. Concordance monitoring and pilot tests

Last but not least, the IFAConc project extends earlier work in monitoring concordancing with a tool called the PICLE concordancer. In Kaszubski (2006a), I provided a short analysis of public and local search logs and summarised questionnaire responses from a group of seminar students who were revising linguistics BA papers with concordancing support. It was noted that users who returned to the system tended to submit complex queries for collocations and patterns rather than for single words, perhaps reflecting greater ability to notice, interpret and apply corpus information. However, the development of this ability could not be traced individually due to the limited character of the logs.

IFAConc's History interface now provides most of the facilities needed for effective user tracking, whether in order to inform annotation feedback or to assess users' level of involvement on tasks. Monitoring facilities are also extremely important for planning and optimising the tool's further development.

5.3.1. The ESAP pilot study

To date, IFAConc has been tested in several different EAP contexts involving EGAP and ESAP writing. It was first used for ESAP with two one-semester seminar groups in corpus linguistics and concordance reading (winter 2007/2008; initially fourteen students, two of whom dropped out). The students' higher-than-average familiarity with corpus technology made them an unrepresentative sample of ESAP writing respondents, but a suit-able team of testers at this launch stage. IFAConc was introduced towards the end of the course, in a 30-minute computer lab activity, after which two major tasks and an evaluation questionnaire were administered as three successive weekly home-assignments. Given that occasional technical problems may have affected the students' performance and opinions, the overall positive outcome was interpreted as promising.

In Task 1 the students worked with link-initiated searches provided from within the History interface. They had to locate annotated queries containing specified key words, read instructions in the annotations, activate the search links, manipulate the concordances as needed and annotate their work. Search patterns were varied, illustrating *inter alia* disciplinary variation and textual positioning (see Figure 5.15).

In Task 2 the students were requested to investigate two or three prob-lems of their own and to annotate them in accordance with the guidelines being constructed at the time (see Figure 5.11). Compared with the first task, more single-word searches were performed, although final annota-tions mostly focused on more complex (i.e. non-single-word) searches. In most cases (11 out of 12 students) the number of searches surpassed that from the link-driven Task 1. This, along with a high proportion of

User	Search Type	Conc Mode	Corpora	Query	Text Pos	Text Segm	Exclude	Id	Link	Query CS	Sorting	Sort CS	Left span	Right span	Line
przemka [Annotated]	Cont.		LEX	remarks [Select] [More]				10887	LINK						1250

fTask: This is an example of a research paper section heading. Which part of the paper does it signal? Is this a single instance, or rather a more widespread use in this and other corpora? What is the typical collocation in which this word is used in section titles? Does this collocation recur in other parts of texts? How would you classify/characterise the behaviour of this collocation, applying Michael Hoey's priming terms?

User	Search Type	Conc Mode	Corpora	Query	Text Pos	Text Segm	Exclude	Id	Link	Query CS	Sorting	Sort CS	Left span	Right span	Line
przemka [Annotated]	Coll.	S	POP INT PCF PRG LEX SL2 L1B	improve_ [Select] [More]				10495	LINK	No	By frequency				

fTask: What sort of improvement is typically described in lexicography as opposed to SLA?

fTask

User	Search Type	Conc Mode	Corpora	Query	Text Pos	Text Segm	Exclude	Id	Link	Query CS	Sorting	Sort CS	Left span	Right span	Line
przemka [Annotated]	Conc.	E	PCF PRG LEX SL2 L1B PRL	+2MD+1VBN [Select] [More]				10359	LINK	No	Node + Right	No	35	45	

fTask: This (non-lexical) pattern favours two different pronouns at its beginning. What are they? What kind of meaning or function is associated with these two versions - is it more or less the same meaning/function or not? Explore the patterns in question and leave your answers in annotations to the most informative (in your opinion) search history links.

fTask ESAP

FIGURE 5.15 ESAP pilot tasks administered as Shared entries through IFAConc History

Table 5.1 ESAP study: independent searches

Total searches	over 1,400 (c. 900 concordance searches; 450 wide-context views; 70 collocation views)
One-word searches	c. 400 (250 concordance searches; 110 wide-context views; 40 collocation searches)
Average searches per user	117
Standard deviation	112.4
Examples of annotated patterns	among|amongst; compile*; snow; when *ing|in *ing; all in all; be+VBN+1 (sentence initial); albeit; in case of|in the case of; we+VB; moreover

wide-context views (see Table 5.1) and the considerable length and depth of most annotations, testified to the intensity of the concordancing processes. There was, however, considerable individual variation (between 40 and over 500 searches per user), which appears to endorse earlier reports of DDL's evoking mixed responses from testees (e.g. Mauranen 2004).

In the Evaluation stage (in which ten students took part), ten closed (5-step Likert-scale) and two open-ended questions were given. IFAConc's overall functionality as an EAP tool was generally assessed as 'useful' on the scale *not useful – don't know – somewhat useful – useful – very useful*. More detailed questions included:

(3) How useful do you find the search options implemented in IFAConc?

(4) How useful did you find the link-driven tasks, that is, the IFAConc activities initiated from annotated links?

(9) Which did you find *easier* to do: pursuing your own investigations or completing the link-driven investigations?

(10) Which did you find more *fruitful*: pursuing your own investigations or completing the link-driven investigations?

For questions 3 and 4, a majority (6–7 votes) of the answers clustered in the 'useful' category, where they had been expected. For question 9, a bimodal pattern emerged, with four students in each of the 'perhaps' categories on the scale *definitely own – perhaps own – no major difference – perhaps link-driven – definitely link-driven*; (the distribution correlated with group assignment, possibly indicating that tutorials had not been equally successful in both groups). For question 10, five students appeared undecided, but four chose the 'perhaps link-driven' and the 'definitely link-driven' options, which I found an encouraging signal of the potential of this technique of encouraging DDL. Appreciation for the link-led discoveries was also reflected in students' open-ended responses.

It should also be noted that many annotations had to be moderated towards the pedagogically useful and away from the 'merely' descriptive. Most students in this pilot group had in fact approached IFAConc as a language research tool rather than as a language-learning aid, and this indicated the need for changes in the online tutorials. The overall benefit of IFAConc was often perceived in terms of discoursal, grammatical or disciplinary awareness being raised, rather than in terms of direct knowledge gains concerning particular language uses.

5.3.2. The EGAP pilot study

In the second pilot study the original plan was to offer a group of fifteen first-year BA-level writing students a series of activities that would gradually prepare them for the role of independent DDL EAP researchers. Following on from the ESAP study, link-driven concordancing had been intended as an integral component of the 'breaking-in' process. Unfortunately, the level of the students proved considerably lower than expected, forcing a refocus on more basic grammatical problems rather than on stylistic naturalness. Under these circumstances, the objective of the study became one of optimising link-driven feedback. The complexity of the links offered

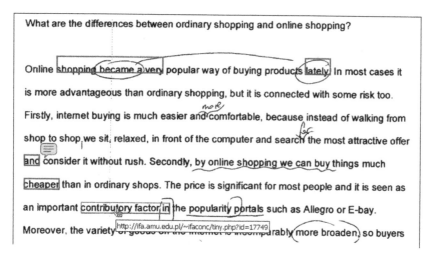

FIGURE 5.16 IFAConc link-supported marking of students' texts

Table 5.2 EGAP study: basic search statistics

Relevant Teacher/Admin searches	c. 3000
Number of links offered as feedback	450 (incl. 27 single-word searches)
Total student searches	931
Students' feedback-link-driven searches	272
Student self-initiated searches	655 (incl. 307 single word searches)

(single words, lemmatised searches, POS searches and the like) was not controlled in any way. As a result, a mini database of annotated searches accumulated in the Administrator's History, which, as Shared entries, later provided a range of authentic training examples for new users and courses. Reused feedback links have also provided valuable information as to local EAP language needs.[3]

From a few training examples through to personalised feedback, a combination of manual and link-based correction was gradually developed, with some links being occasionally balloon-tipped (see Figure 5.16). Overall, during the course of the Spring 2008 term, students were given links for eleven different assignments. Statistics are presented in Table 5.2.

From the evidence provided by the History tracking facility, the students appeared to fall into 3 groups: 6 'adopters' (three continuing to this day), 5 'minimalists' and 3 'refusers' (cf. Gaskell and Cobb's 2004 'persisters' vs.

'non-persisters'). The 'adopter' status was assigned when users conducted at least twice as many searches as the number of hyperlinks received, and also showed independent activity (i.e. from the Corpora Search panel). In contrast, 'minimalists' clicked on the received links and carried out the correction tasks, taking little or no initiative to discover or learn more. The presence of the final 'refuser' category came as a surprise, as some tasks had been set as obligatory. Subsequent studies confirmed, however, that unless specially encouraged and trained to do so, a small fraction of users would claim to be unable to overcome technological inhibitions or negative first experiences. Winning over such users remains a challenge for the Project, and for DDL.

Other interesting observations included:

- students who undertook more link-driven searches, especially adopters, tended to develop a greater liking for self-initiated searches. While there were more word- than pattern-oriented ones, the latter appeared regularly and were generally preferred as insight providers (see the questionnaire results below);
- students had greater difficulty in noticing less visible aspects of patterning and priming (e.g. textual distance, semantic characteristics, frequency differences) unless specifically guided by the co-annotating Teacher/Administrator;
- students were generally reluctant to annotate, despite continual encouragement (only 10% of searches were annotated, mostly from obligatory tasks);
- the length and depth of annotation was less advanced than in the ESAP group in the first pilot study;
- there appeared to be a positive correlation between the adopter-minimalist-refuser classification and students' writing ability and final course grades.

The evaluation questionnaire was slightly longer in this study. The overall user-friendliness of IFAConc was undecided, although most students found the tool useful for the course. Feedback links were also received positively or very positively, while other valued features included the counting of collocates (which had not however been much used), and, importantly, the opportunity to compare multiple and varied corpora. One confusing finding was a lack of appreciation for History, while considerable value was attached to the exchanges with the teacher in the annotations. This result proved decisive for subsequent uses of the tool and updates to its online profile.

No particular connection was perceived between link-driven searches and self-initiated investigations, thus failing to corroborate the mildly positive effect reported by the ESAP group. This may have been partly due to the EGAP students' mostly relying on feedback links rather than practising independent searches. Similarly, when asked to choose and justify the most valuable findings, the students mostly pointed to feedback cases; unlike the ESAP group, they stressed specific language gains rather than increased awareness or skills.

5.4. Interim conclusions

Not all the features of IFAConc described in the first part of this paper were fully utilised in the pilot studies. Some functions were not ready at the time, although most had been tested all along. Despite the limited scope of these pilot attempts, important lessons were learned, some of which determined enhancements for the following academic year (to the extent allowed by programming support).

First, the personal feedback procedures developed for the EGAP pilot, while fruitful and prolific, were judged too labour-intensive to replicate, and it was decided to use fewer feedback links and to optimise their administration. As well as reusing existing annotated History items, many new Shared entries were thus prepared, categorised and made browsable from the new Quick Search links panel (see Figure 5.3) and the Resources Textbook. We also began to distinguish and tag the different needs of ESAP and EGAP students.

Capitalising on the reported value of co-annotations, the new version of History, launched in late 2008, began supporting rtf-formatting, admin annotations and user administration facilities. Commenting and email notification features count among the most recently tested additions.

Most importantly, however, the visibility and centrality of the History and Resources interfaces were greatly enhanced in order to enable learners to take greater advantage of 'top-down' concordancing by themselves – both as part of (self-)training and for regular use. These developments are ongoing, as further tests have shown the insufficiency of link-driven training. Video tutorials and the introduction of interactive tips for adjusting searches have thus been added to the current priorities.

Cobb (2003) has argued that learners have certainly more questions to ask than traditional reference tools can hold answers to. In the approach outlined in this paper, particular inspired by Cobb's ideas, DDL solutions are sought to make students themselves help in discovering, registering and solving relevant questions. As noted in a number of studies (e.g. Frankenberg-Garcia 2010; O'Keeffe and Farr 2003), the key to successful DDL remains effective, and efficient training and continued research is needed, using monitoring facilities such as those shown in this paper, to determine the kinds of tools, interfaces, features and approaches that are most amenable in particular learning contexts. Such research is probably best conducted in realistic quasi-experimental conditions with many diverse users. IFAConc is a tool which aims both to be of practical value to its users and to illuminate some of the pedagogic dilemmas which surround DDL.

Notes

[1] The corpora are small (most within the 200–300,000 word range) and include excerpts of texts from the Web and from resources available to IFA under institutional subscription, thus broadly falling under 'fair use'. Those corpora considered public (including the PICLE learner corpus, i.e. EGAP EFL, Kaszubski 2003) are available in the sampler version of IFAConc for registered public use.

[2] The processing and preprocessing of corpus files is performed typically with the help of additional tools. Full details can be provided upon request.

[3] Integration with the error-tagged sample of the PICLE corpus was also considered in the early design stage (http://ifa.amu.edu.pl/~kprzemek/concord2adv/errors/errors.htm). However, since overexposure to student corpus data could inadvertently 'entrench' native-unlike patterns, further consideration and testing is called for before any final decision is made.

References

Aston, G. (1998), 'What corpora for ESP?', in M. Pavesi and G. Bernini (eds), *L'apprendimento linguistico all'universita: Le lingue speciali*. Roma: Bulzoni, pp. 205–26.

Aston, G. (2004), 'Corpus upon corpus: a bout of indigestion?', Plenary speech at TALC 2004, Granada, Spain, 6–9 July. [Online abstract]. <http://www.ugr.es/~talc6/> (accessed 15 September, 2005).

Braun, S. (2006), 'ELISA: a pedagogically enriched corpus for language learning purposes', in S. Braun, K. Kohn and J. Mukherjee (eds), *Corpus Technology and Language Pedagogy: New Resources, New Tools, New Methods*. Frankfurt am Main: Peter Lang, pp. 25–47.

Cobb, T. (2003), 'Do corpus-based electronic dictionaries replace concordancers?', in B. Morrison, C. Green and G. Motteram (eds), *Directions in CALL: Experience, Experiments, Evaluation*, Hong Kong: Hong Kong Polytechnic University, pp. 179–206.

Cobb, T. (2006), 'Constructivism', in K. Brown (ed.), *Encyclopaedia of Language and Linguistics* (second edn., vol. 3, *Foundations of Linguistics*). Oxford: Elsevier, pp. 85–88.

Cobuild Concordance and Collocations Sampler [Online]. <http://www.collins.co.uk/Corpus/CorpusSearch.aspx> (acessed 13 June, 2009).

Coniam, D. (2004), 'Concordancing oneself: constructing individual textual profiles'. *International Journal of Corpus Linguistics,* 9, (2), 271–298.

Coxhead, A. (2008), 'Phraseology and English for academic purposes: challenges and opportunities', in F. Meunier and S. Granger (eds), *Phraseology in Foreign Language Learning and Teaching.* Amsterdam and Philadelphia: John Benjamins, pp. 149–161.

Frankenberg-Garcia, A. (2010), 'Raising teachers' awareness of corpora', *Language Teaching,* doi: 10.1017/S0261444810000480, published online by Cambridge University Press.

Gaskell, D. and Cobb, T. (2004), 'Can learners use concordance feedback for writing errors?'. *System,* 32, (3), 301–319.

Gavioli, L. (2005), *Exploring Corpora for ESP Learning.* Amsterdam and Philadelphia: John Benjamins.

Gavioli, L. and Aston, G. (2001), 'Enriching reality: language corpora in language pedagogy'. *ELT Journal,* 55, (3), 238–246.

Hoey, M. (2005), *Lexical Priming: A New Theory of Words and Language.* London: Routledge.

Horst, M. and Cobb, T. (2001), 'Growing academic vocabulary with a collaborative on-line database', in B. Morrison, D. Gardner, K. Keobke and M. Spratt (eds), *ELT Perspectives on IT & Multimedia: Selected Papers from the ITMELT Conference 2001.* Hong Kong: Hong Kong Polytechnic University, pp. 189–225.

Hunston, S. (2002), *Corpora in Applied Linguistics.* Cambridge: Cambridge University Press.

Hyland, K. (2006), *English for Academic Purposes: An Advanced Resource Book.* London: Routledge.

Hyland, K. and Tse, P. (2007), 'Is there an "Academic Vocabulary"?' *TESOL Quarterly,* 41, (2), 235–253.

Johns, A. M. (1997), *Text, Role and Context: Developing Academic Literacies.* Cambridge: Cambridge University Press.

Johns, T. (1991), 'Should you be persuaded – two samples of data-driven learning materials', in T. Johns and P. King (eds), *Classroom Concordancing. English Language Research Journal,* 4. Birmingham: University of Birmingham, pp. 1–16.

Johns, T. (2000), *Tim Johns EAP Page.* [Online]. <http://www.eisu2.bham.ac.uk/johnstf/timeap3.htm> (accessed 15 February, 2008).

Kaszubski, P. (2003), *About PICLE.* [Online]. <http://www.staff.amu.edu.pl/~przemka/picle.html> (accessed 23 January, 2007).

Kaszubski, P. (2006a), 'Konkordancer internetowy w nauce języka: w stronę optymalizacji', in A. Duszak, E. Gajek and U. Okulska (eds), *Korpusy w angielsko-polskim językoznawstwie kontrastywnym: Teoria i praktyka.* Kraków: Universitas, pp. 329–59. [English version of manuscript available]

Kaszubski, P. (2006b), 'Web-based concordancing and ESAP writing'. *Poznań Studies in Contemporary Linguistics,* 41, 161–93.

Mauranen, A. (2004), 'Speech corpora in the classroom', in G. Aston, S. Bernardini and D. Stewart (eds), *Corpora and Language Learners.* Amsterdam and Philadelphia: John Benjamins, pp. 195–211.

O'Keeffe, A. and Farr, F. (2003), 'Using language corpora in initial teacher education: pedagogic issues and practical applications'. *TESOL Quarterly,* 37, (3), 389–418.

Widdowson, H. (2000), 'On the limitations of linguistics applied'. *Applied Linguistics,* 21, (1), 3–25.

Part II

Corpora for language learners: tools

Chapter 6

A corpus-based approach to automatic feedback for learners' miscollocations

Anne Li-E Liu, David Wible and Nai-Lung Tsao

This chapter reports a novel statistical method applied to corpora to achieve automatic correction of miscollocations. Our approach borrows the notions of 'collocation cluster' and 'intercollocability' from Cowie and Howarth (1996). A collocation cluster is a set of semantically similar collocations in which the various collocates and focal words in the cluster exhibit a limited degree of substitutability. Limits on this intercollocability within a cluster can lead to language learners' miscollocations arising from overextending intercollocability. Our statistical method for automatic correction of miscollocations shows superior performance when compared with mutual information as a criterion, and significantly improves results yielded by MI when the two are combined. Some applications in pedagogy are suggested for further research.

6.1. Introduction

Collocation has been widely considered a criterion to gauge the language proficiency of L2 learners. Studies that compare the language of L1 speakers and L2 learners suggest that the collocations learners are capable of employing are not only fewer than L1 speakers' but are also limited to a small set (Howarth 1998a; Kaszubski 2000; Nesselhauf 2004). The underlying causes of learners' miscollocations are believed to be eclectic, ranging from L1 interference and the use of near-synonyms to creativity. One issue that arises in the language classroom is that unlike idioms, which are introduced to learners as a whole and are frequently highlighted, collocations are less conspicuous and less commonly targeted for learners' attention; yet when assessing proficiency, particularly in writing, correct collocation is usually seen as a performance criterion L2 learners are expected to meet.

Howarth (1998a, 1998b) compared the academic writing of advanced L2 learners and native speakers by exploring collocational density and use of each collocation. Although he found no correlation between the general proficiency of a learner and the number of collocations a learner used, the fact that miscollocation remains an issue even for advanced learners is worthy of note. In a 4-million word corpus of English writing produced by L2 learners in Taiwan (English Taiwan Learner Corpus), Liu (2002) found that the most frequent error was word choice, and verb-noun miscollocations constituted the bulk of lexical collocation errors.

Researchers have applied statistical techniques to corpora to create a range of resources for teaching and learning collocations (Curado Fuentes 2001; Kita and Ogata 1997; Shei and Pain 2000; Wible et al. 2004; Wible et al. 2006; Wible 2008). Such resources, however, mainly aim to provide authentic input rather than to make suggestions with regard to miscollocations in learners' output. We propose a method which not only retrieves lexical collocations from the BNC, but also uses this information to suggest corrections of learners' miscollocations.

6.2. The larger problem and its parts: computing miscollocations

There is an extensive literature on the retrieval of collocations from large, machine-readable corpora. This work has continued apace since Church and Hanks (1990) proposed mutual information as a statistical means that could be applied to detect association strength among words and discover notable associations. Work on automatically identifying miscollocations, however, has developed more slowly. One reason is that the evidence needed to infer that a certain proximal co-occurrence of two words is a miscollocation is not simply the converse of that needed to infer that it is a collocation. Detection and correction of miscollocations is not just a matter of extrapolating or tweaking the measures that detect positive collocations. If we find that two words co-occur with a frequency that exceeds some threshold of what we would expect by chance, given the frequency of occurrence of each of the two words independently in the same corpus, this is broadly taken as evidence that the pair is a collocation (when occurring typically in some syntagmatic configuration). As Church et al. (1991) point out, however, to demonstrate the converse state of affairs (that is, co-occurrence of a pair of words at an actual rate which is far below what would be expected by chance given the frequency of each word independently) would require a prohibitively large corpus before the judgement that the pair is a miscollocation could be statistically warranted. Thus we can pinpoint the problem of sparseness as one of the fundamental obstacles to automatic miscollocation detection. One brute force approach to this problem would obviously be to use ever larger corpora. Even so, corpus size is not a simple matter, as the rarer the words in the candidate (mis)collocation, the larger the corpus needed.

There is currently no simple solution to the sparseness problem that we are aware of, and therefore we explore in this chapter an alternative approach which circumvents it. We partition the miscollocation issue into two parts: detection and correction. Somewhat counter-intuitively, perhaps, the challenge of correction appears to be more tractable than that of detection. That is, it seems to be easier computationally to find correct collocation candidates for a miscollocation given as input (correction) than it is to determine whether a word pair constitutes a miscollocation (detection). In this chapter we directly address the correction problem and, incidentally, offer an approach for further research into the detection problem.

Our approach to the sparseness problem is to frame the issue of miscollocations as an issue of substitutability. What sets miscollocations apart from errors of lexical choice in general, is that in a miscollocation one of the words is wrong because, in co-occurrence with the focal word of the pair, another choice is conventionally preferred. We do not *eat medicine*, because the focal word *medicine* constrains the verb to *take* rather than *eat*, even though the latter makes sense semantically. That is, there is a restricted substitutability that can not be accounted for by the violation of productive grammatical or semantic rules, but rather by violation of the conventional restricted substitutability of the verb in the presence of *medicine* – a restriction that prohibits, for example, the usually permissible substitution by synonyms. We can not have *big respect* for someone, but only *great respect*.

Statistical measures applied broadly are too coarse-grained to detect such nuances of substitutability. The approach we are proposing is roughly to provide a means of statistically identifying narrow 'pockets' of substitutability and, within these, limits on that substitutability. As pockets of substitutability, we borrow Cowie and Howarth's (1996) notion of collocation clusters, that is, sets of verbs and nouns (or other POS combinations) that exhibit what they call 'intercollocability'. We implement a means of discovering such clusters computationally (described below). It is then within the limited scope of a collocation cluster that many (but not all) of the verbs in that cluster show high association strengths with many (but not all) of the nouns in that cluster. It is precisely within such a cluster that verb-noun (VN) pairs without a high association strength become conspicuous and can be seen as candidate miscollocations. The same low association strength for another VN pair with the same respective frequencies would not be indicative of a miscollocation if that second VN pair were not part of the collocation cluster.

To provide automatic correction of miscollocations identified through our use of collocation clusters, it is exactly within the same cluster that we can identify another verb that shows a strong association with the same noun and which we can thus identify as a candidate correction.

6.3. The study

This study focuses on finding correct collocation suggestions for VN miscollocations via the notion of intercollocability. Collocation formation involves the knowledge of word meaning as well as that of possible neighbouring words. That is, dealing with miscollocations, intuitively, will require a knowledge of semantics. Our approach differs from others in relying solely on the concepts of collocation cluster and intercollocability, without reference to other semantic knowledge sources (such as WordNet).

6.4. Intercollocability, collocation cluster and miscollocation

Based on their observations of L2 writers' academic writing, Cowie and Howarth (1996) proposed that certain collocations form clusters on the basis of the shared meaning they denote, and that these collocation clusters cause L2 writers difficulties. Collocations in a collocation cluster exhibit a certain degree of intercollocability, that is, the collocates of some of these collocations are substitutable. For example, a collocation cluster sharing the sense 'pass on message from this person to another' includes the related expressions *convey a point*, *get across a message* and *express an opinion*. The shared intercollocability implies that collocations such as *convey a point*, *convey a message; get across a point, get across a message* are all acceptable. Cowie and Howarth proposed that collocation errors occurred when a learner overgeneralised the intercollocability within a cluster or from one cluster to an adjacent cluster. That is, learners may overlook the fact that some verbs collocate with some but not all of the nouns in a cluster, or only appear in one cluster whereas others occur in more than one and thus co-occur with two different groups of noun collocates. They suggested this is the underlying cause of the miscollocation *communicate condolences*. This is seen as an overextension of the shared intercollocability of the verbs *communicate* and *convey: convey a point/idea, communicate a point/idea* but *convey condolences;* overgeneralisation gives rise to *communicate condolences*.

Another miscollocation that may be due to overgeneralisation of intercollocability is *reach* their *purposes* (English Taiwan Learner Corpus). *Fulfil goal/dream, achieve ambition/dream, realise goal* and *reach goal* can be clustered to express 'improving a longed-for condition with success'. Figure 6.1 shows the collocation cluster formed for this concept. The key here is that not all the VN combinations in Figure 6.1 are acceptable since the intercollocability is not complete. While *fulfil* and *achieve* collocate with all four nouns on the right, *realise* collocates with *dream* and *goal* but not with *purpose* (as is indicated by the dotted line). *Reach* shares with the verbs in this cluster the property of collocating with *goal,* yet the similarity ends there since it does not collocate with *dream, ambition* or *purpose.* The complex intercollocability may lead L2 learners to assume that *realise* and *reach* also collocate with *purpose* and thus produce *reach* their *purposes,* where the miscollocation can be seen as an overgeneralisation of shared intercollocability within the cluster.

While Cowie and Howarth see limitations on intercollocability within a collocation cluster as a cause of learner miscollocations, we also view collocation clusters as a means for correcting them. A cluster can serve as a bridge that links miscollocations back to the correct collocates. This approach requires, then, that for a particular miscollocation, we determine a collocation cluster that it belongs to which could contain the correct collocation.

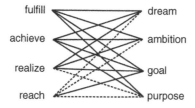

FIGURE 6.1   Collocation cluster for improving a longed-for condition with success

6.5. Methodology

We used learner miscollocations as our starting point. Take the attested miscollocation *improve problems in 'She tries to *improve* her students' *problems*'. Hypothesising that a miscollocation arises from overextending the intercollocability in a collocation cluster, we assumed that if this cluster could be determined, the correct collocation would be found in it. Thus, the first step was to take the miscollocation *improve problem as a seed to generate the relevant collocation cluster. To do this, we used Collocation Explorer,[1] a search engine that showed possible co-occurring words by retrieving collocates in the BNC, listing these on the basis of their MI ranking. This generated fifty-two noun collocates for *improve* and eighty-six verb collocates for *problem*. To find correct replacements for *improve* in the miscollocation *improve problems we determined which of these eighty-six verbs share noun collocates with *improve*. That is, through the notion of overlapping nouns, we assumed the link between the wrong verb and the correct ones would be created. It was found that two verbs, *resolve* and *reduce*, fell into this category (*resolve/improve* + *situation/matter/way*; *reduce/improve* + *quality/efficiency/effectiveness*). This constituted the relevant collocation cluster of the concept 'making better a condition' and provided a link among *improve*, *resolve* and *reduce* by virtue of their shared noun collocates (see Figure 6.2).

Unlike *improve*, both *resolve* and *reduce* have high MI scores with *problem*, so we take them as acceptable substitutes for *improve* in the miscollocation *improve problem. These two verbs will thus be offered to learners as suggested corrections for the miscollocation *improve her students' *problems*.

To test the robustness of this approach, eighty-four miscollocations found in Liu's study (2002) were used. We randomly chose half as training data and the other half as testing data. Two experienced English teachers (one native and one non-native English speaker) offered possible suggestions for the eighty-four miscollocations. We used these suggestions to evaluate any corrections our approach found.

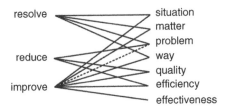

FIGURE 6.2   Collocation cluster for making better a condition

6.6. Results and discussion

In dealing with learner miscollocations, we are interested in whether collocation clusters and intercollocability are plausible sources for correcting miscollocations. Table 6.1 shows some examples of miscollocations and of corresponding correct collocations provided by the two experts. Where our approach found VN combinations that matched the correct collocations proposed by human experts, we treated such matches as true positives.

Since one of the traditional methods of retrieving collocations is by statistical measures of word association strength, we compared results using our method (ON – overlapping nouns) with results using one of the most common of these measures, mutual information (MI). We indicate the performance of K-best suggestions in the first two columns in Table 6.2.[2] Our approach consistently outperformed the MI approach. We then combined the two approaches to construct a hybrid model (third column in Table 6.2).

The hybrid model, which combined the two features (MI + ON), provided the highest proportion of true positives at every value of K. It is clear

Table 6.1 Examples of miscollocations and the corresponding correct collocations

Miscollocation	Correct collocations
pay time	spend time, devote time
make damage	cause damage
pay effort	spend effort, make effort
get knowledge	gain knowledge, acquire knowledge
make conclusion	draw conclusion, form conclusion, lead conclusion

Table 6.2 Precision of K-best suggestions for MI and ON approaches and the hybrid model

K-Best	MI	ON	MI+ON
K=1	16.67	22.62	29.76
K=2	36.9	38.1	44.05
K=3	47.62	50	59.52
K=4	52.38	63.1	72.62
K=5	64.29	72.62	78.57
K=6	65.48	75	83.33
K=7	67.86	77.38	86.9
K=8	70.24	82.14	89.29
K=9	72.62	85.71	92.86
K=10	76.19	88.1	94.05

that our approach not only outperforms MI on its own but improves the performance of MI when used in combination with it.

We will now look at some miscollocations with the correction candidates in Tables 6.3–6.6 and discuss the intercollocability in more detail. These tables show the K-best suggestions provided by the MI and ON models for

Table 6.3   K-Best suggestions for *get knowledge*

K-Best	MI	ON
K=1	impart knowledge	provide knowledge
K=2	+acquire knowledge	+obtain knowledge
K=3	broaden knowledge	increase knowledge
K=4	detail knowledge	secure knowledge
K=5	possess knowledge	+gain knowledge

Table 6.4   K-Best suggestions for *pay time*

K-Best	MI	ON
K=1	bide time	+invest time
K=2	waste time	date time
K=3	+spend time	+spend time
K=4	idle time	occupy time
K=5	while time	last time

Table 6.5   K-Best suggestions for *make conclusion*

K-Best	MI	ON
K=1	jump (to) conclusion	support conclusion
K=2	+reach conclusion	+form conclusion
K=3	+draw conclusion	base conclusion
K=4	leap conclusion	+arrive (at) conclusion
K=5	+lead (to) conclusion	+reach conclusion

Table 6.6   K-Best suggestions for *fill ambition*

K-Best	MI	ON
K=1	+fulfil ambition	+fulfil ambition
K=2	harbour ambition	+achieve ambition
K=3	+achieve ambition	harbour ambition
K=4	lack ambition	lack ambition
K=5	+realise ambition	have ambition

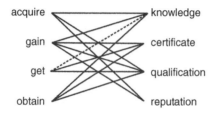

FIGURE 6.3 Collocation cluster for gaining possession of something

K=1–5 for the miscollocations *get knowledge, *pay time, *make conclusion and *fill ambition.* The plusses (+) indicate the true positives. Each model found the correct suggestions for the corresponding miscollocations but at different rankings in the K-best results.

The two approaches seemed to perform equally well since the total number of true positives found for the four miscollocations was nearly the same (eight for MI and nine for ON). When K was 5, our approach found *gain knowledge* for *get knowledge, reach conclusion* for *make conclusion,* whereas the MI approach found *lead (to) conclusion* for *make conclusion* and *realise ambition* for *fill ambition.* However, ON found more suitable alternatives than MI at K=1 and K=2.

The collocation cluster shown in Figure 6.3 expresses the concept 'gaining possession of something'. Despite the fact that *knowledge, certificate, qualification* and *reputation* co-occur with *gain,* the verb *acquire* shares only *knowledge, qualification* and *reputation,* whereas *get* shares only *certificate* and *qualification.* While it is impossible to determine from this data whether this incomplete intercollocability is the cause of the learning difficulty which gives rise to the miscollocation *get knowledge,* it clearly provides us with a computational bridge from the miscollocation to candidate corrections under these stricter criteria. A further search in our learner corpus found 115 collocations relating to the 'gaining possession of something' cluster. Seventy-five of these were instances where 'get' was employed, rather than the correct *gain, acquire* or *obtain.* This error ratio suggests that, on six out of every ten occasions, learners wrongly assume that *get* co-occurs with *knowledge.* With this information, the path to the corresponding corrections can be generated automatically.

Figure 6.4 shows the cluster created for the concept of 'using up or giving one's time, attention, or money entirely to a particular activity' from which the miscollocation *pay time*[3] derives. The intercollocability suggests that when expressing this concept, different nouns require different verb collocates. While one can *spend energy/time/effort,* one cannot *spend attention*

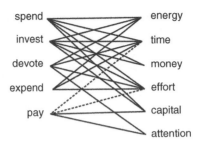

FIGURE 6.4 Collocation cluster for using up one's time/attention/money for a particular activity

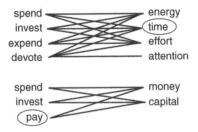

FIGURE 6.5 Two sub-clusters for using up one's time/attention/money for a particular activity

but *pay attention.* Likewise, we *pay capital* and *pay attention* to someone or something but by no means can we *pay time* or *effort.*

As a matter of fact, this cluster is a merged version of two separate clusters (see Figure 6.5). When what is being exerted is related to individuals' mental and physical state, such as *energy, time, effort* and *attention,* verbs used to describe the activities are *spend, invest, expend* and *devote.* On the other hand, if what is being used up is detachable from individuals, like *money* and *capital,* then *spend, invest* and *pay* are the correct collocates. The two clusters, although similar, reflect two different semantic sets. By constructing such neighbouring clusters, we not only have found a plausible explanation for learner miscollocations, but we have taken a further step towards offering solutions to such miscollocation problems.

Another example of overgeneralising intercollocability is *make conclusion,* for which the corresponding cluster is shown in Figure 6.6. All the collocations in this cluster denote more or less 'act of reasoning'. The word 'conclusion' connotes the attributes of inferences being made, comparisons

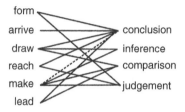

FIGURE 6.6   Collocation cluster for the act of reasoning

Table 6.7   K-Best suggestions for *communicate condolences*

K-Best	MI	ON
K=1	+express condolences	+offer condolences
K=2	+offer condolences	+send condolences
K=3	+send condolences	+express condolences

being drawn or judgments being reached. In other words, a *conclusion* can be 'formed' only after the above processes. 'Arriving at a conclusion' is not an action that is done exclusively but a result or outcome of a reasoning process. Language learners might neglect these subtle semantic properties on the one hand and draw too general conclusions on the other, thus producing a miscollocation like *make a conclusion.*

As a final example, let us return to Cowie and Howarth's (1996) miscollocation *communicate condolences.* Our model successfully found the correct alternatives shown in Table 6.7 (both MI and ON approaches yielded the same results though with different rank orderings). With only a few verbs in this cluster, the K-best suggestions only showed up to K=3. Viewed from another perspective, the small set of results for this specific miscollocation has no false positives; it shows perfect precision.

6.7. Future research

At the beginning of this chapter, we partitioned the miscollocation problem into the two sub-problems of detection and correction. Here we have focused on the issue of correction. As pointed out, however, the use of collocation clusters derived from intercollocability shows promise for detection as well. Taken in isolation, it is extremely difficult to judge by statistical means whether a particular VN pair is a miscollocation. Even if a VN pair were completely unattested in the standard reference corpus, this would be insufficient grounds in itself to categorise the pair as a miscollocation. It would require a prohibitively large corpus to infer that the absence of a specific word pairing qualifies it as a miscollocation. What is more to the point for detecting miscollocations is evidence of resistance to substitutability. The problem then becomes one of framing this notion. We are suggesting that we have grounds for judging a word pairing to be a miscollocation if the V and the N in that pairing are members of the same collocation cluster, but show an MI score which is conspicuously lower than the other pairings in that cluster. It is this approach to miscollocation detection that we intend to explore in the next stages of our research.

6.8. Conclusion

Collocations which can be clustered show a certain level of intercollocability, and restrictions on this intercollocability have been called upon to account for language learners' collocation errors (Cowie and Howarth 1996). We have borrowed from this account in order to develop a computational means of finding corrections to miscollocations via the notion of intercollocability. The eighty-four miscollocations tested in this study have shown that without incorporating semantic knowledge, our approach offers a promising means of correcting miscollocations.

The analysis of miscollocations helps researchers and teachers to better understand the underlying causes of language learners' lexical difficulties. What would help learners, however, is a tool which can provide collocational information as and when they need it. Our next step will be to implement our approach as an application in the digital writing environment of IWiLL, an online language learning platform (Wible et al. 2001). The main issue of interest there will be to assess the utility of such a tool for second language writers and in the feedback process of teachers. To what extent this can affect learners' writing will shed further light on the pedagogical benefits of corpora in language teaching and learning.

Acknowledgments

The work reported in this chapter was supported by grants from the National Science Council, Taiwan (Grant Nos. 96–2524-S-008–003- and 97-2631-S-008–004-)

Notes

1. Collocation Explorer. *http://research.iwillnow.org/project/bncrce/default.htm*
2. By 'K-best' we are referring to a variable value for the number of top correction candidates automatically generated by the correction algorithm. So, for example, if the algorithm performance is evaluated at K=3, only the top three candidates generated are considered in looking for true positives; if evaluated at K=5, then the top five candidates are examined for true positives. Obviously, the larger the value of K, the looser the criteria for evaluating the algorithm.
3. Although we do not include **pay effort* in the discussion, fifteen instances of **pay effort* are found from English TLC. Thus the miscollocation *pay effort* is also indicated in the cluster.

References

Church, K., Gale, W., Hanks, P. and Hindle, D. (1991), 'Using statistics in lexical analysis', in U. Zernik (ed.), *Lexical Acquisition: Exploiting On-line Resources to Build a Lexicon*. Englewood Cliffs, NJ: Erlbaum, pp. 115–164.

Church, K. and Hanks, P. (1990), 'Word association norms, mutual information, and lexicography'. *Computational Linguistics*, 16, (1), 22–29.

Cowie, A. P. and Howarth, P. (1996), 'Phraseological competence and written proficiency', in G. M. Blue and R. Mitchell (eds), *Language and Education*. Clevedon: BAAL/Multilingual Matters, pp. 80–93.

Curado Fuentes, A. (2001), 'Lexical behavior in academic and technical corpora: implications for ESP development'. *Language Learning & Technology*, 5, 106–129.

Howarth, P. (1998a), 'Phraseology and second language proficiency'. *Applied Linguistics*, 19, (1), 22–44.

Howarth, P. (1998b), 'The phraseology of learners' academic writing', in A. P. Cowie (ed.), *Phraseology: Theory, Analysis and Applications*. Oxford: Clarendon Press, pp. 161–186.

Kaszubski, P. (2000), *Selected Aspects of Lexicon, Phraseology and Style in the Writing of Polish Advanced Learners of English: a Contrastive, Corpus-based Approach*. Unpublished PhD Thesis. Poznań: Adam Mickiewicz University.

Kita, K. and Ogata, H. (1997), 'Collocations in language learning: corpus-based automatic compilation of collocations and bilingual collocation concordancer'. *Computer Assisted Language Learning*, 10, (3), 229–238.

Liu, A.L.E. (2002), *A Corpus-Based Lexical Semantic Investigation of Verb-Noun Miscollocations in Taiwan learners' English*. MA Thesis, Tamkang University, Taipei County, Taiwan.

Nesselhauf, N. (2004), *Collocations in a Learner Corpus*. Amsterdam and Philadelphia: John Benjamins.

Shei, C.C., and Pain, H. (2000), 'An ESL writer's collocational aid'. *Computer Assisted Language Learning*, 13, (2), 167–182.

Wible, D. (2008), 'Multiword expressions and the digital turn', in F. Meunier and S. Granger (eds), *Phraseology in Language Learning and Teaching*. Amsterdam and Philadelphia: John Benjamins, pp. 163–181.

Wible, D., Kuo, C.H., Chen, M.C., Tsao, N.L. and Hung, T.F. (2006), 'A ubiquitous agent for unrestricted vocabulary learning in noisy digital environments'. *Lecture Notes on Computer Science*, 4053, 503–512.

Wible, D., Kuo, C.H., Chien, F.Y., Liu, A.L.E. and Tsao, N.L. (2001), 'A web-based EFL writing environment: exploiting information for learners, teachers, and researchers'. *Computers and Education*, 37, 297–315.

Wible, D., Kuo, C.H. and Tsao, N.L. (2004), 'Contextualizing language learning in the digital wild: tools and a framework'. *Proceedings of IEEE International Conference on Advanced Learning Technologies*. Joensuu, Finland.

Chapter 7

Multimodal functional-notional concordancing

Francesca Coccetta

This chapter reports on the latest theoretical and technical innovations which have taken place in the field of multimodal corpus linguistics (Baldry and Thibault 2001, 2006a, 2006b, forthcoming) and shows how they can be applied to spoken texts. In particular, the chapter suggests how the online multimodal concordancer MCA (Baldry 2005) can be used to create, annotate and concordance spoken corpora in terms of functions and notions (van Ek and Trim 1998a, 1998b, 2001), and illustrates the kind of information the concordances and their associated film clips provide. In so doing, the paper introduces the multimodal functional-notional concordancing technique (Coccetta 2008b), which is based on the notional-functional tradition (e.g. Wilkins 1976), and presents two multimodal data-driven-learning activities which show how established theory and new tools can be combined to create a novel approach to the analysis of spoken texts and enhance language learning.

7.1. Introduction

Spoken corpora are particularly useful for the classroom exploration of oral discourse because they 'can achieve high authenticity, serve as communication aids, and provide irreplaceable models of the target language' (Mauranen 2004a: 208). However, the common practice of applying approaches borrowed from the investigation of corpora of *written* texts has greatly limited their potential for doing so. This is partly due to the need to develop appropriate concordancing software tools, although some headway in this direction *has* been made (see, for example, Widmann et al., this volume). In the light of the recent theoretical and technological developments regarding the analysis of multimodal corpora (Baldry and Thibault

2001, 2006a, 2006b, forthcoming), this paper investigates multimodal functional-notional concordancing, a new approach to the analysis of spoken corpora, which focuses on language and on the ways speakers express things, but also considers how language combines with other semiotic resources such as gesture, facial expressions and gaze to create meaning. This approach is facilitated by the use of the online multimodal concordancer MCA (Multimodal Corpus Authoring System), available at http://mcaweb.unipv.it/.

This paper analyses a small selection of texts in the Padova Multimedia English Corpus (hereafter: Padova MEC) (Ackerley and Coccetta 2007) and in so doing demonstrates how MCA can be used to investigate spoken corpora for functions and notions. It also describes the ties existing between verbal and non-verbal information that the individual concordances and their related video clips reveal. We may recall that functions are defined as 'the kind of things people may *do* by means of language' (van Ek and Trim 1998a: 28), while notions are 'the concepts we may refer to while fulfilling language functions'. The authors also distinguish between general and specific notions. The former can be expressed in any situation and include concepts such as space, quantity and time. The latter are topic-related and can be expressed only in particular situations. They include thematic categories such as education, travel and personal identification. The last part of the paper gives examples of teaching materials developed for language learners at various levels of proficiency designed to promote communicative language competence and raise their awareness of the multimodal nature of spoken texts. The teaching materials adopt a data-driven-learning (DDL) approach 'which gives the learner access to the facts of linguistic "performance"' (Johns 1991: 2), and which, through deductive and inductive reasoning, encourages the learner to discover patterns in the target language.

7.2. The Padova Multimedia English Corpus

The Padova MEC is a corpus of in-house audio and video texts that the Language Centre of the University of Padua is creating for teaching, research and testing purposes. In particular, the texts are used for the development of interactive multimedia materials for *Le@rning Links* (Ackerley and Cloke 2005; Ackerley and Coccetta, in press), one of the online courses produced and distributed online by the Language Centre. The corpus is free from copyright issues, as all the speakers involved in the recordings gave signed permission for the use of the texts for the purposes indicated above.

The speakers come from different English-speaking countries, such as the United Kingdom, America and Australia, but also include non-native and bilingual speakers. The difficulties in creating a corpus of English in a country where English is not the official language led the developers of the corpus to include Erasmus and other bilateral-agreement students attending Italian courses organised by the Language Centre, and English speakers working and living in Italy as well as their relatives and friends (Ackerley and Coccetta 2007). This heterogeneity of speakers, with different backgrounds and experiences, is reflected in the individual texts making up the corpus in terms of the topics discussed and stories told.

In the compilation of the Padova MEC, the Common European Framework of Reference (CEFR) (Council of Europe 2001) and the Council of Europe publications *Waystage* (van Ek and Trim 1998b), *Threshold 1990* (van Ek and Trim 1998a) and *Vantage* (van Ek and Trim 2001) were used as a starting point when making decisions about the kind of oral interactions to record, the topics, the functions and respective linguistic forms the texts should include.

The corpus is not very big in terms of the number of words it includes – currently about 120,000 words, from approximately 11 hours of film – but it offers a wealth of information on the different linguistic forms the speakers use to express themselves and on visual elements such as facial expressions, gaze and posture. This raises some questions: (1) how can we make the corpus more easily accessible to language learners for hands-on activities and to material developers for the creation of online learning materials for Le@rning Links? (2) How can we make the corpus available for corpus investigations without losing sight of the visual elements the texts contain and the way in which they interact with language? (3) How can we use the corpus to promote communication? The following sections try to answer these questions, suggesting all the time that the ways in which we define the nature and dimensions of a multimodal corpus of spoken texts are fundamentally different from classic conceptions of corpora as assemblies of monomodal written texts.

7.3. Using a scalar-level approach to study spoken corpora

Adolphs (2008) has raised the issue that to study the functions that an utterance can have, we need an extended unit of analysis which goes beyond the utterance level and explores the surrounding discourse. To do this, the study presented in this chapter adopts a scalar-level approach to text analysis developed within multimodal corpus linguistics (Baldry and Thibault 2001, 2006a, 2006b, forthcoming). In a scalar-level system, a text is seen as a hierarchical structure where large-scale units contain smaller-scale units and provide them with integrating contexts. All the units in the system interact with each other in the meaning-making process of the text.

With the aim of analysing language functions in this study I adopt the following four levels, arranged in descending order of size: whole text; phase; subphase; utterance. Each text is divided into functional units called phases. Thibault (2000: 320) defines phases as pieces of text 'characterised by a high level of metafunctional consistency or homogeneity among the selections from the various semiotic systems that comprise that particular phase in the text'. A phase may contain two or more subphases, characterised by the same properties typical of a phase, but relating to a specific aspect of it. Finally, each phase/subphase may contain one or more utterances.

In the study presented here, the scalar-level approach allows us to analyse the language functions produced in each utterance and, by moving to the next level in the system, to see how these functions relate to others in the same phase/subphase. For example, in the extract given in concordance 1, this approach enables the user to analyse the sequence of functions 'enquiring about likes' and 'expressing likes' realised respectively by 'What kind of music are you into?' and 'I like all kind of music . . . ' and see the speakers' different linguistic choices. In this extract, Timothy uses the expression *to be into something*, whereas Giove uses the verb *to like:* the two register different degrees of intensity and involvement with music.

Table 7.1 Adjacent functions

Phase	Speaker	Text
	Timothy:	What kind of music are you into?
1	Giove:	I like all kinds of music. I like a lot of modern music, pop music, but also a lot of Latin music. [. . .]

The use of a scalar-level approach is particularly useful where, unlike those in the example in concordance 1, functions are *not* adjacent, as in concordance 2. Sarah asks Daniel to turn down/off the air conditioning by dropping a hint ('It's a bit cold in here, isn't it?') and Daniel's compliant ('Should I turn up? Should I turn down?') is 'interrupted' by his question 'Do you think so?' and Sarah's answer 'Yeah'.

Table 7.2 Non-adjacent functions

Phase	Speaker	Text
	Sarah:	It's a bit cold in here, isn't it?
1	Daniel:	Do you think so?
	Sarah:	Yeah.
	Daniel:	Should I turn up? Should I turn down?

By moving one level up in the scalar-level system, the learner soon realises that s/he needs to consider not so much the individual utterance but the utterance in relation to its phase/subphase.

7.4. Multimodal concordancing

This section reports on research into multimodal concordancing and the way it relates to the scalar-level approach. The research carried out into the field of multimodal corpus linguistics in the last ten years offers both the conceptual and software tools required to examine a variety of multimodal texts, such as advertisements (Baldry 2004; Baldry and Thibault 2006a), conversational texts (Coccetta 2008a, 2008b; Dalziel and Metelli, in press) and websites (Baldry and O'Halloran, forthcoming; Baldry and Thibault 2006a). As regards the study of spoken texts, the development of the online multimodal concordancer MCA, capable of creating, annotating and concordancing multimodal texts, has overcome some of the limitations imposed by concordancers such as *WordSmith Tools* (Scott 2008) and *AntConc* (Anthony 2005), which arise as a result of the process of transposing a speech event to a written medium (Coccetta 2008a, 2008b), a process which deprives spoken texts of such distinguishing features as the speakers' tone of voice and stress patterns, along with visual elements such as facial expression, gesture and posture (Kress and van Leeuwen 2006). In MCA multimodal texts are made available in the form of film clips so that they are preserved in, more or less, their original format; for each concordance the system provides contextualised access to specific parts of these texts, thus allowing the investigation of what Baldry (2008a) calls a concordance's *multimodal co-text*, which extends beyond the concordance itself and includes, besides language, other semiotic resources featured in the part of the text to which the concordance relates. This concordancing practice is inter-semiotic in its orientation, as it considers language as integrated with, rather than isolated from, other semiotic modalities; in other words, language

Table 7.3 *Concordance Matrix* to investigate multimodal corpora

Concordance types	Concordancing procedures
1. monomodal form-oriented concordances	a. default type (i.e. KWIC concordancing)
2. monomodal meaning-oriented concordances	b. media-indexed type
3. multisemiotic form-oriented concordances	c. tabulated type
4. multisemiotic meaning-oriented concordances	d. overlay/captioned type

constantly interacts with other resources in the meaning-making process within the scalar organisation of texts.

Extensive research into multimodal concordancing within the MCA project has led to the development of a Concordance Matrix (Baldry 2007b, 2008a; Baldry and Thibault 2008), which combines four concordance types, each associated with four concordancing procedures within this scalar approach. This is based on the hypothesis that multimodal concordances can explore interactions across different textual levels in multimodal texts (Baldry 2008a; Baldry and Thibault 2006b, 2008). Table 7.3: (Baldry 2007b, 2008a) outlines this matrix and indicates how, from a theoretical standpoint, any of these concordance types can be combined with any of the procedures implemented in the MCA system.

The multimodal functional-notional concordancing approach presented in this paper is an example of Option 2b in the *matrix,* namely the *monomodal meaning-oriented, media-indexed* concordance. This concordancing technique is monomodal in the sense that the concordance only provides information about one semiotic resource, namely language, and excludes an analysis of, say, gaze or gesture; it is meaning-oriented because it focuses on a specific language function/notion and investigates the different language forms which enact this function/notion; finally, it is media-indexed because it gives access to the film sequence indexed in each concordance, that is, its multimodal co-text. For example, as regards the 'expressing dislikes' function, this concordancing technique allows us to see its different linguistic realisations in Padova MEC, such as 'I can't stand opera', 'I tend to really despise Italian pop music. And techno, no I can't stand it. It's horrible', and 'Well and the rest of the world hates America', but it also allows us to see how language interacts with the other semiotic resources. As for 'And techno, no I can't stand it', the video shows that when the speaker says this, he simultaneously shakes his head. The word 'multimodal' included in the expression 'multimodal functional-notional concordancing' thus refers to the multimodal co-text rather than the concordance itself. By way of further clarification, we can mention that, for example, Option 2d is identical, except that the individual concordances (i.e. the written part of the concordance or traditional concordance) are displayed as a sequence of 'subtitles' on the multimodal co-text, that is, the part of the film to which the concordance relates. Similarly, Option 3b means that, thanks to the application of the relational database accessed by MCA, a concordance relates to the forms of at least two semiotic resources (e.g. language and gaze) presented by the software in the form of a vertical table rather than in terms of horizontal lines, while Option 4b does the same but specifies the functions that the selected forms carry out.

The following sections illustrate how MCA can be used to construct, annotate and concordance spoken texts for functions and notions, that is, Option 2b in the *matrix*.

7.5. Annotating a spoken corpus for functions and notions with MCA

The MCA system adopts a manual approach to tagging which allows users to: (a) segment texts into functional units; (b) create mini-grammars, namely the sets of descriptors which specify the features to be investigated in texts; and (c) annotate texts. To do so, users have to follow five steps. These are summarised in Figure 7.1 (top row) in relation to the tools used to implement the process (bottom row).

To be searchable, an MCA corpus needs to have at least one mini-grammar. This is created through the Grammar Definition tool. To annotate the linguistic features of the texts in the Padova MEC, three mini-grammars have been developed: one for language functions, one for general notions and one for specific notions. These are based on the specifications given by van Ek and Trim in *Threshold 1990* (1998a) and *Vantage* (2001), with some modifications to meet users' needs. For example, 'replying to good wishes'

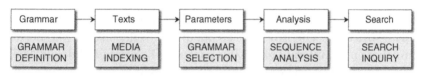

FIGURE 7.1   Basic organisation of MCA (adapted from Baldry 2007a: 181)

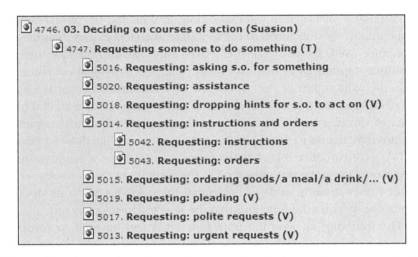

FIGURE 7.2 Excerpt from the mini-grammar for the 'requesting someone to do something' function

is not included in the list of functions, but was added in the tagging adopted in this project. In fact, if learners are required to express good wishes (van Ek and Trim 2001), similarly they should be able to reply to them. An excerpt from the mini-grammar for the function 'requesting someone to do something' is given in Figure 7.2.

As Figure 7.2 exemplifies, MCA mini-grammars are hierarchically organised on the basis that the deeper you go into the hierarchy, the more specific the descriptors are. For example, the function in question belongs to the functional category 'suasion' (Wilkins 1976) and comprises subfunctions such as 'polite requests', 'pleading' and 'instructions and orders', which are more specific than the function 'requesting someone to do something'. Similarly, the function 'requesting: instructions and orders' comprises the more specific subfunctions 'requesting: instructions' and 'requesting: orders'. The hierarchical organisation of the mini-grammars allows users to decide how deeply into the analysis of the texts they want to go – that is, using concordancing's text microscope functionality (Baldry 2008b).

Once the tagging system has been created, in the Media Indexing tool the corpus is divided into functional units of any length within a prototypically scalar approach to concordancing that divides texts into macro and micro structures. The structures are identified by the analyst, who needs to find those more relevant to her/his purposes (Baldry and Thibault 2006b). Thus, in the Padova MEC, texts are divided into the functional units previously identified as phases, subphases and utterances.

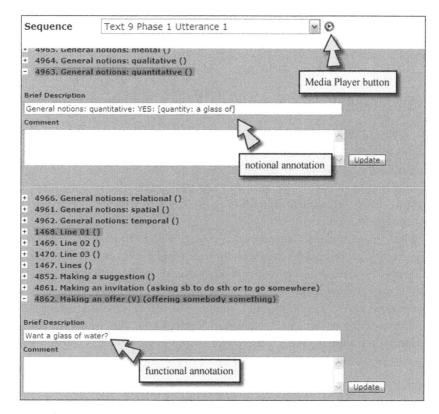

FIGURE 7.3 Example of functional-notional annotation

Finally, once the parameters required for corpus annotation have been selected using the Grammar Selection tool, each sequence is associated to the descriptors that characterise it. Figure 7.3 shows the Sequence Analysis tool used to annotate texts, which also contains the tagging systems created.

The manual annotation method adopted requires the utterance 'Want a glass of water?' to be associated explicitly with the 'making an offer' function. Similarly, to tag the general notion of quantity 'a glass of' the descriptor 'general notions: quantitative' is selected and 'a glass of' is written in the empty box below it. By convention, 'a glass of water' is in square brackets along with the type of quantitative general notion it realises, that is, 'quantity'. In addition, the annotation also includes the selected parameter followed by 'YES:' indicating that the parameter is present in the sequence. The Media Player button at the top of the page facilitates the annotation of the sequence, as it allows users to watch it.

The following section illustrates the last step identified in Figure 7.1, the retrieval of sequences containing a given function and a notion using the Search Inquiry tool.

7.6. Multimodal concordancing for functions and notions

The use of a spoken corpus to learn about typical ways of expressing something has been called for by Mauranen (2004b). With reference to the functional tagging system described above and the use of the search engine incorporated in MCA, this section exemplifies how the Padova MEC can be investigated for functions and, in particular, how a function and a notion can be combined.

MCA incorporates a search engine, the Search Inquiry tool shown in Figure 7.4, which allows users to find and isolate sequences in a corpus sharing the same characteristics. For example, to see if the 'declining an offer' function is expressed in a Padova MEC subcorpus relating to requests, invitations and offers, and to find what linguistic forms realise this function, the respective parameter is selected from one of the three drop-down menus included in MCA's search engine. Concordance 1 presents the results retrieved.

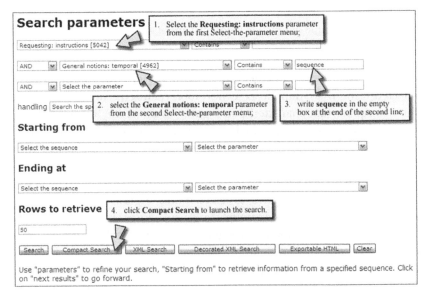

FIGURE 7.4   Instructions to find specific utterances using MCA's Search Inquiry tool

Concordance 1.   Results with MCA for the 'declining an offer' function

---

1. No thanks.
2. No thanks.
3. No thanks. I mean, that – that water's been there for ages.
4. No.
5. No thanks. I'm not – I'm not hungry.
6. Uh, no thanks.
7. I've already had one, thanks.

Access to the film clip for each concordance gives information about the multimodal co-text which might turn out to be useful for language learners. Research has shown the relevance of texts that use many semiotic resources in helping language learners, in particular lower level ones (Mueller 1980; Hoven 1999), to understand spoken texts (Kellerman 1992; Sueyoshi and Hardison 2005). For example, in the majority of the concordances presented in concordance 1, the speaker shakes her/his head when s/he says 'No', thus showing the synchronisation that exists between gesture and speech in the meaning-making process, and giving learners clues as to how these resources are typically co-deployed and used concurrently.

We may illustrate the capacity for integration of textual levels and resources in this approach to language learning and teaching with a further example. As MCA allows users to combine up to three descriptive parameters, it is easily possible to analyse adjacency pairs (Schegloff and Sacks 1973). For example, by selecting the 'requesting someone to do something' function and the 'responding to a request' function in the subcorpus relating to requests, invitations and offers, users see that, rather surprisingly, none of three requests are accepted or denied. To find out why this happens, users need to go beyond the utterance level in the scalar-level system and watch the respective phases. By watching the videos, users can note that the request is complied with non-verbally. In the specific case the listener (1) whips some eggs, (2) stops pouring the water and (3) turns off the air conditioning.

In the same vein, users can combine a language function with one or two general or specific notions. With reference to a cooking demonstration taken from the Padova MEC, Figure 7.4 shows how MCA's search engine can be set in such a way as to find utterances expressing the 'requesting: instructions' function which contains a temporal notion of the sequence type (e.g. *then, first* and *afterwards*). Figure 7.5 shows the results of this search.

The following section further exemplifies this approach through sample DDL activities which analyse language functions and notions.

132   *Francesca Coccetta*

		25.17	29.56
Text 1 Phase 3 Subphase a Utterance 2			
Requesting: instructions	You take yogurt and then you mix it with tandoori special blend.		
General notions: temporal	General notions: temporal: YES: [reference without time focus: simple present] [sequence: then]		
Text 1 Phase 4 Utterance 3		74.82	107.99
Requesting: instructions	we cut it first [...] Do that and you do some slabs on the chicken, [ ] And do the same on the other bit.		
General notions: temporal	General notions: temporal: YES: [reference without time focus: simple present] [sequence: first] [present reference: now]		
Text 1 Phase 2 Subphase a Utterance 1		134.38	144.1
Requesting: instructions	after you've left this for 30 minutes which we haven't done, but it doesn't matter, um, you coat it with this marinade.		
General notions: temporal	General notions: temporal: YES: [sequence: after + sub-clause] [duration: for] [divisions of time: minutes] [past reference: present perfect]		
Text 1 Phase 2 Subphase c Utterance 1		168.96	213.88
Requesting: instructions	then you put this on. [ ] You put this on and, um, you turn the oven on at 170 degrees [...] And then you put salt all over it.		
General notions: temporal	General notions: temporal: YES: [reference without time focus: simple present] [sequence: then]		

FIGURE 7.5.   Results with MCA for the search set in Figure 7.4

7.7. Multimodal DDL activities for functions and notions

Giving personal details about name, age, profession, family and address is one of the first things learners learn to do in a language (see the specifications for the A1 level in the global scale of the CEFR, Council of Europe 2001: 24). The exercise in Figure 7.6 illustrates how a Padova MEC subcorpus relating to short introductions can be used to help A1 learners express their age. Given the learners' level, the exercise instructions are given in the native language (Italian). Learners are given the elements used to express age and are asked to put them in the correct order. To do so, they are required to search the corpus for the 'stating' function and the specific 'personal identification: age' notion. This produces the concordances presented in Figure 7.7.

By analysing the concordances, learners are able to place the elements in the correct order. In addition, by accessing the original text they get used to hearing numbers in utterances. The results are typically used to develop follow-up exercises. For example, the concordance 'I'm a 19-year-old student here at the University of Padova' illustrates the use of a compound adjective to express age. The concordances 'I – I have 20 . . . 21 years' and 'I've got 25 years', produced by non-native speakers of English, on the other hand, illustrate the incorrect use of the verb *to have* to express age, a mistake which is very common among language learners, and Italians in particular. Drawing learners' attention to this potential mistake helps them avoid it. Similarly, learners can be encouraged to combine the 'stating' function and the specific 'personal identification: name' notion to find out how to express their names, or the specific 'personal identification: address' notion to learn how to say where they live. In this regard, by analysing the concordances retrieved (concordance 2) learners can infer the meaning of the verb *to live*.

Esprimere l'età

Per esprimere la propria età vengono utilizzati i seguenti elementi linguistici

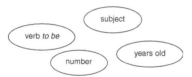

Cerca nel corpus gli enunciati nei quali i parlanti esprimono la loro età e riordina adeguatamente gli elementi presenti.

Per far questo, esegui la seguente ricerca:

1. seleziona il parametro **Stating** nel primo menù "Select the parameter";
2. seleziona il parametro **Personal identification: age** nel secondo menù "Select the parameter";
3. clicca **Compact Search**;
4. guarda 2 or 3 clip a tua scelta.

FIGURE 7.6   Exercise on expressing age

		2.37	6.71
Stating	I'm 20 years old and I'm a student at Boston University.		
Personal identification: age	Personal identification: age: YES: [I am ... years old]	111.9	114.37
Stating	I - I have 20 ... 21 years.		
Personal identification: age	Personal identification: age: YES:	122.01	127.9
Stating	I'm 27 years old and I'm third year student in University of Padova, foreign languages.		
Personal identification: age	Personal identification: age : YES: [I am ... years old]	129.89	139.1
Stating	I enrolled in University when I was 25 because I lived, something like, 4 or 5 years abroad before coming back to Italy		
Personal identification: age	Personal identification: age: YES: [I was ...]	208.17	214.14
Stating	My name is Diana Gosciewski, and I'm a 19-year-old student here at the University of Padova.		
Personal identification: age	Personal identification: age: YES: [adjective]	250.08	257.49
Stating	I'm 24 years old and I'm a student here at the University of Padua. And I study Linguistics and various foreign languages.		
Personal identification: age	Personal identification: age: YES: [I am ... years old]	330.33	333.14
Stating	I've got 25 years.		
Personal identification: age	Personal identification: age: YES:	345.25	349.84
Stating	I'm 23 years old and I study English and German here in Padua.		
Personal identification: age	Personal identification: age: YES: [I am ... years old]	386.27	391.3
Stating	I'm twenty years old and I'm in Padova, studying Geography.		
Personal identification: age	Personal identification: age: YES: [I am ... years old]	399.7	404.37
Stating	I am 25 years old.		
Personal identification: age	Personal identification: age: YES: [I am ... years old]	406.76	410.17
Stating	I'm 23 years old and I'm studying Archaeology in Padova.		
Personal identification: age	Personal identification: age: YES: [I am ... years old]	480.79	484.85
Stating	I'm 27 years old.		
Personal identification: age	Personal identification: age: YES: [I am ... years old]	484.84	486.78
Stating	I'll be 28 in October		
Personal identification: age	Personal identification: age: YES: [I'll be ...]		

FIGURE 7.7   Results with MCA for the 'stating' function and the specific 'personal identification: age' notion

Concordance 2.   Results with MCA for the 'stating' function and the specific 'personal identification: address' notion

---

1. I live here in Vicenza.
2. My parents and both of my sisters still live in Ireland.
3. I live about 10 minutes from Gatwick airport.
4. I have 3 half-siblings that live in New York.

Thanks to tagging for functions and notions, the results with MCA are neither 'messy' (Meunier 2002: 129), nor ambiguous or misleading in comparison with traditional KWIC concordancing (Option 1a in the *matrix*). In all these concordances, the speaker expresses where s/he, or someone else lives (e.g. 'I live here in Vicenza' and 'I have three half-siblings that live in New York'). On the contrary, a KWIC concordance for *live** using a text-based concordancer also includes examples where *live* is used as an adjective, or in conjunction with a preposition or an adverb (thus forming a phrasal verb which at the very least is problematic for A1 learners of English). If they have to focus on computer strategies to isolate grammatical categories, then they are not focusing, as they should be, on learning how words function in context. This is exemplified in the concordance lines taken from the British National Corpus, BNC (concordance 3).

Concordance 3.   Selected results from BNC for *live**

---

1. Where do you live?
2. Now you can't even rely on seeing a live performance at a live concert!
3. An agent deals with live gigs, concerts and touring.
4. Are you sure you can live through another summer without air conditioning?
5. I still don't live up to my standards.

Access to the original text allows learners to practise listening, and provides information which might be difficult to retrieve when only a linguistic co-text is available. The exercise in Figure 7.8 was created with reference to the cooking demonstration mentioned above, and focuses on the use of deictic elements, and demonstrative pronouns in particular, when giving instructions.

Because the participants in the cookery demonstration share the same context, the speaker uses a large number of deictic elements whose referent can most often be identified only by watching the video. For example, by watching the sequence where the utterance 'do that and you do some slabs on the chicken' is produced, learners come to realise that the demonstrative pronoun *that* refers to the action of cutting the chicken. In the same way, while watching the sequence where the utterance 'so you keep that and, uh, you leave it there for 30 minutes' is produced, they realise that here *that*

Deixis

Deixis is reference by means of linguistic items such as personal pronouns (subject forms and object forms), demonstrative adjectives and pronouns (e.g. *this*, *that*, etc.), definite and indefinite articles, etc. Deixis is dependent upon the liguistic and non-liguistic context of the utterance.

Consider the demonstrative pronouns Chiara uses when she gives instructions and match them with the referents they refer to. To do so, carry out the following search:

1. select the **Requesting: instructions** parameter from the first Select-the-parameter menu;
2. select the **General notions: deixis** parameter from the second Select-the-parameter menu;
3. write **personal pronoun** in the empty box at the end of the second line;
4. click **Compact Search**;
5. then, watch the clips.

Utterances	Referents
1. So you just do **that**	a. chicken in the Pyrex
2. before you actually put **that** on the, uh, on the chicken, you have to	b. cutting the chicken
3. Do **that** and you do some slabs on chicken	c. sticking tandoori special blend in the yoghurt
4. so you keep **that** and, uh, you leave it there for 30 minutes	d. chicken in the Pyrex
5. after you've left **this** for 30 minutes	e. marinade in the bowl
6. then you put **this** on.	f. marinade in the bowl
7. you take **this**	g. chicken in the Pyrex

FIGURE 7.8   Exercise on using deictic elements when giving instructions

The demonstrative pronoun *that* refers to the action of cutting the chicken

The demonstrative pronoun *that* refers to the chicken in the Pyrex placed away from the speaker

The demonstrative pronoun *this* refers to chicken in the Pyrex the speaker is holding in her hands

FIGURE 7.9   Use of *this* and *that* in the cooking demonstration

refers to the chicken in the bowl. Thus the video clips-cum-multimodal co-texts reveal the difference in use between *this* and *that* in this context. In the utterance 'after you've left this for 30 minutes', *this* refers to the chicken in the bowl that the speaker is holding in her hands, while in 'so you keep that and, uh, you leave it there for 30 minutes' *that* refers to the chicken in the bowl closer to the listener's space. This is shown in Figure 7.9.

7.8. Conclusions

This chapter has briefly illustrated how spoken corpora can be annotated for functions and notions and how they can be investigated accordingly through the use of the multimodal concordancer MCA. In so doing, the chapter has introduced the concept of multimodal functional-notional concordancing, recovering an applied linguistic theory that was historically important for the definition of the *Council of Europe CEFR* scale (2001). The chapter has recontextualised this theory in relation to the different concordancing techniques developed in multimodal corpus linguistics, and has also exemplified some DDL activities which focus on the ways in which speakers express things and the ways in which speakers and listeners interpret the multimodal co-text. In so doing, it has illustrated some of the benefits that this approach to the study of spoken texts can bring to language teaching and learning, in particular in the early stages of the latter. The chapter has highlighted the critical nature of oral discourse and listening strategies in these early stages and suggests that corpus techniques which are specific to oral discourse need to be developed. All this raises the question of how we define a corpus. The size of a corpus in terms of number of words seems not to be particularly useful in the current context. One alternative might be to consider the number of hours of film in a corpus and the number of hours for which it is used by language learners as automatically recorded by the software. This is however a topic that needs to be discussed in another paper.

References

Ackerley, K. and Cloke, S. (2005), 'A web of choices: integrating language learning resources in an online English course', in A. Moražikova, C. Taylor Torsello and T. Vogel (eds), *University Language Centres: Broadening Horizons, Expanding Networks*. Bratislava: CercleS, pp. 257–268.

Ackerley, K. and Coccetta, F. (2007), 'Enriching language learning through a multimedia corpus'. *ReCALL*, 19, (3), 351–370.

Ackerley, K. and Coccetta, F. (in press), 'Multimodality in an online English course', in A. Baldry and E. Montagna (eds), *Interdisciplinary Perspectives on Multimodality: Theory and Practice*. Campobasso: Palladino.

Adolphs, S. (2008), *Corpus and Context. Investigating Pragmatic Functions in Spoken Discourse*. Amsterdam and Philadelphia: John Benjamins.

Anthony, L. (2005), 'AntConc: design and development of a freeware corpus analysis toolkit for the technical writing classroom', in G. Hayhoe (ed.), *2005 IEEE International Professional Communication Conference*. Piscataway, NJ: IEEE, pp. 729–737.

Baldry, A. (2004), 'Phase and transition, type and instance: patterns in media texts as seen through a multimodal concordancer', in K. O'Halloran (ed.), *Multimodal Discourse Analysis*. London and New York: Continuum, pp. 83–108.

Baldry, A. (2005), *A Multimodal Approach to Text Studies in English. The Role of MCA in Multimodal Concordancing and Multimodal Corpus Linguistics*. Campobasso: Palladino.

Baldry, A. (2007a), 'The role of multimodal concordancers in multimodal corpus linguistics', in T. Royce and W. Bowcher (eds), *New Directions in the Analysis of Multimodal Discourse*. Mahwah and London: Erlbaum, pp. 173–193.

Baldry, A. (2007b), 'What are concordances for? Getting multimodal concordances to perform neat tricks in the university teaching and testing cycle', in A. Baldry, M. Pavesi, C. Taylor Torsello and C. Taylor (eds), *From Didactas to Ecolingua. An Ongoing Research Project on Translation and Corpus Linguistics*. Trieste: Edizioni Università, pp. 35–50.

Baldry, A. (2008a), 'Turning to multimodal corpus research for answers to a language-course management crisis', in C. Taylor Torsello, K. Ackerley and E. Castello (eds), pp. 226–237.

Baldry, A. (2008b), 'What is multimodality for? Syllabus construction in English text studies for communication sciences', in M. Solly, M. Conoscenti and S. Campagna (eds), *Verbal/Visual Narrative Texts in Higher Education*. Bern: Peter Lang, pp. 229–250.

Baldry, A. and O'Halloran, K. (forthcoming), *Multimodal Corpus-based Approaches to Website Analysis*. London: Equinox.

Baldry, A. and Thibault, P.J. (2001), 'Towards multimodal corpora', in G. Aston and L. Burnard (eds), *Corpora in the Description and Teaching of English*. Bologna: CLUEB, pp. 87–102.

Baldry, A. and Thibault, P.J. (2006a), *Multimodal Transcription and Text Analysis. A Multimedia Toolkit and Coursebook*. London and New York: Equinox.

Baldry, A. and Thibault, P.J. (2006b), 'Multimodal corpus linguistics', in G. Thompson and S. Hunston (eds), *System and Corpus: Exploring Connections*. London and Oakville: Equinox, pp. 164–183.

Baldry, A. and Thibault, P.J. (2008), 'Applications of multimodal concordances in the university teaching and testing cycle'. *Hermes*, 41, 11–41.

Baldry, A. and Thibault, P.J. (forthcoming), *Multimodal Corpus Linguistics*. London: Routledge.

Coccetta, F. (2008a), 'First steps towards multimodal functional concordancing'. *Hermes*, 41, 43–58.

Coccetta, F. (2008b), 'Multimodal corpora with MCA', in C. Taylor Torsello, K. Ackerley and E. Castello (eds), pp. 81–91.

Council of Europe (2001), *Common European Framework of Reference for Languages: Learning, Teaching, Assessment*. Cambridge: Cambridge University Press.

Dalziel, F. and Metelli, M. (in press), 'Learning about genre with a multimodal concordancer', in A. Baldry and E. Montagna (eds), *Interdisciplinary Perspectives on Multimodality: Theory and Practice*. Campobasso: Palladino.

Hoven, D. (1999), 'A model for listening and viewing comprehension in multimedia environments'. *Language Learning and Technology*, 3, (1), 88–103.

Johns, T. (1991), 'Should you be persuaded: two examples of data-driven learning materials', in T. Johns and P. King (eds), *Classroom Concordancing*.

English Language Research Journal, 4. Birmingham: University of Birmingham, pp. 1–16.

Kellerman, S. (1992), '"I see what you mean": the role of kinesic behaviour in listening and implications for foreign and second language learning'. *Applied Linguistics*, 13, (3), 239–258.

Kress, G. and van Leeuwen, T. (2006), *Reading Images. The Grammar of Visual Design*. London and New York: Routledge.

Mauranen, A. (2004a), 'Speech corpora in the classroom', in G. Aston, S. Bernardini and D. Stewart (eds), *Corpora and Language Learners*. Amsterdam and Philadelphia: John Benjamins, pp. 195–211.

Mauranen, A. (2004b), 'Spoken corpus for an ordinary learner', in J. Sinclair (ed.), *How to Use Corpora in Language Teaching*. Amsterdam and Philadelphia: John Benjamins, pp. 89–105.

Meunier, F. (2002), 'The pedagogical value of native and learner corpora in EFL grammar teaching', in S. Granger, J. Hung and S. Petch-Tyson (eds), *Computer Learner Corpora, Second Language Acquisition and Foreign Language Teaching*. Amsterdam and Philadelphia: John Benjamins, pp. 119–141.

Mueller, G. (1980), 'Visual contextual cues and listening comprehension: an experiment'. *Modern Language Journal*, 64, 335–340.

Schegloff, E. and Sacks, H. (1973), 'Opening up closings'. *Semiotica*, 6, (4), 289–327.

Scott, M. (2008), *WordSmith Tools Version 5*. Oxford: Oxford University Press.

Sueyoshi, A. and Hardison, D.M. (2005), 'The role of gestures and facial cues in second language listening comprehension'. *Language Learning*, 55, (4), 661–699.

Taylor Torsello, C., Ackerley, K. and Castello, E. (eds) (2008), *Corpora for University Language Teachers*. Bern: Peter Lang.

The British National Corpus, version 3 (BNC XML Edition) (2007). Distributed by Oxford University Computing Services on behalf of the BNC Consortium.

Thibault, P. J. (2000), 'The multimodal transcription of a television advertisement: theory and practice', in A. Baldry (ed.), *Multimodality and Multimediality in the Distance Learning Age*. Campobasso: Palladino, pp. 311–385.

van Ek, J.A. and Trim, J.L.M. (1998a), *Threshold 1990*. Cambridge: Cambridge University Press.

van Ek, J.A. and Trim, J.L.M. (1998b), *Waystage*. Cambridge: Cambridge University Press.

van Ek, J.A. and Trim, J.L.M. (2001), *Vantage*. Cambridge: Cambridge University Press.

Wilkins, D.A. (1976), *Notional Syllabuses: A Taxonomy and its Relevance to Foreign Language Curriculum Development*. Oxford: Oxford University Press.

Chapter 8

Academic corpus integration in MT and application to LSP teaching

Alejandro Curado Fuentes

Corpus use in machine translation has seen various linguistic approaches (parallel, statistical, example-based, etc). In Content-Based Machine Translation (CBMT), corpus size and the role of general-purpose corpora are also significant aspects. In our CBMT project, we focus on the distribution of linguistic data, searching functions to provide high database performance, and use a specific corpus of academic writing to test our procedures. The architecture is based on a massive general target language corpus (in Spanish), a huge fully inflected bilingual dictionary (English/Spanish) and a smaller source language corpus (English). Frequency-based lexicogrammatical information derived from the corpus concerning collocations, colligations, semantic associations and text-related colligations can also be incorporated. Initial prototypes suggest that such resources have potential uses not only for machine translation, but also for the teaching and learning of languages for specialised purposes (LSP).

8.1. Introduction

Kay (1997) observed that high-quality Machine Translation (MT) would not be produced in the near future by any single linguistic approach (statistical, rule-based, etc.), and proposed that the best practical solutions would involve Machine-aided Human Translation (MAHT). Over the past decade, Kay's claim seems to have been proved both right and wrong. The proliferation of automatic translation on the web and the crucial need for MT systems in the global economy have become important stimuli for the improvement of MT methods and implementations. However, it also seems that MT has delivered its best results in conjunction with other resources, such as online dictionaries, thesauri and word processors (Wilks 2009). Current hybrid approaches to MT also demonstrate the lack of consensus as to a specific methodology, with a combination of both linguistic and symbolic theories (e.g. statistical methods with Artificial Intelligence).

One approach seldom mentioned in MT research is reliance on context from one corpus alone. In Sin-wai's dictionary of translation technology (2004), for example, CBMT (Context-based Machine Translation) is absent. Unlike methods which draw on parallel corpora, CBMT adapts chunks of translated input to corpus-based context in the form of inter-connected n-grams. In their initial discussion of CBMT, Abir et al. (2002: 216) argued that effective MT systems would work with an infinite numbers of sentences, but with 'a finite number of discreet ideas'. This limited amount of information takes the form of n-gram pairs regarded as 'pieces of DNA' (Abir et al. 2002: 217). A crucial process of connecting these DNA blocks would enable their weaving and interlocking along the translated text.

If not originally conceived as a revolutionary idea in MT, Abir's system at least opened up access to new experimental developments. While Abir's initial work still relied on parallel corpora of source and target languages, Carbonell et al. (2006) used a massive target language corpus (between 50 GB and 1 terabyte of electronic text), along with a fully inflected bilingual dictionary instead. With the aid of an optional smaller source language corpus for synonym finding, they implemented a Spanish to English MT system which outperformed other rule- or statistically-based systems on the BLEU (Bilingual Evaluation under Study) scale. The bigger the corpus, the higher were the scores achieved.

This line of work and results motivate our own project, which aims to produce machine translations of written English into Spanish which can significantly reduce human effort and cost. In this paper, we focus on CBMT of academic written discourse, particularly in relation to specific lexical/ rhetorical items with high frequency rates. We demonstrate that the CBMT approach can easily store frequency-based information on collocations, colligations, semantic associations and text-related colligations derived from the target language corpus. The system can thus not only improve the machine translation of specialised text, but can also serve as a reference for teaching LSP (Languages for Specialised Purposes). For example, Spanish students enrolled in ESP (English for Specific Purposes) courses may benefit from resources and strategies from the CBMT approach to learn more about the specialised discourse of the target language.

8.2. The CBMT system

The first key resource in our English-Spanish CBMT system is Lozano Palacios's (2008) fully inflected dictionary containing mapping tables for English to Spanish translation (e.g., gerunds in English can give rise to infinitives and passive forms in Spanish). The dictionary is searched for each word, compound, or phrase (if listed) contained within n-grams of the source text, determined by a sliding window of four to eight words from left to right (i.e., the n-gram span).

The other key resource used here is a massive Spanish corpus built using web-crawling techniques (Boleda et al. 2006), with multilayered inverted indexing for the dynamic identification of n-grams (Badia et al. 2005). However, unlike the statistical approach used in the latter study, the present indexation does not require POS tagging, only plain text. Our research group has currently indexed up to 40 GB of text (approximately 400 million words), taken randomly from the web. However, current testing is done with a smaller portion of academic texts (nearly seven million words, as shown below). The larger general corpus will be uploaded on the server in a future stage so that the system performance of general-purpose translation can be compared with our current academic corpus-based results.

Because readers and writers tend to rely on certain aspects of discourse more than on others, machine translation into Spanish should use as much context as possible. Examples are the use of indirectness and discourse markers, hedges and paraphrasing, all of which are important in academic Spanish (Lahuerta Martínez 2004; Morales et al. 2007; Cademártori et al. 2007). In written English, according to Biber et al. (2004), co-occurring lexical items often signal academic stance (e.g. impersonal statements with 'seem', or nominal phrases as subject with 'consequence', etc.). The register is often determined by degrees of collocational strength in the two languages — in terms of content, grammatical-discursive position, semantic space and text-item relationships (Hoey 2005).

The CBMT approach can integrate resources for the identification of specific linguistic-discursive traits. The corpus and the dictionary can be linked via different database tables, similarly to the way translation memory systems store translation units or segments (Somers 2003). The MT system retrieves such data as a first step in the case of existing translation pairs, along the lines originally proposed by Abir et al. (2002). The information is stored according to co-occurrence, in the form of collocations, colligations, semantic associations and text-related colligations, as defined below.

Collocation refers to the statistically significant co-occurrence of two or more words in the texts. An example is the verb lemma APPEAR with 'to be' (20.4% probability of co-occurrence in the academic texts of the BNC Sampler: Burnard and McEnery (1999)). Colligation may involve frequency of use of a given word class, such as nouns, or may include a lexical item where a grammatical aspect is related to it (e.g., 'BE + asked to' in the present tense). Semantic association refers to those collocations that have a recurrent semantic attachment. For instance, in the BNC Sampler, the expression 'to be seeking' typically associates with the semantic group of 'work' (e.g., 'employment', 'job', etc.).

Text-related colligation is a phenomenon similar to Hoey's definition of textual colligation. In Hoey's theory of lexical priming 'Every word is primed for use in discourse as a result of the cumulative effects of an individual's encounters with the word' (Hoey 2005: 13). According to Hoey, a lexical item (or combination of lexical items) is primed to occur in certain positions within the sentence, paragraph, text, speaking turn or conversation; this positioning within the discourse is said to be a word's 'textual colligation'. Our concept of text-related colligation consists of two types. Type 1, characterised by the positioning of a lexical item or pattern in a given location in the sentence and/or paragraph, accords with Hoey's definition of textual colligation. An example is 'one of the most + adjective' at the beginning of sentences. Type 2 extends Hoey's definition as it refers to a pattern found at a specific location of sentences and/or paragraphs that also demonstrates a good deal of grammatical co-occurrence. For example, in Academic Spanish, *a continuación* [*next*] followed by a future tense verb within an impersonal statement generally occurs at the beginning of a sentence. Further examples of significant lexical information are given in Table 8.1.

Table 8.1 Examples of co-occurrence types from the Spanish corpus

Collocations	Colligations	Semantic associations	Text-related colligations (Type 1)	Text-related colligations (Type 2)
razón por la cual	*¿por qué no +* present simple	*La mayor parte de* + 'people'	*. En la medida en que*	*, para lo que +* reflexive verb
lo que se denomina	*necesidad de +* infinitive	'collected' + *en la tabla* #	*. Por lo que respecta a*	*. Teniendo en cuenta* + NP
hay que tener en cuenta que	*en el proceso de +* noun-*ción*	*en el marco +* 'institution'	*. Contrariamente a lo que*	*. Desde el punto de vista* + adjective

The linguistic-discursive information from the corpus should enable the system to extract enough contrastive data to optimise the retrieval of such lexical-grammatical information. In the sample corpus of academic Spanish, appropriate texts were found using the WebBootCat utility in Sketch Engine (Baroni et al. 2006) to download articles, reports and textbook chapters. The key words used in the search were content words taken from word frequency lists, in groups of six to eight words including adjectives, verbs and nouns. Wikipedia and www.urumedia.org/formarse were used to find various other academic texts, such as books and reports.

Words and/or multi-word units are managed by comparing the inflected dictionary equivalences with the linguistic information in the corpus. Thus, *way* receives the Spanish equivalence *modo* from the dictionary, while *thus* receives *de este modo*. All the occurrences of *modo* in the corpus are labeled with the same number, except those appearing in the unit *de este modo*, to which a different number is assigned. As the resources grow, new information may result that 'contradicts' already stored words. For instance, if the idiom *raining cats and dogs* is introduced with its dictionary translation *llueve a cántaros*, the numbers previously assigned to *llueve* followed by *cántaros* must be replaced with the new number for the idiom. Consequently, updates of the dictionary database will revise the indexation of the corpus.

8.3. The case study

The sample corpus contains 1540 Spanish texts and a total of 6,898,481 running words. Standardised Type-to-Token Ratio (i.e., lexical density) is 40.21 per 1000 words, and the average number of words per sentence is 31.19. These scores are similar to those calculated for the academic English texts from the BNC Sampler: 41.54 and 26.23 respectively. Given these initial similarities, it seems that the academic register of the Spanish texts may parallel English discourse proportions of word use. It should be found, then, that the five types of co-occurrence described above (collocation, colligation, semantic association, text-related colligation Type 1 and text-related colligation Type 2) are similarly significant in Spanish academic texts. Competence in an academic discipline relates to 'mastery of collocations, colligations and semantic associations of the vocabulary (. . .) of the domain-specific and genre-specific primings' (Hoey 2005: 182).

Figure 8.1 displays the number of lexical features found with the first twenty-five grammatical words from the frequency word list. The results are

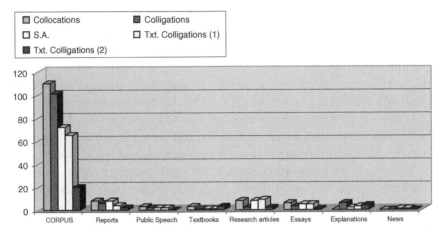

FIGURE 8.1   Number of features in entire corpus and in specific genres

classified according to appearance across the whole corpus, and according to distribution within specific genres.

Figure 8.1 shows that overall there are most instances of collocations. These are generally easy to record and label for the provision of fitting translation options. For example, the construction *al mismo tiempo* [*at the same time*] accounts for 80% of the cases of *al mismo* (actually, a very close figure to *at the same time* in relation to *at the same* in the BNC Sampler texts: 79.1%).

CBMT would work with a segmenting tool that takes n-grams of four to eight words and matches them against the information in the cache database. In the process, collocations and other combinations can work as basic items to find alternatives in the form of prefabricated language. These items are inserted as approved items in the database before the CBMT segmentation analysis takes place, or even when some lexical items may not be found in the dictionary. For instance, when the system encounters *at the same time*, the database should offer *al mismo tiempo*, given the approved information stored (*at the same time¬al mismo tiempo*). This collocation would then be selected even if it is not in the dictionary database.

Other statistically noteworthy examples from the corpus include colligations such as *al objeto de* [*with the objective of*] + infinitive verb (86.6%), *una vez* [*once*] + past participle (73%), *si no se* [*should he/she/it*] + present simple indicative (86.6%), etc. In such cases, the information should be labeled as obligatory (for example if a specific verb tense is favoured, the system should check and select it from lists/tables of conjugations).

In the case of the semantic associations, a similar process can take place with particular semantic sets which have been arranged in the database. For example, the form *se sitúa en* [*to be located in*] + 'physical location' appears in 42% of the instances of the lemmas *situarse en*. Some items can be associated with particular genres, and this information too can be entered on the database. An example is *se encuentra en* [*it is found in*] + 'virtual space', which only occurs in textbooks.

Text-related colligations (Types 1 and 2) would operate a bit differently, as they may involve changing the arrangement of the translated sentences. For instance, the item *en este trabajo* [*in this paper*] should be positioned at the beginning of the sentence and followed by a comma. This would be done after checking the information regarding this item, where it appears as a text-related colligation (Type 1) with sentence initial position in 72% of the occurrences. Similarly with instances of text-related colligation Type 2 (see Table 8.1), such as the form *por más que* [*no matter what*], in sentence initial position followed by the present simple subjunctive (71% of instances).

The reason for this classification is to allow the system to anticipate established translations in academic discourse, working with likely co-occurrences before using the dictionary and corpus databases. Obviously, the dictionary can and should include idiomaticity at all levels (i.e., fixed and semi-fixed word combinations), but these items should be managed after checking the cache database.

Once the retrieved translations are sent from the dictionary to the corpus, many different n-gram options can be measured, since there may be any number of n-grams found across the whole corpus, and many different possible combinations of the words within them. The classification of best translation options should be done according to statistical formulae that check the number of words in the given n-grams, co-occurrence within the four to eight word span, and distances between such words. In this process of n-gram word identification, the system should only work with content words (nouns, verbs, adjectives and adverbs). The main purpose is to establish co-occurrences. An n-gram like *the research paper focuses* would first be identified as – *research paper focuses*, and then, because *research paper* is an item in the dictionary, only two possible translated items would be sought from the n-gram: *trabajo de investigación* with one indexed number, and all the possible translations of *focuses* with various numbers throughout the corpus.

In our sample corpus, there are already many candidates for the combinations between *trabajo de investigación* and verb forms and nouns derived

Table 8.2   Some n-gram translation options for *research paper focuses* found in the corpus

7772#9# Para Bwin, - trabajo de investigación - - enfoque - muestra - verdadera
19393#14# - trabajo de investigación - - - perfectamente clara - - - enfoques alternativos
11171#19# - wagner, - - - instrumento internacional avala - trabajo de investigación - -
8763#17# - - - ocurrencia principal - - trabajo de investigación, enfocado - - servicio -
17612#23# pielografía - - - - inyectado oxígeno - - pelvis renal neumoquisis - centra
11334#17# aclimatación conjunto – centran - incluidos - - selección - adaptación, - - - -
19952#13# - objetivo - - monografía - - - - - - - trabajo de investigación - enfoca - -

from *focuses* (e.g., *enfoca / acerca / centra / centre / enfoques,* etc). Text and sentence labels (#) in the indexed corpus indicate where these occur (see Table 8.2). The statistical formula should enable the system to automatically recognise the best options in terms of number of words and proximity. Some options may contain a long distance between the items, (e.g. 7 or 8 words in the second line), or may not include both (third line), and such options should be given less priority. In this process, preliminary machine-based results should be manually checked to discern best options, so that weightings in the formulae can be adjusted.

For the items in Table 8.2, the system yields the best scores for the last line, followed by the first one (0.98 and 0.86 respectively). This order must then be confirmed (or not) with the insertion of functional items to complete the n-gram. Hyphens indicate functional words which must be retrieved from other tables in the system (based on corpus-based word frequency lists). For instance, in the last line, the word missing is the reflexive form *se,* while in the first line, the two hyphens point to the need to insert *tiene el* [*has the*]. The first option would be confirmed because the 4-unit n-gram [*el*] *trabajo de investigación [se] enfoca* matches the source text n-gram better (in number of words and proximity) than [*el*] *trabajo de investigación [tiene el*] *enfoque.*

The following step is that of connecting n-grams. This too is supported by statistical formulae that measure numbers of words, sentences and text identification numbers where the n-grams occur, so that connections based on these labels can be made. An example would be the connection between *research paper focuses* and the next n-gram identified by the sliding window, i.e., *on the.* Because in this case, two function words follow, the process is less complicated: as we can observe in Table 8.2, there are already sentence and text matches in the last and first lines from which we can draw this data. A more challenging step is that of finding the next context word(s). Here, the bigger the corpus, as Carbonell et al. (2006) note, the better the possibility of finding suitable matches. As these authors explain, where insufficient content information is available from either dictionary or corpus n-grams, both source and target language corpora may be exploited via synonym finding tools. Such devices would search for other options that match the co-text to the left and right of the unfound lexical item. Such co-text items, called signatures by Carbonell et al. (2006), would enable the system to provide more candidates that behave similarly. The unfound word would be replaced by the best similar option, that is, that appearing most times in those signatures.

8.4. CBMT and LSP teaching

The integration of specific lexicogrammatical information into the CBMT system seems to enhance the results that can be obtained in academic discourse. As a potential LSP teaching/learning tool, the CBMT approach may help learners in their study of effective English/Spanish translations along with corpus-driven tasks. Both ESP teachers and learners can profit from the approach, while readers and writers in a given discipline can appreciate a good translation of English discourse in their studies by relying on such utilities.

As mentioned in the introduction, most recent MT scholarship tends to acknowledge the fact that MT can work especially well when used for specific discourse. In CBMT, the case of academic discourse illustrates an efficient translation of linguistic chunks. For instance, an item like *There is no need for* or *There is no point in* may have different translation alternatives, but in academic Spanish, we find that *No se trata de* followed by infinitives is a more likely match, given the corpus data, and a human translator's evaluation. The translation becomes clear for the reader, who can perceive the solid relationship between the source and target items as well as their common use (the expression actually appears at the beginning of sentences in about 80% of instances within the academic texts).

The approach can be exploited in ESP courses by means of both corpus tools and database tables. As Bhatia et al. (2004: 205) state, increased linguistic-discursive awareness of basic generic principles and lexicogrammatical resources strengthens text processing and production competence. These tenets should be kept in mind in the integration of CBMT resources and strategies. The n-gram serves as the key linguistic unit for the study of academic lexical-rhetorical features, fundamental for the comprehension (and cohesion) of academic discourse. If the student can effectively recognise and identify specific lexicogrammatical relationships in translation, he/she can adapt certain learning mechanisms to the production of academic language at a subsequent stage.

The targeted range of lexical items may differ not only depending on the types of texts used, but also on topic and subject area. As Sin-wai (2004: 233) notes, 'conventions of highly conventionalised text types should be observed in the translation because readers expect to read texts in a recognisable form'. An example would be a greater focus on instructional language in textbook chapters, or on research language in journal articles or abstracts.

Examples of different cases of translation and equivalence can be shown to students to foster and strengthen their awareness of academic stance. With access to translations derived from corpus-based information, learners can figure out how and why their own previous (human) translation of the English items into Spanish should be changed and/or revised. Frequency-based lists of academic English/Spanish equivalences for collocations, colligations, semantic associations and text-related colligations (Types 1 and 2) can be useful in the task. The items should result from the actual corpus analysis performed in CBMT, and provide contrastive feedback for LSP translation output assessment.

Big differences can exist in the frequencies of academic (or semi-technical) items from one language to another. Therefore, corpus work in the LSP class should unveil and point to the evidence of such variations. For example, in the English corpus, more expressions are found with the first person pronoun *we* than in Spanish, which tends to present instead a higher rate of impersonal statements with the reflexive *se*. Items like *presentamos a continuación* [*we will describe*] and *llevamos a cabo* [*we will develop*] are rare by comparison. This type of contrastive exercise can show the students the way academic discourse may differ from one language to another, especially in the case of the more research-oriented type of discourse, such as that which is typical in Engineering (Hyland 2008).

A significant task in the process can be the classification of items in terms of translation quality evaluation. The use of tables can help the learners in the decision-making stage to distinguish effective equivalences. The teacher can direct the procedure by using the corpus-based frequency information from CBMT as reference data. Figure 8.2 displays some examples of classified items. The ones in the left-hand columns ('English corpus ok'/'Spanish corpus ok') have been approved as effective translations, and appear as such in the CBMT database. The items in the two columns on the right ('English corpus no'/'Spanish corpus no') have high frequencies in their respective corpora, but do not have the same translation quality level. The (v) sign in some items means that the item is repeated in upwards of 50% of all node word instances.

While in the 'ok' columns the items reflect equivalent frequency proportions and positive evaluation, the case differs for the 'no' columns. All items are ordered according to their frequency-based positions in each academic corpus. For instance, at position # 11, the 'ok' categories show suitable matching of the collocations. In contrast, the items do not match at this position in the 'no' categories, since the parallel Spanish item is a text-related colligation (Type 1) occurring at the beginning of sentences. In other cases, for example at positions # 14 and 15, there are no optimal matches according to the corpus information, but approximate equivalences listed in the 'no' categories. Finally, a row with a blank cell indicates that there was no parallel item found with a similar frequency for that group.

This task helps students to make sense of, and come to terms with, effective translations in the academic context. The classification, based on the corpus information and cache database obtained from the CBMT system, is then analysed and discussed in class, giving learners the opportunity to offer possible translation solutions in the process. An important aspect that arises is poor translations due to L1 (first language) transfer. For instance, at position # 8 in the 'no' categories (Figure 8.2),

Id	english corpus ok	spanish corpus ok	english corpus no	spanish corpus no
1	more than #	con más de / en más de#	more likely to (v)	lo más probable es que
2	more and + more	cada vez + más	more and more + adj	cada vez más + adj (v)
3	in order to + verb	con el fin de + verb / a fin de + verb		
4	. In other words,	. Dicho de otro modo,		
5	in terms of	en relación con, en función de + N		
6	in the field of + area / study	en el ámbito de + área / estudio		
7	in the case of	en el caso de		
8			in this sense, (v) / in this res	. En este sentido, (v)
9	in reference to / referred to	en lo que respecta a		
10	. According to + data	. De acuerdo con + datos		
11	in relation to / related to	en relación con	with regard to	. En cuanto a + NP (v)
12	in regard to	en lo que concierne a		
13	for example,	, por ejemplo,		
14			for this reason,	razón por la cual (v)
15			on the basis of (v)	en el marco de [v]
16	as far as (...) concerned	en lo que se refiere a		
17	. As a result,	. Por todo ello,		
18	as well as	al igual que	as well as to (v)	. Al igual que + NP (v)
19	defined as	se define como		
20	the fact that	el hecho de que		
21			stated / argued (...) that (v)	
22	it is difficult to + verb	no es fácil + verb + D.O.		. Por lo que respecta a
23	so that	para que	this means that (v)	lo cual significa que (v)
24	to ensure that	para asegurar que		

FIGURE 8.2   Example of approved item classification and storage in the ESP class

the Spanish equivalent checked is a text-related colligation (Type 1), recurrent in academic Spanish, but very seldom used in academic English. This finding encourages the learners to look for other options in the corpus to express the same thing at this position in the sentence, or, alternatively, to identify the same English item at other positions within sentences.

Having learners work concurrently with the corpus and these tables can make them aware of discourse variations and help to prevent common L1 transfer mistakes in academic writing. One example is the Spanish collocation at position # 14 (Figure 8.2), which sometimes appears to cause the ungrammatical English equivalent *reason by which**. The juxta-position in the table of the more valid, highly frequent item *for this reason* should serve to alert students to use the item in its appropriate context. As Hoey (2005) states, the function that these frequencies will play in the future writer's mind, especially those amply recognised in their L1, can be key for the correct selection and reproduction of linguistic items in the L2 text type.

8.5. Conclusions

CBMT requires huge amounts of linguistic information (dictionaries and corpora) in order to cope with as many candidate translations as possible. Still, for certain types of text/discourse, the linguistic information can be translated effectively using less computer effort and smaller resources. The n-grams (4 to 8 words) constitute the basic unit or structure where the lexical items are managed.

In this paper we have only described an initial prototype for the CBMT approach with English and Spanish. We have highlighted the importance of dealing with academic discourse as a starting point for the comparison of further linguistic analyses. The more dictionary and corpus information is entered in the databases, the greater the number of possible translation candidates to be managed, and the more possibilities for translation that will have to be filtered and examined. The statistical formulae will have to be fine tuned to enable the system to distinguish between very similar candidates. This task will be a great challenge for translation when there is little fixed or semi-fixed language, and the machine-based results will have to be manually checked. But the ultimate goal of machine translation is to approach human translation quality (Carbonell et al. 2006).

The final remarks and observations in this paper mainly concern possible developments and applications to EAP/ESP teaching, especially for academic translation and writing skills. Obviously enough, this paper can serve as a first step or basis for further corpus-based contrastive examination. The analysis may aim at the description of stylistic choices and guidelines where students may find clear information on those linguistic-discursive items characteristic of academic stance in their domains. To check discourse variation, the material should include not only the target English items in their field, but also in Spanish. The scope would entail a descriptive, and not prescriptive, approach to the material in such a way that, for example, textual considerations may be made as regards native versus non-native use, genre, subject and topic. The use of DDL (Data-Driven Learning) techniques (Johns 1993) can also play a significant role to foster the completion of schemata often formed by lexical relationships, which would thus meet specific linguistic needs in the academic context, not necessarily exclusive of the subject field encompassed. To some extent, the use of n-gram information in CBMT can provide the LSP learner with a direct observation of the primings of lexical items within academic discourse, and ample evidence of how fixed and semi-fixed language can convey such primings.

References

Abir, E., Klein, S., Miller, D. and Steinbaum, M. (2002), 'Fluent Machines' EliMT system'. *Association of Machine Translation in the Americas*, 2002, 216–219.

Badia, T., Boleda, G., Melero, M. and Oliver, A. (2005), 'An n-gram approach to exploiting a monolingual corpus for Machine Translation', in *Proceedings of the Second Workshop on Example-based Machine Translation*. Phuket, Thailand. [Online]. http://mutis.upf.es/glicom/Papers/gboleda/MTsummit2.pdf (accessed September 20, 2008).

Baroni, M., Kilgarriff, A., Pomikálek, J. and Rychly, P. (2006), 'WebBootCaT: instant domain-specific corpora to support human translators', in *Proceedings of EAMT 2006 – 11th Annual Conference of the European Association for Machine Translation*. Oslo: The Norwegian National LOGON Consortium and The Deparments of Computer Science and Linguistics and Nordic Studies at Oslo University, pp. 247–252. [Online]. http://www.sketchengine.co.uk (accessed September 16, 2008).

Bhatia, V.K., Langton, N.M. and Long, J. (2004), 'Legal discourse: opportunities and threats for corpus linguistics', in U. Connor and T.A. Upton (eds), *Discourse in the Professions: Perspectives from Corpus Linguistics*. Amsterdam and Philadelphia: John Benjamins, pp. 203–234.

Biber, D., Csomay, E., Jones, J.K. and Keck, C. (2004), 'A corpus linguistic investigation of vocabulary-based discourse units in university registers', in U. Connor and T.A. Upton (eds), *Applied Corpus Linguistics. A Multidimensional Perspective*. Amsterdam and Philadelphia: Rodopi, pp. 53–72.

Boleda, G.S., Bott, S., Castillo, C., Meza, R., Badia, T. and López, V. (2006), 'CUCWeb: a Catalan corpus built from the web', in *Proceedings of the Second Workshop on the Web as a Corpus at EACL'06*. Trento, Italy. [Online]. http://www.citeulike.org/bibtex_options/user/ChaTo/article/501628 (accessed October 17, 2008)

Burnard, L. and McEnery, T. (1999), *The British National Corpus Sampler*. Oxford: Oxford University Press.

Cademártori, Y., Parodi, G. and Venegas, R. (2007), 'El discurso escrito y especializado: las nominalizaciones en manuales técnicos', in G. Parodi (ed.), *Lingüística de Corpus y Discursos Especializados: Puntos de Mira*. Valparaíso, Chile: Ediciones Universitarias de Valparaíso, pp. 79–96.

Carbonell, J., Klein, S., Miller, D., Steinbaum, M., Grassiany, T. and Frey, J. (2006), 'Context-based machine translation'. *Association of Machine Translation in the Americas*, 2006, 19–28.

Hoey, M. (2005), *Lexical Priming: A New Theory of Words and Language*. London: Routledge.

Hyland, K. (2008), 'Academic clusters: text patterning in published and postgraduate writing'. *International Journal of Applied Linguistics*, 18, 1, 42–57.

Johns, T. (1993), 'Data-driven learning: an update'. *TELL & CALL*, 3, 23–32.

Kay, M. (1997), 'The proper place of men and machines in language translation'. *Machine Translation*, 12, 3–23.

Lahuerta Martínez, A.C. (2004), 'Discourse markers in the expository writing of Spanish university students'. *Ibérica*, 8, 63–80.

Lozano Palacios, A. (2008), *Diccionario Inglés – Español*. Granada: Servicio de Publicaciones.

Morales, O.A., Cassany, D. and González-Peña, C. (2007), 'La atenuación en artículos de revisión odontológicos en español: estudio exploratorio'. *Ibérica*, 14, 33–58.

Sin-wai, C. (2004), *A Dictionary of Translation Technology*. Hong Kong: The Chinese University Press.

Somers, H.L. (2003), 'Translation memory systems', in H.L. Somers (ed.), *Computers and Translation: A Translator's Guide*. Amsterdam and Philadelphia: John Benjamins, pp. 31–47.

Wilks, Y. (2009), *Machine Translation. Its Scope and Limits*. New York: Springer.

Chapter 9

Using corpora in the learning and teaching of phraseological variation

Martin Warren

This chapter restates the case that phraseology is central to meaning creation and that phraseological variation, in particular, remains under-researched. In the past, the absence of the means to fully explore phraseology and its variations has prevented comprehensive investigations, but, with the arrival of a new program, ConcGram (Greaves 2009), and a new corpus linguistics methodology (Cheng et al. 2009), they are now possible. Concgramming provides the raw data to identify phraseologies and this study describes the three main types of phraseology which the program is particularly well-suited to find. The implications of foregrounding phraseological variation in language learning and teaching are also discussed.

9.1. Introduction

In the 1960s, Sinclair led the first computer-mediated, corpus-driven study of English collocation (Sinclair et al. 1970). This study, and Sinclair's subsequent research, has greatly impacted corpus linguistics, especially our understanding of the importance of phraseology. Sinclair's work established the primacy of lexis over grammar in terms of meaning creation and, crucially, that meaning is created through the co-selection of words. This led him to outline his well-known 'idiom principle' (1987) and, by placing the study of phraseology at the heart of corpus linguistics, Sinclair was emphatic that language study is about the study of meaning creation.

While the importance of collocation was firmly established in the 1960s (Halliday 1966; Sinclair 1966; Sinclair et al. 1970), the study of phraseology has only relatively recently become more widespread. Studies have looked, for example, at extended units of meaning, n-grams, pattern grammar, phraseology and phrasal constructions (see, for example, Biber et al. 1999; Biber et al. 2004; Carter and McCarthy 2006; Cheng and Warren 2008; Granger and Meunier 2008; Hoey 2005, 2009; Hunston 2002; Hunston and Francis 2000; Louw 1993; O'Keeffe et al. 2007; Partington 1998; Scott and Tribble 2006; Sinclair 1987, 1996, 2004, 2005, 2007; Stubbs 2002, 2009; Tognini Bonelli 2001).

This paper explores the importance of examining phraseological variation, and the means available to now do this more thoroughly than in the past. It also examines the implications of such findings for the learning and teaching of phraseology.

9.2. Phraseology and corpus linguistics

Most of the studies of phraseology are based on analyses of frequently occurring n-grams (also variously termed 'chunks', 'clusters' and 'lexical bundles' in the literature). An n-gram is made up of two or more words which co-occur contiguously (e.g. *I know, at the, it is, end of a*). While such studies are quite commonplace, Sinclair (2001: 351–353) questions the extent to which the concentration on examining n-grams has led to other forms of phraseology being unintentionally overlooked. He points out that in studies of n-grams 'there is no recognition of variability of exponent or of position or of discontinuity' (2001: 353).

It should be pointed out that the deficiency in the study of n-grams highlighted by Sinclair has not gone completely unnoticed by at least some of the researchers in the field. Nesi and Basturkmen (2006: 285), for example, state that the identification of n-grams alone 'does not permit the identification of discontinuous frames (for example, *not only . . . but also . . .*)'. Biber et al. (2004: 401–402) state that a future aim needs to be 'to extend the methods used to identify lexical bundles to allow for variations on a pattern', but they make the point that the problem blocking a more comprehensive study, which also accounts for variation, is 'trying to identify the full range of lexical bundles across a large corpus of texts'.

These limitations of n-gram searches have led to the development of searches for gapped n-grams, or 'skipgrams', in NLP (Wilks 2005).

Skipgrams include a certain amount of constituency variation (i.e. *hard work* and *hard detailed work*). A skipgram search also has its limitations, however, because it is currently limited to three-word skipgrams and four 'skips' (Wilks 2005). As a result, co-occurring words which are more than four words apart are not found. A skipgram search is also limited in that it does not find instances of positional variation (i.e. *hard work* and *work hard*). Another example of a skipgram-like search is Fletcher's (2006) program which finds 'phrase frames'. Phrase frames are based on an initial automated search for n-grams up to eight words long. A subsequent search finds phrase-frames which are 'sets of variants of an n-gram identical except for one word' (Fletcher 2006). Phrase frames, then, are constrained by narrower search parameters than those for skipgrams, with the result that non-contiguous co-occurrences of the same words go undiscovered if they differ by more than one word, along with instances with positional variation.

Sinclair's criticism of relying solely on studies of n-grams to describe phraseology raises fundamental issues with regard to what he terms the phraseological tendency in language (Sinclair 1987), and he proposes his own model for identifying and describing 'extended units of meaning', or 'lexical items'[1] (Sinclair 1996, 1998, 2004). A lexical item is made up of five categories of co-selection: the core word(s), semantic prosody, semantic preference, collocation, and colligation (Sinclair 2004: 141–142). The core and the semantic prosody are obligatory, whereas collocation, colligation and semantic preference are optional. The core is 'invariable, and constitutes the evidence of the occurrence of the item as a whole' (p. 141), in other words the core word(s) is always present. Semantic prosody is the overall functional meaning of a lexical item, while collocation and colligation are related to the co-occurrences of words and grammatical choices with the core. The semantic preference of a lexical item is 'the restriction of regular co-occurrence to items which share a semantic feature, e.g. about sport or suffering' (p. 142).

It is evident that Sinclair's five categories of co-selection comprising a lexical item are not going to be found in studies which are confined to n-grams, but the problem remains: how do we find these co-selections in a corpus without any prior knowledge of them? Cheng et al. (2006) have developed a program, ConcGram (Greaves 2009), which is able to fully automatically retrieve the co-selections which comprise lexical items, and other forms of phraseological variation, from a corpus. The outputs from this program are described and exemplified below.

9.3. Identifying phraseological variation in a corpus

The original idea for the ConcGram program came from a desire to be able to fully automatically retrieve the co-selections which comprise Sinclair's meaning shift units (MSUs) (Sinclair 2007) from a corpus. The central aim was to be able to identify MSUs without relying on potentially misleading clues in single word frequency lists or lists of n-grams or any form of user-nominated search. It was felt that single word frequencies are not the best indicators of frequent phraseologies in a corpus, and there was also the concern that studies based on n-grams miss phraseologies that have constituency (e.g. *work hard, work so hard, work very very hard* etc.) and/or positional variation (e.g. *work hard, hard work, hard detailed work* etc.). It was decided that a program was needed which could identify all of the co-occurrences of two or more words irrespective of constituency and/ or positional variation in order to more fully account for phraseological variation and provide raw data for identifying MSUs (see Cheng et al. 2006; Cheng et al. 2009) and other forms of phraseology. In addition, as mentioned above, it was critical that the program be able to identify these co-occurrences fully automatically in order to support corpus-driven research (Tognini Bonelli 2001), without requiring the user to input any prior search parameters. The final product, ConcGram (Greaves 2009), meets these demands and it is hoped that researchers, teachers and learners can all benefit from the new insights into what Sinclair (1987) terms 'the phraseological tendency of language' which the program makes possible.

It is important to note that in its fully automatic mode, ConcGram finds co-occurrences of words in a wide span, and therefore not all of them are necessarily meaningfully associated. Consequently, it is necessary to make a distinction between 'co-occurring' words (i.e. concgrams) and 'associated' words (i.e. phraseology). It has been found that determining the parameters of 'associatedness', and classifying instances of a concgram accordingly, are useful activities for language learners to engage in (Greaves and Warren 2007).

In order to get a sense of how ConcGram's outputs differ from traditional concordances, sample concordance lines for the two-word concgram 'provide/services' are given in concordance 1 which illustrate how the program finds the full range of phraseological variation. (All examples of concgrams in this paper are from a 5-million word sample of the British National Corpus comprised of 3 million written words and 2 million spoken.)

Concordance 1. Sample concordance lines of the two-word concgram 'provide/services'

```
1    London. Erm basically to say that elsewhere can provide services on a cheaper basis than those hospitals
2         forms, the home health authority does not provide any services at all directly, but puts out
3    government also permitted local authorities to provide extra services in addition to the ones covered
4         to pay sensible attention to the need to provide essential public services economically, but
5       adapt its internal organisation in order to  provide a set of integrated services to the local
6    distinguishes them from the state agencies that provide health, education or other services on the
7    [unclear] employer. We in the public services provide a higher standard of efficiency and quality,in
8    over the last decade to improve the services we provide for the people we serve and  the environment in
9    to do derive a profit from the services that you provide to, I don't know, public bodies.  <u
10         goods and services. Export credit agencies provide insurance against certain defaults to the
```

The various concgram configurations for 'provide/services', when 'provide' is centred, begin with contiguous words to the right, and subsequent lines show instances ordered according to the distance between the words in the concgram in terms of character spaces. Once all of the instances to the right of the centred word have been displayed, those to the left are similarly displayed. As the program is designed to uncover all of the instances of phraseology irrespective of variation, this display aims to show the extent of the variation in as orderly and manageable a manner as possible. In Concordance 1, line 10 is a good example of the need to distinguish between instances of 'provide' and 'services' which simply co-occur and ones which are meaningfully associated; this instance is classified as a co-occurrence while all the other instances in Concordance 1 are classified as associated.

Concgrams present a very different view of word co-occurrences compared with KWIC (key-word-in-context) displays. A KWIC concordance highlights the node (i.e. the centred search word) and the result is that there is a tendency to adopt an analytical approach taking the node as the centre of attention and any co-occurring words as subordinate to it. By highlighting the co-occurring words as well as the node, ConcGram shifts attention from the node to all of the words in the concgram. To underline this difference, the term 'origin' rather than 'node' is used for the word or words which are the source of automated concgram searches. In its automatic mode, the program starts by finding all the two-word concgrams and then builds up iteratively to five-word concgrams. In such a process, the notion of a 'node' is misleading and that of an 'origin' (one-word, two-word, three-word or four-word) better captures the fact that the focus is on co-occurring words.

9.4. Types of phraseological variation

In the research conducted to date on concgrams, phraseological associations can be categorised as one of three main types: 'meaning shift units (MSU)' (Sinclair 2007) (also termed 'lexical items', Sinclair 1996, 1998, 2004), 'collocational frameworks' (Renouf and Sinclair 1991) and 'organisational frameworks'. Each of these is described and exemplified below.

The original idea for identifying concgrams in a corpus was to find and describe MSUs (Sinclair 2007). Cheng et al. (2009) illustrate an analytical procedure for identifying and fully describing MSUs using concgram outputs. Here the identification of an MSU is illustrated using this procedure in the analysis of the two-word concgram 'hard/work' in Concordance 2. The sample of instances of 'hard/work' in Concordance 2 has been selected to illustrate the steps involved.

Concordance 2. Sample concordance lines for the meaning shift unit 'hard/ work'

```
1        side of  life and who's nevertheless, through hard work and perseverance and so on,  triumphed over
2              quality football  in their performances. Hard work, 10 man defending, clearing the ball as far
3        at Baltusrol  NICK FALDO, never afraid of hard work in his pursuit of golfing perfection, has
4        collectively for the  tremendous amount of hard work and dedication put in during the year, and
5        to my business than my wife. Determination, hard work, commitment and family unity got us where we
6        selling comes from careful preparation  and hard work. It comes from taking a genuine interest in
7        am also in no doubt about the amount of devoted hard work that has gone on  during the last four
8        and its  display, because this reflects hard work and thrift. Hard work, thrift, and the
9        trendy and affluent. This affluence comes from hard work in a well paid job, and permits the
10       such as  loyalty, confidentiality, dynamism, hard work, the ability to sell a product,  and so on.
11       of responsibility requires good preparation and hard work in sharing,  adjusting and reaching agreed
12       community, and because of their  reputation for hard work and honesty, Goans have always be able to
13       and the Managing Director paid tribute to the hard work and  positive attitude of the Company's
14       a fag I   need something I've worn out, had a hard day's work. The other guy will rea really get
15       in middle management,  where all the hard detailed work had to be done.  Walsh, lecturing
16       TAURUS: Apr 21 to May 21    You'll find it hard to turn off today and work colleagues will not be
17       I'm not trying to make it hard for you, I'm trying to work out what is useful
18       "They've been amazing," he said. "It's hard to believe the amount of work that's gone on and
19       child's internalising, I'm loved because I work hard, and this is what I have to do. If you work
20       earn, then  it really is an incentive to work hard and perform well, says Tony, 28. "Tipping - or
21       this is your opportunity  in life, and you work hard. You're what we want, you work hard at school,
22       wants to be free: free to fall in love, work hard and have fun. All she is asking for, she says,
23       no (they do, though most of them have to work hard for it), and whether parents  should go and fuck
24       late 1987.  Mr Louis-Dreyfus will have to work hard to recover the company's standing. He may also
25       genuine changes in our erm willingness to work hard  at our family life and not to give in easily at
26       brightest in the year and I had  to work very hard, but God always  was with me as I always passed
27       and  constructive. People still work very hard during meetings, but their conversation begins to
28       the equity of those exchanges. If we work extra hard for our employers we expect some kind of reward
29       what I expect for you to be able to work, really hard, get your homework  done, work hard in your
30       workers may work in industries particularly hard-hit in the recession, or  there may be a high
```

The first step in identifying an MSU is to find the canonical form in terms of both frequency and meaning. The canonical form is then used as the benchmark for all of the other concgram configurations. In the corpus studied, there are 130 instances of this concgram. Of the 130 occurrences, 85 have the positional variation 'hard.. work' and 45 are 'work.. hard'. Of those 85 instances of the positional variation 'hard.. work', 72 are the contiguous 'hard work' with the remaining 13 having constituency variation. Of these 13, 9 are classified as co-occurrences and 4 are associated. In Concordance 2 examples of co-occurrences can be seen in lines 16–18 and examples of those deemed to be associated are in lines 14 and 15. Of the 45 instances with the positional variation 'work.. hard', 21 are the contiguous 'work hard' and 25 have constituency variation, which is typically a one word modifier such as 'very' or 'so'. Of these 25, 15 are associated, such as those in lines 26–29, and ten are co-occurrences, for example line 30. This means that, based on frequency, the canonical form of 'hard/work' is the contiguous form 'hard work'.

The next step is to determine the extent of the adherence of the other configurations of 'hard/work' to the meaning of the canonical form and these configurations can then be ranked relative to it. Here it is argued that all of the associated forms adhere to the canonical form with what is termed increasing levels of 'turbulence' (Cheng et al. 2009) as words intervene between the core words of this MSU or positional variation occurs. By then studying the patterns of collocation, colligation and semantic preference it is possible to build up a profile of this MSU's co-selections. The consistent pattern of co-selections, such as 'perseverance', 'perfection', 'determination', 'affluence', 'dedication', 'devoted', 'dynamism', 'reputation', 'honesty', 'tribute', 'incentive' 'love', 'fun', 'willingness', 'careful/good preparation', 'perform well', 'company's standing', 'opportunity' and 'positive attitude', provides the evidence for the semantic prosody of this MSU. The semantic prosody is of a cause and effect relationship in which hard work brings the hard worker, or the organisation in which s/he works, positive rewards of various kinds. This semantic prosody is further confirmed by a speech by UK politician Gordon Brown at a Labour Party Conference in September 2006. In his speech, Mr Brown thanked his parents for the values they instilled in him as a young boy and one of the values is 'hard work': 'They believed in duty, responsibility and respect for others. They believed in honesty and hard work, and that the things that matter had to be worked for'. By means of the analytical procedure illustrated above, an MSU together with the extent of its variation and its co-selections is fully identified and described.

It is well known that 'grammatical' or 'function' words top the single word frequency lists generated from corpora, and so it is not surprising to find that the co-occurrences of these words dominate concgram frequency lists. The co-selections of grammatical words are termed 'collocational frameworks' (Renouf and Sinclair 1991) and, despite their high frequencies, this form of phraseology remains under-researched. Concgramming makes the study of collocational frameworks easier because they typically exhibit considerable constituency and positional variation. Studies of collocational frameworks using ConcGram show that the five most frequent are 'the . . . of', 'a/an . . . of', 'the . . . of the', 'the . . . in' and 'the . . . to' in a 5-million word sample of the British National Corpus (Li and Warren 2008). Examples of the collocational framework 'the/of' are given in Concordance 3.

Concordance 3. Sample concordance lines for the collocational framework 'the/of'

1	(1974) indicate that, in both the USA and UK, **the** mix **of** public goods and tax rates has an effect
2	into Iran, and I saw the whole situation with **the** aid **of** erm the United States mass media, so
3	is intended to work through from Stage One at **the** age **of** 5-7 to Stage Four at the age of 14-16,
4	Before I kick off I to reply to them I put at **the** top **of** my scribbled notes three words poverty
5	and there will be a bucket collection at **the** end **of** this session. A victory for the G M B is
7	are ripening, much like the olives growing in **the** Department **of** Energy's new atrium at the centre
8	by your format variety and, wherever possible, **the** right kind **of** sparkle. You inform by making
9	6 PLANNING AND THE ENVIRONMENT As we approach **the** last years **of** the 20th century, environmental
10	social" railway, were the commuter services in **the** south east **of** England, centred on the metropolis

The prevalence of collocational frameworks such as the one illustrated above suggests that they deserve more attention from researchers and in the language classroom. Sinclair and Renouf (1988) argue that they should be included in a lexical syllabus, but, so far, they are still ignored. Some new grammars (Carter and McCarthy 2006) now list and discuss n-grams as do other studies by corpus linguists. For example, Scott and Tribble (2006: 139) list the most frequent three-word n-grams found across spoken and written corpora. Their lists include, *the end of, the number of, the use of* and *the rest of* among many similar phraseologies. It could be argued that descriptions of these n-grams should begin with a description of their shared collocational framework; namely 'the/of'.

Hunston (2002) briefly describes 'clause collocation' which derives from the tendency for particular types of clause to be co-selected. She provides one example of a clause collocation, 'I wonder . . . because', where 'I wonder' and 'because' are co-selected to link clauses in the discourse (2002: 75) and notes that such collocations can be hard to find because the size of the 'I wonder' clause can be any number of words. Sinclair and Mauranen (2006) distinguish between 'organisation-oriented' elements and 'message-oriented' elements in their linear unit grammar, and this distinction has been adopted to denote this type of phraseology as an 'organisational framework' (Greaves and Warren 2008). This choice of terminology captures how organisational elements, such as conjunctions, connectives and discourse particles, are sometimes co-selected to link sections of a discourse. ConcGram is particularly good at finding organisational frameworks because it finds co-occurring words across a wide span. Sample concordance lines of the organisational framework 'but/so' are shown in Concordance 4.

Concordance 4. Sample concordance lines of the organisational framework 'but/so'

```
1      give it to Ian  to take to college tonight, but he's not in so I can't, so I've gotta send it
2      it. I know it will hurt for a little while, but I'll get better, so why worry? I don't see why I
3    he going to College tonight? <u who=PSOK8> Yeah, but he's not in today  so I can't give it to him. <u
4  And I said well you haven't even met me. Said no but you come from Essex so you can't be too  bad .
5        not ever counted amongst the statistics. But nobody keeps statistics, so nobody really knows.
6   me. She could say nothing. So she said nothing. But she was almost choking with emotion. And not with
7    to let us stay in bed, so it was a bit tough. But it was also great, because we didn't know any
8      it had started. So I've looked after myself but I've worked hard as well because I like a
9    Nobody bought them so I began to repair fridges. But nobody has their fridges repaired any more, they
10     French, so they've sent him to study in France. But they're missing him badly, they say.   Quote of
```

There are some well-known organisational frameworks and these are usually described in grammars as 'correlative conjunctions' (e.g. 'both . . . and', neither . . . nor', 'not only . . . but also', 'if . . . then'). There are others, however, such as 'but/so', which are not included in such descriptions, and others that are probably still unknown, which merit attention. For those who tend to restrict the search for collocations to within sentence boundaries, it is interesting to note that some instances of the organisational framework 'but/so' transcend sentence boundaries (see lines 6, 7, 9 and 10). It is also of interest that this organisational framework exhibits both constituency and positional variation and this is found in other organisational frameworks as well.

9.5. Conclusions and implications for learning and teaching

It is hard to overstate the key role of phraseology in meaning creation.

By far the majority of text is made of the occurrence of common words in common patterns, or in slight variants of those common patterns. Most everyday words do not have an independent meaning, or meanings, but

are components of a rich repertoire of multi-word patterns that make up
a text.

Sinclair (1991: 108)

We now better understand that when we speak and write, on almost all
occasions, we select words in combination. This is the phraseological
tendency in language, whereby individual words are not selected separately but are co-selected (Sinclair 1987). While these co-selections are
now starting to be described in new corpus-based grammars of the English
language (e.g. Carter and McCarthy 2006), they are still not sufficiently
foregrounded. Attention has been largely confined to n-grams, which
while a frequently occurring type of word association, provide only
a partial picture of the extent of phraseology. Phraseology has not only
become a new frontier which is of interest to researchers, but it also presents new challenges and opportunities for learners and teachers of the
English language. While its importance is not disputed, this is currently a
relatively neglected area in the learning and teaching of applied English
language studies and English language proficiency. Exceptions to this
general observation are recent textbooks on phraseology and collocation
(see for example, McCarthy 2005; Sinclair 2003; Stubbs 2002). This paper
argues that greater emphasis should be placed on phraseology and
advocates concgramming to introduce and promote it in learning and
teaching. This proposal builds on the work of those who have promoted
the use of corpora and corpus linguistics in language learning (see for
example, Aston 1997; Bernardini 2002; Braun 2005; Kennedy and Miceli
2002; Sinclair 2004) and, in particular, the use of concordancing (see for
example, Bernardini 2000; Cobb 1997; Gaskell and Cobb 2004; Johns
1991; Sinclair 2003; Stevens 1991).

The findings from studies of phraseology to date have impacted dictionary
writing as well as the writing of some English language grammars, and, to a
lesser extent, English language textbooks. They also have the potential to
further influence English language teaching, and comparisons of the use of
phraseologies by expert and novice writers and speakers are increasingly
common. Cortes (2004), for example, finds that the use of phraseology, in
the form of collocations and fixed expressions associated with particular
registers and genres, is a sign of proficient language use. Similarly, in a
study of longer (four-word) n-grams, Hyland (2008: 5) states that the use of
these phraseologies signals 'competent participation in a given community'.
Hyland finds that this is often not the case for novice members of a speech

community, and the absence of discipline-specific n-grams can indicate a lack of fluency. The conclusion is that learners need to acquire 'an appropriate discipline-based lexical repertoire' of n-grams (Hyland and Tse 2007: 235). This conclusion, based on a study of the use of n-grams, can also be expected to hold true for the three broad categories of phraseology described and discussed in this paper. There are at least three ways in which concgramming may contribute significantly in language learning and teaching. It can be used as a tool for textual analysis (see, for example, Carter and McCarthy 1994; Stubbs 2002, 2009) and it can be used to help raise learners' awareness of the idiom principle by helping them to identify associated words and phraseology in general (Sinclair and Mauranen 2006). Lastly, concgramming can be used to enable learners to have a better understanding and command of the discourse of specialised fields and their specific genres (see, for example, Bhatia 2004; O'Keeffe et al. 2007; Scott and Tribble 2006; Swales 2004). Further work on the identification of all the potential variation in patterns of phraseology will contribute to a better understanding of the co-selections that constitute the full extent of the phraseological tendency in language which Sinclair (1987) outlined. Both learners and teachers stand to benefit from a better knowledge of phraseologies, particularly with regard to collocational frameworks and organisational frameworks which have generally been overlooked. Sinclair (1996: 95) argues that 'a start can be made on an inventory of the units of meaning of English'. It is hoped that further analysis of concgrams will contribute to building up a comprehensive inventory of phraseologies.

Acknowledgements

The author is grateful to John Sinclair for his invaluable input as consultant to the first concgram-related project. Thanks are also due to Winnie Cheng, Chris Greaves and Elena Tognini Bonelli who all work on the current project. The work described in this paper was substantially supported by a grant from the Research Grants Council of the Hong Kong Special Administrative Region (Project No.: PolyU 5459/08H, B-Q11N).

Notes

[1] Sinclair later suggests the term 'meaning shift unit' rather than 'lexical item' (Sinclair 2007; Sinclair and Tognini Bonelli, 2010).

164   *Martin Warren*

References

Aston, G. (1997), 'Small and large corpora in language learning', in B. Lewandowska-Tomaszczyk and J. P. Melia (eds), *Practical Applications in Language Corpora*. Łodz: Łodz University Press, pp. 51–62.

Bazell, C. E., Catford, J. C., Halliday, M.A.K. and Robbins, R. H. (1966) (eds), *In Memory of J. R. Firth*. London: Longman.

Bernardini, S. (2000), 'Systematising serendipity: proposals for concordancing large corpora with language learners', in L. Burnard and T. McEnery (eds), *Rethinking Language Pedagogy from a Corpus Perspective*. Frankfurt: Peter Lang, pp. 225–234.

Bernardini, S. (2002), 'Exploring new directions for discovery learning', in B. Kettemann and G. Marko (eds), pp. 165–182.

Bhatia, V. K. (2004), *Worlds of Written Discourse*. London: Continuum.

Biber, D., Conrad, S., and Cortes, V. (2004), ' "If you look at . . ." ': lexical bundles in university teaching and textbooks'. *Applied Linguistics*, 25, 371–405.

Biber, D., Johansson, S., Leech, G., Conrad, S., and Finegan E. (1999), *Longman Grammar of Spoken and Written English*. London: Longman.

Braun, S. (2005), 'From pedagogically relevant corpora to authentic language learning contents'. *ReCALL*, 17, (1), 47–64.

Carter, R. and McCarthy, M. (1994), *Language as Discourse: Perspectives for Language Teaching*. London: Longman.

Carter R. and McCarthy, M. (2006), *Cambridge Grammar of English*. Cambridge: Cambridge University Press.

Cheng, W., Greaves, C. and Warren, M. (2006), 'From n-gram to skipgram to concgram'. *International Journal of Corpus Linguistics*,11, (4), 411–433.

Cheng, W., Greaves, C., Sinclair, J. and Warren, M. (2009), 'Uncovering the extent of the phraseological tendency: towards a systematic analysis of concgrams'. *Applied Linguistics*, 30, (2), 236–252.

Cheng, W. and Warren, M. (2008), '// → ONE country two *SYS*tems //: the discourse intonation patterns of word associations', in A. Ädel and R. Reppen (eds), *Corpora and Discourse: The Challenges of Different Settings*. Amsterdam and Philadelphia: John Benjamins, pp. 135–153.

Cobb, T. (1997), 'Is there any measurable learning from hands-on concordancing?' *System*, 25, (3), 301–315.

Cortes, V. (2004), 'Lexical bundles in published and student disciplinary writing: examples from history and biology'. *English for Specific Purposes*, 23, (4), 397–423.

Fletcher, W. H. (2006), 'Phrases in English'. [Online]. http://pie.usna.edu/ (accessed February 15, 2006).

Gaskell, D. and Cobb, T. (2004), 'Can learners use concordance feedback for writing errors?' *System*, 32, (3), 301–319.

Granger, S. and Meunier, F. (eds) (2008), *Phraseology in Foreign Language Learning and Teaching*. Amsterdam and Philadelphia: John Benjamins.

Greaves, C. (2009), *ConcGram 1.0: A phraseological Search Engine*. Amsterdam and Philadelphia: John Benjamins.

Greaves, C. and Warren, M. (2007), 'Concgramming: a computer-driven approach to learning the phraseology of English'. *ReCALL Journal*, 17, (3), 287–306.

Greaves, C. and Warren, M. (2008), 'Beyond clusters: a new look at word associations', Paper presented at *IVACS 4, 4th International Conference: Applying Corpus Linguistics.* University of Limerick, Ireland, 13–June 14, 2008.

Halliday, M.A.K. (1966), 'Lexis as a linguistic level', in C. E. Bazell, J.C. Catford, M.A.K. Halliday and R.H. Robins (eds), pp. 148–162.

Hoey, M. (2005), *Lexical Priming: A New Theory of Words and Language.* London: Routledge.

Hoey, M. (2009), 'Corpus-driven approaches to grammar: the search for common ground', in U. Römer and R. Schulze (eds), pp. 33–47.

Hunston, S. (2002), *Corpora in Applied Linguistics.* Cambridge: Cambridge University Press.

Hunston, S. and Francis, G. (2000), *Pattern Grammar: A Corpus-driven Approach to the Lexical Grammar of English.* Amsterdam and Philadelphia: John Benjamins.

Hyland, K. (2008), 'As can be seen: lexical bundles and disciplinary variation'. *English for Specific Purposes*, 27, (1): 4–21.

Hyland, K. and Tse, P. (2007), 'Is there an "Academic Vocabulary"?'. *TESOL Quarterly*, 41, (2), 235–253.

Johns, T. (1991), 'Should you be persuaded: two samples of data-driven learning materials', in T. Johns and P. King (eds), pp. 1–16.

Johns, T. and King, P. (eds) (1991), *Classroom Concordancing. English Language Research Journal*, 4. Birmingham: University of Birmingham.

Kennedy, C. and Miceli, T. (2002), 'The *CWIC* project: developing and using a corpus for intermediate Italian students', in B. Kettemann and G. Marko (eds), pp. 183–192.

Kettemann, B. and Marko, G. (eds) (2002), *Teaching and Learning by Doing Corpus Analysis.* Amsterdam and New York: Rodopi.

Li, Y. and Warren, M. (2008), '*In . . . of:* what are collocational frameworks and should we be teaching them?'. Paper presented at the *4th International Conference on Teaching English at Tertiary Level.* Zhejiang, China, 11–12 October, 2008.

Louw, B. (1993), 'Irony in the text or insincerity in the writer? The diagnostic potential of semantic prosodies', in M. Baker, G. Francis and E. Tognini Bonelli (eds), *Text and Technology: In Honour of John Sinclair.* Amsterdam and Philadelphia: John Benjamins, pp. 157–176.

McCarthy, M. (2005), *English Collocations in Use.* Cambridge: Cambridge University Press.

Nesi, H. and Basturkman, H. (2006), 'Lexical bundles and signalling in academic lectures'. *International Journal of Corpus Linguistics*, 11, (3), 283–304.

O'Keeffe, A., McCarthy, M., and Carter, R. (2007), *From Corpus to Classroom.* Cambridge: Cambridge University Press.

Partington, A. (1998), *Patterns and Meanings.* Amsterdam; John Benjamins.

Renouf, A.J. and Sinclair, J.McH. (1991), 'Collocational Frameworks in English', in K. Aijmer and B. Altenberg (eds), *English Corpus Linguistics.* London: Longman, pp. 128–143.

Römer, U. and Shulze, R. (eds) (2009) *Exploring the Lexis-Grammar Interface.* Amsterdam and Philadelphia: John Benjamins.

Scott, M. and Tribble, C. (2006), *Textual Patterns: Key Words and Corpus Analysis in Language Education*. Amsterdam and Philadelphia: John Benjamins.

Sinclair, J. (1966), 'Beginning the study of lexis', in C. E. Bazell, J.C. Catford, M.A.K. Halliday and R.H. Robins (eds), pp. 410–431.

Sinclair, J. (1987), 'Collocation: a progress report', in R. Steele and T. Threadgold (eds), *Language Topics: Essays in Honour of Michael Halliday*. Amsterdam and Philadelphia: John Benjamins, pp. 319–331.

Sinclair, J. (1991), *Corpus Concordance Collocation*. Oxford: Oxford University Press.

Sinclair, J. (1996), 'The search for units of meaning', *Textus* 9, (1), 75–106.

Sinclair, J. (1998), 'The lexical item', in E. Weigand (ed.), *Contrastive Lexical Semantics*. Amsterdam and Philadelphia: John Benjamins, pp. 1–24.

Sinclair, J. (2001), 'Review'. *International Journal of Corpus Linguistics*, 6, (2), 339–359.

Sinclair, J. (2003), *Reading Concordances*. London: Pearson Longman.

Sinclair, J. (2004), *Trust the Text*. London: Routledge.

Sinclair, J. (2005). 'Document relativity'. Manuscript, Tuscan Word Centre, Italy.

Sinclair, J. (2007), 'Collocation reviewed'. Manuscript, Tuscan Word Centre, Italy.

Sinclair, J., Jones, S. and Daley, R. (1970), *English Lexical Studies*. Report to the Office of Scientific and Technical Information. Birmingham: The University of Birmingham.

Sinclair, J. and Mauranen, A. (2006), *Linear Unit Grammar*. Amsterdam and Philadelphia: John Benjamins.

Sinclair, J. and Renouf, A. (1988), 'A lexical syllabus for language learning', in R. Carter and M. McCarthy (eds), *Vocabulary and Language Teaching*. London: Longman, pp. 140–160.

Stevens, V. (1991), 'Concordance-based vocabulary exercises: a viable alternative to gap-fillers', in T. Johns and P. King (eds), pp. 47–63.

Stubbs, M. (2002), *Words and Phrases: Corpus Studies of Lexical Semantics*. Oxford: Blackwell.

Stubbs, M. (2009), 'Technology and phraseology: with notes on the history of corpus linguistics', in U. Römer and R. Schulze (eds), pp. 15–31.

Swales, J. (2004), *Research Genres: Explorations and Applications*. Cambridge: Cambridge University Press.

Tognini Bonelli, E. (2001), *Corpus Linguistics at Work*. Amsterdam and Philadelphia: John Benjamins.

Tognini Bonelli, E. (ed.) (2010). *John Sinclair on Essential Corpus Linguistics*. London and New York: Routledge.

Wilks, Y. (2005), 'REVEAL: the notion of anomalous texts in a very large corpus'. Tuscan Word Centre International Workshop: Dial a Corpus. Certosa di Pontignano, Tuscany, Italy, June 31–July 3, 2005.

Chapter 10

The SACODEYL search tool – exploiting corpora for language learning purposes

Johannes Widmann, Kurt Kohn and Ramon Ziai

SACODEYL is a EU project that has created pedagogically motivated spoken language corpora in seven European languages: English, French, German, Italian, Lithuanian, Romanian and Spanish. The corpora consist of video interviews with 13–17-year-old secondary school pupils, which have been aligned with their transcripts and pedagogically annotated. Enrichment materials, such as learning packages, have also been incorporated. This chapter describes the development and the features of the SACODEYL search tool, which is currently in a piloting and validation phase. Focus is given to the design of the search tool and to how it enables the teacher or language learner retrieve materials and annotations in pedagogically useful ways. The innovative features for corpus access and exploitation are discussed, and it is shown how these features can be used in language learning scenarios of secondary schools to create a fruitful, authentic and varied learning environment.

10.1. Introduction

The EU-funded SACODEYL project has created pedagogically motivated spoken language corpora in seven European languages: English, French, German, Italian, Lithuanian, Romanian and Spanish. Each language has its own corpus and each corpus consists of 25 interviews with teenagers between 13 and 18 years of age. All the interviews are equally structured, which means that the interviewers use roughly the same questions, based on the same topics. All of the topics were selected on the basis of a survey among secondary school teachers and on the basis of the functional progression of the Common European Framework for languages.[1] Consequently, simple answers were elicited at the beginning of the interviews where the teen-agers present themselves. They then go on to talk about their homes and families. Later, they talk about increasingly complex subjects, such as their hobbies, their school lives, their plans for the future, past holidays, etc. At the end of most interviews, there are open discussion questions where the interviewees are asked to voice their opinions on specific topics that came up during the interviews.

All the corpora have been annotated, bearing in mind the needs of language learners at secondary school level. Thus, most of the annotation focuses on clear examples that do not confuse language learners at this level and that nicely illustrate the point in question. The annotation mainly focuses on well-known lexical and grammatical categories, so that language teachers and language learners can easily familiarise themselves with the annotation system. However, some annotation categories, such as *topic-specific terminology*, go well beyond what is typically available and, taken together with a specific topic, nicely illustrate the additional benefits of a corpus search when compared to what is usually available in schoolbook materials.

All the video recordings have been aligned with the transcript sections, allowing the user to jump to the exact position in the video where the tran-script section starts. In addition, enrichment materials, such as learning packages, have been produced and attached to the relevant sections. All this has been done to help learners and teachers to exploit the corpora in various ways and from various angles. The two theoretical ideas behind the approach are the pedagogical concepts of constructivist learning and language authentication. For constructivist learning to be successful, it is important that learners can find a starting point where they can link new to existing knowledge (Rüschoff 1999). Consequently, the more possible starting points a corpus offers for exploitation, the more likely it is that there exists an appropriate starting point for a specific learner. The idea of language authentication on the other hand originates in the work of Henry Widdowson, who holds that pedagogic mediation of 'real language' mater-ials is necessary so that learners can actually appropriate the materials for themselves (Widdowson 2003). Simply the fact that language is 'real' does not necessarily mean that it is possible for language learners to reconnect to it in their specific classroom situations. Again, the more options for appropriation the corpus offers, the more likely it is that the corpus and the language materials will be perceived as helpful by the learners.

In this paper, we first discuss the design principles of the search tool and briefly review some technical decisions. In the second section we introduce all the features of the search tool and explain their characteristics and relative strengths. The next section is about the kind of usage scenarios we intend the tool to be used in. The paper finishes with a conclusion that puts this work-in-progress report into a larger perspective of desirable future developments.

10.2. Search tool design principles

A survey of existing corpus software made it clear that almost all existing solutions started with a focus on concordance-based searches. The reason for this is clear when you look at the development of corpus linguistics and the origins of concordance application in the area of lexicography. The tools were designed for professional linguistic research and the production of dictionaries and reference books. Their impressive functionality can be quite daunting for the novice user and it usually takes some time to come to grips with the software (Frankenberg-Garcia 2010; Santos and Frankenberg-Garcia 2007). However, for use in the classroom these tools do not seem an ideal starting point. Most teachers do not feel comfortable teaching by just providing concordance lines or frequency lists, and students may have problems understanding KWIC concordances. In a classroom study, Braun (2007) shows that many secondary school students have serious problems with the vertical reading skills that are required to interpret concordances. They simply need a different starting point before they can look at concordance lines and make sense of them. Mukherjee (2004), on the other hand, shows that many teachers are not even aware of the existence of corpus linguistics, partly because it does not have a prominent place in university education. Even if they are aware of it, they consider corpora mainly as a tool for teachers rather than learners. It seems clear that both groups need additional ways to access corpora, which go beyond interpreting concordance lines (cf. Coccetta, this volume). As a consequence, we decided to design our search tool from scratch. First, we wanted a tool whose functions were motivated by the needs of language learners and teachers. Second, we wanted a tool that requires little or no installation and is easily available on all computers without administrator rights, since ease of access is a central issue for most teachers when they decide whether or not to use an eLearning tool (Kohn et al. 2008).

10.3. Pedagogical design decisions

In order to achieve our first aim of pedagogical usability, we have added browse and view functions to the tool that do not rely on 'vertical' reading, as is the case with KWIC concordance lines, but rather support the 'horizontal' reading mode that students and teachers are used to. In order to support this browse and view mode of access efficiently, all the corpus transcripts have been given summaries in their metadata. Moreover, the transcripts have been structured into topic-based sections that were given titles in the annotation process. In the browse mode, these titles are displayed along with the interview summaries. In all other search modes, the search can also be limited to certain sections only, based on topic filters and other annotation filters. These functions are more in line with the 'horizontal' reading that teachers and students are used to. They also allow for easier construction of a discourse context in which the individual search results might make sense. Furthermore, we wanted the search tool to also be able to display the learning packages or other resources developed to enrich a specific corpus. This kind of corpus enrichment, and the various access modes, make the process of searching and exploring the corpus a multimodal activity that offers much more than just concordances and word lists.

10.3.1. Search tool – technical decisions

In order to achieve our second usability aim, the search tool runs online in all browsers that support JavaScript. This makes SACODEYL very easy to use, as no software installation is needed on the client side, that is, on the computer of the user. All you need is a web browser and an internet connection. All seven corpora of the project can be accessed freely. The server end runs with standard Java Enterprise technology, and can be set up on any standard server in a Java Servlet Container. All the tools developed in the project have been made available as open source tools, either for download or as web tools.[2] The data of the corpus files are stored using XML technology, and the coding format follows the TEI P5 guidelines. We chose this format in the hope of having a data format that is highly versatile and reusable in different contexts (Ward 2002).

The video clips have been saved in RealMedia, a popular streaming format (europe.real.com). RealMedia uses the XML-based Synchronised Multimedia Integration Language (SMIL) technology, which enables the search tool to jump to predefined points within the video. This is a very useful feature when you have a particular section in your search results and you want to show exactly this section to your students.

10.3.2. Search tool features

Based on the design decisions, the search tool offers four different modes of corpus access that can be classified according to increasing granularity. The first and broadest is the browse mode.

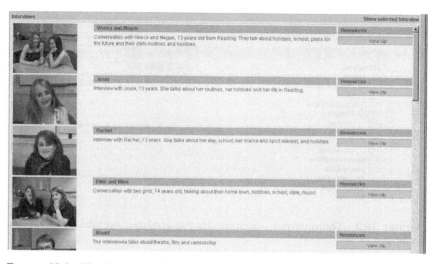

FIGURE 10.1 The browse mode view of the English corpus with a picture and an interview description

The browse mode

In this mode, users get an overview of all the interviews included in the corpus with a picture of each interviewee (see Figure 10.1). Users can browse through the summary descriptions that the annotator has given to each interview (see middle column of Figure 10.1), and they can also view the full text of each interview where the section titles are displayed.

The full video clips for each interview can also be viewed in this mode. These open in a separate window. Thus, the teacher can easily resize the clip and, if they want to show the clip to their class, they can show it in full screen mode. When they are done with the video, they simply go back to the web browser where they can choose further clips.

The section search mode

In addition to the browse mode, there are three other search modes. All of these can be accessed simply via changing tabs (see Figure 10.2). The section search mode allows users to search for certain sections based on what has been annotated. All the categories included during the annotation process can be freely combined as search filters. Users can select whether all of the selected categories must be present in a section, or whether they want all sections with at least one of the selected categories. Based on a search result,

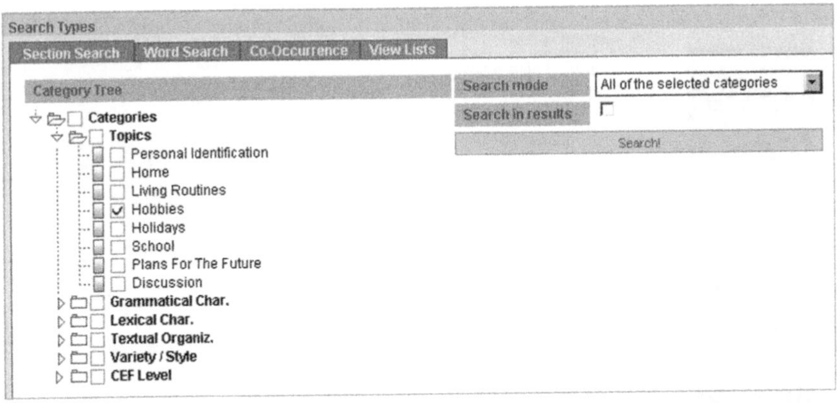

FIGURE 10.2   The different search modes are arranged on tabs in the browser window

they can also do follow-up searches with new filters to further specify the sections they get. In SACODEYL, we defined categories based on topics, grammatical characteristics, lexical characteristics, textual organisation, variety/style and Common European Framework (CEF) levels. Categories are normally assigned at section level, so that the entire section is tagged. If relevant, however, they can also be applied more specifically to individual words or phrases in the section. The search tool can then highlight the specific words/phrases within each section where the annotation has been applied.

Section search results are displayed as full sections with the section titles, as in the browse mode. Moreover, the search tool displays the categories that are returned for each section, and highlights the specific words or phrases where the annotations have been applied within a section. Table 10.1 shows some examples of the categories that the annotators of SACODEYL created during the annotation process. These categories are not hardwired into the search tool. Corpus annotators are free to create and delete their own categories. The search tool will display all the categories that the annotators have created.

The co-occurrence mode

The second search option is the co-occurrence search. In this mode you can enter two or more words and search for the places where they appear in the corpus. You can freely define the span in which the search words are supposed to appear (search scope). This search scope can range from one sentence to the whole interview. This mode is not a collocation search in a statistical sense because in our tool it is the user who defines the search

Table 10.1 The SACODEYL annotation categories

Category type	Examples
Topics	personal identification hobbies plans for the future discussion topics
Grammatical characteristics	tenses passives modality conditionals determiners/quantifiers adjective/adverb comparison
Lexical characteristics	topic specific terminology typical collocations idiomatic expressions
Textual organisation	basic cohesive ties pragmatic markers prosodic markers
Variety/Style	casual/informal language typical of spoken language teenage/youth language taboo/vulgar language
CEF level	A1, A2, B1, B2, C1[3]

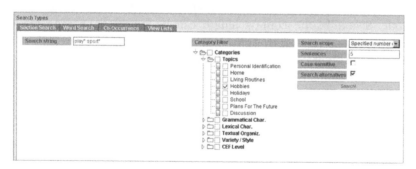

FIGURE 10.3 Specification of a co-occurrence search for [play*] and [sport*]

scope based on the familiar notions of 'whole interview', 'one section' and 'number of sentences'. As in the section search, it is also possible to apply category filters to restrict a co-occurrence search to certain sections only. In the results of the search, the search tool will display the entire text fragments as defined in the search scope.

For example, if you carry out the search in Figure 10.3, it will yield a pretty good impression of all the different kinds of sports that the teenagers talk about in the corpus. As all the search results range over five sentences, it is still possible to read what the section is actually about and understand the context of the search words. This supports the authentication and the discourse comprehension process enormously. It can also serve as a preparation for concordance-based exercises, because in this mode you get a feeling what it means to look at non-consecutive text fragments, but you still have more co-text for orientation than in simple concordance lines. In this search mode (as well as in the word search mode described in the next section), you can use wildcards such as the asterisk (*) to replace any number of characters between two spaces, and the question mark (?) to replace one single character.

The word search mode

This third search option is the closest to traditional KWIC concordancers. While our word search mode is less powerful than that in most other linguistic concordancing software, it offers some carefully selected features that users can apply to filter and sort the search results. However, it should be kept in mind that all the corpora are rather small at the moment, so it is not advisable to use more than two filters at the same time, because this might lead to very few or no results for most lexical words. The first filter option is the topic filter, which can be used to limit the search to certain sections, as in the section search mode and in the co-occurrence search mode. Secondly, the context length can be specified between five and fifteen words to the left or right. Alphabetical sorting of the results can be done to the right or to the left of the search word. You can then decide whether the search is supposed to be case-sensitive or not, which is important for languages such as German, where capitalisation can result in a meaning distinction or can distinguish nouns from verbs. Finally, you can decide whether to search for spelling variations that were entered in the transcription phase, such as 'going to/gonna' or 'because/cos'. This is important because we decided to include standard spelling variants for all words where the transcribers decided to use a transcription variant that is phonetically closer to what is heard in the video recording. All of these options have default values, so novice users have to take no decisions except to type in their search words.[4] In subsequent searches, they can always replace the default options with their own values. Figure 10.4 shows an example of a word search that focuses on the problem of using 'do/make' idiomatically in English. For this, the search words [do*] and [mak*] are entered and the category filters 'Lexical Characteristics – Idiomatic Expressions' and 'Typical collocations' are used. In order to spot typical patterns easily, the

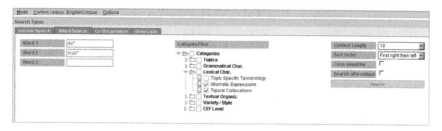

FIGURE 10.4 Word search for [do*] and [mak*] with lexical filters and right-sort turned on

Table 10.2 The different search tool modes and their advantages

Mode	Advantages
Browse mode	Gives a quick overview of available texts and allows whole-text access to the corpus ('horizontal' reading)
	Gives a quick summary of each interview in the corpus
	Allows watching the full videos of all interviews
Section search mode	Allows zoom in on topic-specific sections and on all other annotation categories included in the corpus
	Allows follow-up searches to limit the section results with further categories
	Returns section-based results with titles that still allow for some 'horizontal' reading
Co-occurrence search mode	Allows searching for several words within a certain span
	Returns span-based results that still allow for some 'horizontal' reading
	Gives a good overview of the lexical content of the results
	If needed, the span can be expanded to the full section
Word search mode	Allows word-pattern searches
	Limits word-pattern searches to certain topics, or combines them with other lexical, grammatical, or register categories
	Searches for phrases with wildcards
	If needed, a KWIC concordance can always be expanded to the full section

sort order 'first right then left' is chosen, so the primary sort is to the right of the search word.

While the other three search modes are more useful for zooming in on thematic topics and annotation categories, the word search mode is most useful for detecting the lexical patterns associated with certain words. So the four approaches are complementary to each other, with each one having its specific advantages. Table 10.2 gives a quick overview of the features of the individual tools.

10.4. SACODEYL usage scenarios

The SACODEYL approach is geared to the needs of secondary school education. To this end, the interviews were structured according to those topics that feature in secondary school curricula. The result of this structured approach is that all interviews have roughly the same topic progression. The interviews start with the interviewees presenting themselves, their families and their homes. Then, they talk about their hobbies or their favourite activities. Next, they talk about their everyday routines and their school experiences. These are all typical topics that feature in the regular school curricula of beginners to intermediate level. Almost all the interviews include sections where students talk of their past holidays or of their plans for the future. Both of these topics are very useful for studying the use of tenses. At the end of the interviews there are often discussion questions where the interviewees are asked to voice their opinions in an open-ended way. These topics are more suitable for advanced learners. Thus, all the topics can be integrated seamlessly into existing regular secondary school curricula. Teachers do not have to do extra 'SACODEYL lessons'; they can use the materials to teach the classes they would have been teaching anyway. The only change is that they will have a more varied approach to teaching, and that they can use authentic materials for their thematic topics. SACODEYL does not, however, prescribe any particular way of using the corpora and the enrichment materials. This is still the decision of the teacher.

With its focus on spoken language, SACODEYL is of course most useful in lessons and exercises where the emphasis is on listening or on speaking. To this end, we have developed a range of exploratory and communicative exercises that can serve as a guide to teachers. The video interviews feature different accents and different speech rates, making them an ideal resource for listening activities at different levels of proficiency.

However, the corpora can be useful for writing activities as well, since the search tool will return all the learning packages developed for the individual interviews. These packages include various exercises for written production, where students have to paraphrase typical spoken language utterances, or where they have to write their own opinions on certain topics.

Although as a project SACODEYL has focussed on secondary school education, the approach is open to be used in any kind of topic domain or learning scenario. As mentioned above, annotation categories can be freely defined, so any other kind of annotation can be applied to the corpus transcripts. It is also possible to develop totally new corpora, since the search tool can process any corpus that complies with the TEI XML specifications.

One interesting example is the ELISA project, a forerunner of SACODEYL, which developed comparable interviews based on topics of professional life (www.uni-tuebingen.de/elisa). These interviews are more appropriate to adult education learning scenarios, and can be easily converted into SACODEYL corpora.

10.5. Conclusion

The SACODEYL search tool is a step in the direction of a pedagogically viable type of corpus exploitation which on the one hand does not require too much technical expertise, and on the other, draws systematically on the insights of corpus research to mediate and apply these to language teaching on the basis of pedagogical principles. With its focus on teenage language, it matches the requirements of an authentic classroom where students are engaged in language and tasks that they are really interested in, and that relate to the specific stage of their personal lives.

The concept of topic-based sectioning of the transcripts enables teachers and learners to focus on specific topics more easily than has been the case with professional concordancing software. The SACODEYL search modes allow for a balanced focus between the search for topics and the search for relevant words and phrases for these topics. The topic-based approach is also helpful for a communicatively-oriented teaching approach, where language structures are embedded in topic-driven tasks. The exploratory topic-driven concept of the exercises has been tested in a piloting phase where the learning packages and the different components of the search tool were validated in schools in four European countries (Germany, Lithuania, Romania and Spain). The next step will be to look at user feedback and use this to inform decisions in the follow-up to the project.

Notes

[1] The Common European Framework for languages has established functional descriptors for gauging the proficiency level of language learners, starting at level A1 and ending at level C2. See Council of Europe (2001, p. 24) for an overview.

[2] All the software developed in the SACODEYL project is open source under the GPL, and can be downloaded from www.um.es/sacodeyl. The search tool can be reached at http://purl.org/sacodeyl/searchtool.

[3] The project consortium did not create materials for level C2.

[4] The corpus XML files are stored in Unicode Big-Endian character encoding (16 bit), supporting all the diacritics of the implemented languages.

References

Braun, S. (2007), 'Integrating corpus work into secondary education: from data-driven learning to needs-driven corpora', *ReCALL*, 19, (3), 307–328.

Council of Europe (2001), *Common European Framework of Reference for Languages: Learning, Teaching, Assessment.* Cambridge: Cambridge University Press.

Frankenberg-Garcia, A. (2010), 'Raising teachers' awareness of corpora', *Language Teaching*, doi: 10.1017/S0261444810000480, published online by Cambridge University Press.

Kohn, K., Glombitza, A., and Helbig, G. (2008), 'Perceived Potential of ICT in European Schools – A Survey Report', in *EcoMedia Europe Comenius Network – ICT in European Schools, ePortfolios and Open Content*, pp. 17–42. [Online]. *http://www. ael.uni-tuebingen.de/downloads/index.html* (accessed May 25, 2008).

Mukherjee, J. (2004), 'Bridging the gap between applied corpus linguistics and the reality of English language teaching in Germany', in U. Connor and T. Upton (eds), *Applied Corpus Linguistics: A Multidimensional Perspective.* Amsterdam and New York: Rodopi, pp. 239–250.

Rüschoff, B. (1999), 'Construction of knowledge as the basis of foreign language learning', in B. Mißßler and U. Multhaup (eds), *The Construction of Knowledge, Learner Autonomy and Related Issues.* Tübingen: Stauffenberg, pp. 79–88.

Santos, D. and Frankenberg-Garcia, A. (2007), 'The corpus, its users and their needs: a user-oriented evaluation of COMPARA', *International Journal of Corpus Linguistics*, 12, (3), 335–374.

Ward, M. (2002), 'Reusable XML technologies and the development of language learning materials', *ReCALL* 14, (2), 285–294.

Widdowson, H. (2003), *Defining Issues in English Language Teaching.* Oxford: Oxford University Press.

Part III

Corpora by language learners: learner language

Chapter 11

Oral learner corpora and the assessment of fluency in the Common European Framework

John Osborne

This chapter examines how empirical findings from learner corpora can help inform assessment of foreign language speaking skills within the Common European Framework of Reference. Recordings of learners performing comparable tasks from a parallel corpus of L2 English, French and Italian, along with samples from a project on collaborative assessment of oral language proficiency, were independently rated on the CEF scales. They were then analysed for fluency features such as speech rate, pauses, retracing and length of utterance, in order to establish the degree of convergence between different measures of fluency; and the extent to which they are reflected in raters' perceptions of proficiency. There was much individual subject variation, and no single measure of spoken fluency provided a reliable indication of proficiency. But when fluency was measured as a bundle of these features, there was a satisfactory correlation with proficiency bands, potentially enabling this measure to be used to benchmark different CEF levels.

11.1. Oral production and the CEFR

The descriptors used in the Common European Framework (Council of Europe 2001) combine quantitative criteria (how many things the second language learner can do in the target language) and qualitative criteria (how well he/she can do them). These qualitative aspects of language use are described through carefully formulated 'can do' statements covering, in the case of spoken language use, such things as accuracy, fluency and coherence. However, these qualitative scales are not themselves directly quantifiable, and it is left to the expertise and experience of the evaluator to determine, individually or collectively, whether a given L2 learner is able to express him/herself 'spontaneously at length with a natural colloquial flow' (CEF level C2) or 'fluently and spontaneously, almost effortlessly' (CEF level C1). In practical terms, this may not be of major importance, if the objective of language assessment is to reflect how a learner's speaking skills will be perceived by a potential listener. Nevertheless, as Hulstijn (2007) observes, it seems a shaky ground on which to construct European-wide descriptors of language proficiency.

Specifically, the CEFR illustrative scales for spoken fluency (section 5.2.3.2 of the CEFR; p.129 of the English version) include the following descriptors:

- Can express him/herself at length with a natural, effortless, unhesitating flow. (C2)
- Can express him/herself fluently and spontaneously, almost effortlessly. (C1)
- Can communicate spontaneously, often showing remarkable fluency and ease of expression. (B2+)
- Can produce stretches of language with a fairly even tempo; although he/she can be hesitant as he/she searches for patterns and expressions, there are few noticeably long pauses. (B2)
- Can express him/herself with relative ease. Despite some problems with formulation resulting in pauses and 'cul-de-sacs', he/she is able to keep going effectively without help. (B1+)
- Can keep going comprehensibly, even though pausing for grammatical and lexical planning and repair is very evident, especially in longer stretches of free production. (B1)
- Can make him/herself understood in short contributions, even though pauses, false starts and reformulation are very evident. (A2+)
- Can construct phrases on familiar topics with sufficient ease to handle short exchanges, despite very noticeable hesitation and false starts. (A2)
- Can manage very short, isolated, mainly pre-packaged utterances, with much pausing to search for expressions, to articulate less familiar words and to repair communication. (A1)

The interpretation and application of these descriptors to specific samples of L2 production pose three kinds of problem. Firstly, it is debatable how many native speakers could maintain a 'natural, effortless, unhesitating flow', particularly in the context of an oral examination. Hesitation has long been recognised as a widespread phenomenon in L1 speech; Good and Butterworth (1980) estimate that hesitations account for about one third of speaking time in L1 speech, with some variation according to task. This is similar to the measures we have obtained for the native speaker group in our own corpus (see below), where the average time spent hesitating is just under 32% of total speaking time. Secondly, the distinctions between neighbouring CEF levels often rely on downtoners and semantic niceties ('effortless' vs. 'almost effortlessly'; 'very evident' vs. 'very noticeable'), making it difficult to apply them systematically. It can be a salutary experience to take the fluency descriptors for neighbouring CEF levels – say B2, C1 and C2 – and ask trainee language teachers to put them in the 'correct' order. Thirdly, the descriptors identify a number of disfluency phenomena – pauses, false starts and reformulation – as being more or less 'evident' up to B1 level, but it is not obvious whether this should imply that they will be absent, or at least not 'noticeable' at B2 level and above. False starts and reformulation are by no means an exclusive feature of learner language, as can be seen in this short sequence from a native speaker of French:

(1) donc j'ai vu un appareil qui [/] donc qui sert [/-] donc un objet en haut d'un [/] d'un bâtiment [/] d'un immeuble
     so I saw an appliance which [/] so which is used [/-] so an object at the top of a [/] of a building [/] of a block

This single utterance contains two instances of backtracking, one abandon and one lexical reformulation. Overall, this native speaker has a rate of retracing comparable to that of an average A1-level L2 speaker performing the same task, although in some other respects (words per minute, silent pauses) her speech shows characteristics of greater fluency.

There is thus a need for more information about the extent to which these phenomena are present in oral production at various levels, including native-speaker production. North (2007) remarks that the CEFR fluency descriptors are in fact based on exploratory research, since they are partly inspired by Fulcher (1996). However, the 200–300 word descriptors proposed for each band in Fulcher's fluency scale only appear in a much condensed form in the 20–30 word CEFR descriptors. In addition, Fulcher's descriptors are themselves already based on an interpretive coding system, which codes the data for such things as 'pauses which appear to allow the student to plan the content of the next utterance' (Fulcher 1996: 216).

11.2. Oral production in L2 and L1

The data used for this study came from two related sources: a European project in collaborative assessment of oral language proficiency (*WebCEF*), and a corpus of oral learner language (the *PAROLE* corpus). These two sources are briefly described below.

11.2.1. The *WebCEF* project

The aim of this project, financed under the Socrates-Minerva programme, is to provide web-based tools for evaluating oral language skills with reference to the Common European Framework. The project has two main components: a 'showcase' of selected samples that have been jointly assessed and annotated by a team of language teachers and assessors from various European countries, and an 'assessment tool' which provides a workspace for language teachers throughout Europe to upload samples of oral production, to assess and annotate them and to compare their assessments with those of other European colleagues. The tasks on which the oral samples are based are also available on the workspace, along with any documents used during the task, so that teachers can reuse or adapt existing tasks to record samples produced in similar conditions. Although the central objective of the project is to provide tools for collaborative evaluation of speaking skills, it will also result in a steadily growing database of oral learner language in English, French, Italian, Dutch, German, Finnish, Polish and other languages.[1]

11.2.2. The *PAROLE* corpus

Some of the initial tasks used in the *WebCEF* project were first used to collect data for the *PAROLE* corpus (Parallèle, Oral, en Langue Etrangère) at the University of Savoie. This corpus consists of 15–20 minute recordings of speakers of L2 English (L1 French and German), of L2 French (various L1s) and of L2 Italian (L1 French), along with recordings from native speakers of English, French and Italian carrying out the same tasks. The recordings are transcribed in *CHAT* format (MacWhinney 2000) and annotated for pauses (filled and unfilled), retracings and errors, with a view to comparing (dis)fluency characteristics across languages, between native speakers and non-natives and between non-native speakers at different levels of proficiency. For a fuller description of the corpus, see Osborne (2007), Osborne and Rutigliano (2007), Hilton (2008).[2]

The convergence between these two projects allows previously assessed *WebCEF* samples to be analysed for their fluency features, and previously analysed samples from the *PAROLE* corpus to be collectively assessed on the CEF scales, thus providing for each sample a set of quantitative measures and a measure of perceived fluency as rated by a group of experienced assessors. Comparison of these should then enable us to investigate (a) what degree of convergence there is between different measures of fluency, (b) to what extent these are reflected in the raters' perception of oral language proficiency.

11.3. Measures of oral fluency

The principal problem in evaluating spoken L2 fluency is teasing apart individual, task-related and developmental factors. Hesitation features are frequent in native speech, and native speakers vary considerably in the extent to which they display such features. The additional demands of oral production in an L2 may be expected to constitute extra sources of disfluency, but there is no reason to suppose that individual differences related to a person's speaking style will disappear when the person happens to be speaking another language. Longitudinal studies (Dechert 1980; Towell et al. 1996; Freed et al. 2004) provide useful evidence of how individual and developmental factors may be related; but what is needed for the present purposes is a measure, or set of measures, that will reflect an individual speaker's fluency at a given time. In order to reduce the effect of task-related factors (difficulty, familiarity of topic, setting), the measures need to be based on identical tasks for all speakers.

11.3.1. Quantitative measures of fluency

Various quantitative measures have been used in previous studies of spoken production, including primary variables such as speech rate, articulation rate, length of runs or length of silent pauses, and secondary variables such as filled pauses, drawls, repetitions and false starts (Grosjean 1980; Raupach 1980). Those used in the present study are:

1. Speech rate: measured in words per minute or syllables per minute. For analyses of a single language, it is easier to measure words per minute, but for comparisons across languages it may be necessary to take the syllable rate into account, since the ratio of syllables to words varies between languages.

2. Pauses: measured by the average length of pauses (filled and unfilled) and by the percentage of pause time in relation to the total time used by the speaker.
3. Length of utterances: measured by mean length of utterance (MLU) and by the mean length of fluent runs in between pauses.
4. Retracing: measured by the number of retracings per 100 words, either without modification (simple repetition) or with modification (self-correction).

Including secondary variables such as pauses and retracing in the measurement of fluency does not imply that they are purely parasitic characteristics of oral production. Repairs, repetitions and hesitation phenomena can be seen to fulfil a number of functions in speech management (see Allwood et al. 1990). For Clark and Fox Tree (2002), fillers such as 'uh' and 'um' are 'collateral signals', which speakers use when referring to the performance itself rather than to the topic of discourse. If they are linguistic signals, they argue, it is misleading to call them 'filled pauses'. Rühlemann (2006) takes a similar view, arguing that repeats, pauses and fillers are so much a part of everyday speech that a negatively charged term like 'disfluency' is inappropriate. Recognising these phenomena as normal speech behaviour raises three main questions. First, to use Clark and Fox Tree's terms (2002: 75–76), are they involuntary symptoms of processes occurring in speech, or are they fully conventional signals? Secondly, is it possible to identify a norm for the use of repeats, pauses and fillers by speakers of a language? And thirdly, to what extent does their use by learners deviate from that of native speakers of the language? Each of these questions depends on being able to separate out individual and linguistic factors. To take the case of fillers, the majority of native speakers in the *PAROLE* corpus use both 'uh' (or 'er') and 'um', suggesting that they may indeed be functionally differentiated. However, there is considerable individual variation in the rate of fillers, ranging from 1.14 to 10.66 per 100 words (based on a word count that does not include the fillers themselves), so that rather than trying to determine a norm, it might be more profitable to think in terms of a ceiling, beyond which the use of fillers would be perceived as intrusive. The learners in the corpus not only use 'uh' and – more rarely – 'um', but also, largely according to their level of proficiency, an 'uh'-type filler with L1 phonology. As Levelt (1989: 484) remarks, the universality of 'er'/'uh' should make us suspicious about its status as a word. The rate of fillers in learner production (up to 60 occurrences per 100 words) and their frequent inclusion in longer hesitation groups make it difficult to discern any clear function other than that of signalling difficulty, particularly in the case of monologue production, where speech management functions such as turn-taking or holding the floor are less in evidence.

In learner speech, lack of fluency is clearly a major concern for both teachers and learners, judging from the large number of books, materials and language courses that emphasise fluency as a goal. Ultimately, what matters to learners is how their speech is perceived by other speakers, by teachers and testers and by the learners themselves, bearing in mind that phenomena that are tolerated in native speakers may sometimes be perceived – rightly or wrongly – as inappropriate behaviour in learners (see for example Davies 1991: 157–158). Consequently, the purpose of these quantitative measures is not to determine whether repeats, pauses and fillers are 'normal' or undesirable features of speech, but to what extent their presence in learner speech is related to perceptions of fluency.

11.3.2. Qualitative measures of fluency

Impressions of fluency may not only derive from temporal characteristics of speech, but also from more qualitative factors. These are incorporated into the descriptors for some, but not all of the CEF levels: 'pauses only to reflect on precisely the right words' (C2); 'fluency and ease of expression in even longer complex stretches of speech' (B2+); 'very short, isolated, mainly pre-packaged utterances' (A1). Fillmore (2000: 51) describes this kind of fluency as 'the ability to talk in coherent, reasoned and "semantically dense" sentences'. Its quantification requires a measure of how a speaker packages content into his/her production, and to obtain this it is useful to distinguish between three types of units:

- Utterances: typically an utterance is made up of an independent clause and all its dependent clauses (i.e. a T-unit). We have coded run-on coordinate clauses as a single utterance if the conjunction is not preceded or followed by a pause of more than 300 ms. Isolated clause fragments are counted as utterances.
- Syntactic units: the total number of clauses plus the number of adjunct phrases. A clause is defined following Berman and Slobin (1994: 660) as 'any unit that contains a unified predicate'.
- Information units: this is a measure of the amount of information encoded by the speaker. Three types of unit are distinguished: macrostatements, micro-events and circumstances/attributes. Thus, irrespective

of their syntactic differences, the two following examples would be coded as having the same informational content: (a) *There is a boy. He is in a zoo. He is eating a chocolate. I think it is his last chocolate.* (b) *There is a boy in a zoo, eating his last chocolate.*

Combining these three types of unit, it is possible to calculate measures of the informational and syntactic characteristics of speech. In addition to these features, perceptions of fluency may be affected by what Kormos and Dénes (2004: 160) call 'high-order' fluency features, such as accuracy and lexical diversity, noting that 'accuracy is positively related to temporal variables that are influential in fluency judgements'.

Altogether, we thus have four types of qualitative fluency measures:

1. Informational content: this can be measured either by rate of information (the number of information units per minute) or by density (information units per 100 words). An additional measure of 'granularity' (Noyau et al. 2005) indicates how much detail a speaker provides, by looking at the number of micro-events in relation to the number of macro-statements.
2. Syntactic content: can also be measured by rate or by density (respectively, the number of syntactic units per minute and per 100 words). The number of syntactic units per utterance can also be calculated, to give a measure of 'condensation'.
3. Lexical range: measured by Vocd (Malvern and Richards 1997) and by the proportion of words used which fall outside the first 2000 word frequency band.
4. Accuracy: measured by the rate of errors (per 100 words).

Figure 11.1 summarises the eight types of measure used to investigate the (dis)fluency of spoken production.

These measures were applied to three groups of speakers performing identical tasks for each of the three languages (English, French and Italian) in the *PAROLE* project. The groups were composed, respectively, of L1 speakers of the language (NS), more advanced L2 speakers, who had been assessed at B2 level or above on the *DIALANG*[3] online test (NNS1) and less advanced L2 speakers, who had been placed at B1 level or below (NNS2). For the quantitative measures, a fairly constant picture emerges: whatever single measure is taken, there is dispersion among speakers of the same group and overlap between the groups. Table 11.1, showing the percentage of hesitation time in relation to total speaking time, provides an illustration

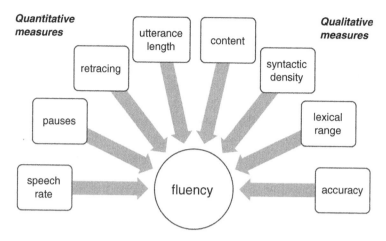

FIGURE 11.1 Quantitative and qualitative measures of fluency

Table 11.1 Percentage of hesitation time in relation to total speaking time

language	group	all speakers	most hesitant	least hesitant
English	L1 speakers	31.9	34.7	12.3
	L2 more advanced	29.6	41.7	23.5
	L2 less advanced	59.0	64.0	34.1
French	L1 speakers	23.1	34.7	15.9
	L2 more advanced	30.5	33.2	27.4
	L2 less advanced	43.6	49.5	38.0
Italian	L1 speakers	17.2	27.0	6.8
	L2 more advanced	34.5	46.0	24.6
	L2 less advanced	51.1	63.4	34.3

of this phenomenon. In each of the native-speaker groups, there is a considerable spread between the least hesitant speaker and the most hesitant, and the most hesitant native speaker hesitates more than the least hesitant of the non-native speakers for the same language. This pattern is repeated for all of the other quantitative measures. The greatest variations among native speakers (up to 4:1) are observed for retracings, percentage of pause time and mean length of runs; the smallest variations (less than 2:1) for words per minute, average length of pauses and mean length of utterances. There is no measure for which there is no overlap between native and non-native speakers (i.e. there is always a non-native speaker who performs 'better' than at least one of the native speakers of the same language).

The qualitative measures show the same general pattern as the quantitative measures; there is individual variation within each group, and overlap between the groups. The greatest overlap is found for granularity, which not only shows considerable variation within groups, but also within an individual speaker, who may choose to present two consecutive macro-events with very different degrees of granularity. Condensation (the number of syntactic units per utterance) appears to increase in the earlier stages of language learning and then level off. The clearest differentiation between groups is found, not surprisingly, for frequency of errors, but even here there is a small overlap, with the most error-free L2 production showing fewer performance errors than some L1 speech. Does this mean that fluency, whether defined by quantitative or qualitative criteria, is so much an idiosyncratic characteristic of speakers that it is fruitless trying to use it as a measure of L2 proficiency? Not necessarily, but if (dis)fluency is manifested in different ways, then we need to know how these ways combine: to what extent do different measures of fluency agree with each other, and is there such a thing as 'overall fluency', which could be measured by taking into account all, or at least several, of its components?

When the measures are compared, the best agreements appear between four features: words per minute, information units per minute, percentage of pause time and mean length of runs. Each one of these measures correlates strongly ($r > 0.8$) with each of the others. The weakest correlations ($r < 0.5$) are between syntactic condensation and all other measures, and between retracing and all other measures except information content and vocabulary range. Condensation and retracing thus appear to be more individual characteristics of speaking style. Their relation to other aspects of fluency – and to language proficiency in general – is also ambiguous. In the case of condensation, the ability to produce utterances containing multiple clauses is a sign of syntactic control, and thus plausibly an indication of proficiency, but the actual use of certain subordinate structures is frequently a strategy to compensate for lexical or other deficiencies. This is particularly the case for utterances containing relative clauses, as in (2), compared with (3) from a more proficient (and more fluent) L2 speaker:

(1) and the [/]the man that [/] that [/-] who is the car [*] is very [/-] is not happy.
(2) and I think the car's owner was screaming

Similarly, retracing may be the result of a learner struggling with morphological, lexical or syntactic difficulties, but it can also be a sign of greater

Table 11.2 Overall fluency index for selected speakers

	Less advanced L2		More advanced L2		Native speakers	
	least fluent	most fluent	least fluent	most fluent	least fluent	most fluent
English	0.18	0.53	0.5	0.94	0.69	1.35
French	0.27	0.58	0.66	0.86	0.8	1.29

awareness and capacity to self-correct, or of an ability to backtrack and reformulate content more precisely. Kormos (2000: 359) found that the number of grammatical or lexical-error repairs decreased with proficiency, while the number of appropriacy repairs – where the speaker decides to encode the original information in a different way – increased. Consequently, references in the CEF descriptors to 'repair' and 'reformulation' may need to be interpreted with caution.

To answer the second question – is there a measurable overall quality of fluency in L1 and L2 speech – it is possible to combine the different measures by calculating z-scores, or by calculating a 'fluency index' based on the average native-speaker values for each measure. There is no practical difference between the two methods in terms of ranking samples in order of fluency, and the fluency index has the advantage of being more immediately interpretable, in that scores close to 1.00 will indicate an overall fluency comparable to that of an average native speaker. Table 11.2 gives the results for the least fluent and the most fluent speaker in each group, for English and for French.

There is little or no overlap between the less advanced and the more advanced groups of L2 speakers, so that if fluency is measured as a bundle of features, then it does appear to be a real characteristic of more proficient speakers. A second conclusion that can be drawn is that it is entirely possible for a proficient L2 speaker to be as fluent as a native-speaker, if not more so. We have so far no cases of L2 speakers who are more fluent than the average for native speakers, but in principle this seems possible.

11.4. Perception of fluency

The next question is to what extent these measures of fluency coincide with the way listeners perceive the quality of non-native speech. A number of studies (Freed 2000; Kormos and Dénes 2004; Lennon 1990; Mizera

2006; Molholt et al. 2009; Rossiter 2009 for L1 speech) have investigated relationships between perceived fluency, as indicated by native-speaker judgements, and various temporal or other quantifiable measures of fluency. Two studies are of particular interest, in that they explicitly compare fluency measures with the ratings given by expert assessors on oral proficiency tests. Fulcher's (1996) study, already mentioned above, related learners' disfluency phenomena to the bands they achieved on the ELTS oral test. A more recent study, by Iwashita et al. (2008), analyses data collected during piloting of the speaking section of the TOEFL iBT test. Seven spoken language features were examined, grouped into three categories: linguistic resources (grammatical accuracy and complexity, vocabulary), phonology (pronunciation, intonation and rhythm) and fluency, measured by filled pauses, unfilled pauses, repair, total pausing time, speech rate and mean length of runs. Of these fluency measures (similar to those used in the present study), three – speech rate, number of unfilled pauses and total pause time – were found to be clearly related to proficiency level, while three others – filled pauses, repair and mean length of runs – were not.

In order to compare the results of fluency measures with perceived fluency, thirty-five samples from the English part of the *PAROLE* corpus were independently rated on the CEF scales by fifteen raters from three European countries, France, Belgium and the Netherlands. Two of the raters were experienced language teachers and examiners; the others were trainee language teachers. They were asked to rate each of the samples with reference to the CEF descriptors for 'overall oral production' and for 'fluency'. The CEF levels attributed to each recording were converted to a numerical value (A1=2, A1+=2, etc.), and in cases of disagreement between the raters the average was taken. This was done separately for the CEF grades given by the 'expert' and by the 'novice' raters, which were then compared with the fluency measures discussed above. The results of the comparisons are shown in Tables 11.3 and 11.4.

Table 11.3 Correlation with CEF levels for fluency: 'expert' assessors

quantitative measures	r	qualitative measures	r
speech rate	0.835	info. units per min.	0.729
% pause time	-0.790	condensation	0.483
retracings	-0.507	VocD	0.710
MLR	0.789	errors /100 words	-0.800
combined quantitative	0.841	combined qualitative	0.845
all measures combined			0.896

Table 11.4 Correlation with CEF levels for fluency: 'novice' assessors

quantitative measures	r	qualitative measures	r
speech rate	0.601	info. units per min.	0.394
% pause time	0.520	condensation	0.483
retracings	-0.334	VocD	0.480
MLR	0.481	errors /100 words	-0.410
combined quantitative	0.558	combined qualitative	0.584
all measures combined			0.608

Agreement between the two 'expert' raters was good (r = 0.837). The principal cases of divergence between the raters appear, on the limited evidence available, to be atypical speakers (specifically, speakers with an unusually high rate of syntactic subordination). When the CEF-based assessments made by these two raters are compared with the fluency measures discussed above, the weakest correlations are found, as might be expected, for retracings and for syntactic condensation. The strongest correlations, r = 0.835 and r = -0.79 respectively, are for the two quantitative measures of speech rate (in words per minute) and pause time. Combining all the quantitative measures gives a slightly stronger correlation with the CEF ratings. Among the qualitative measures, the strongest correlations are for errors and rate of information. However, the coding of errors is very dependent on annotators' judgements, and time-consuming cross-checking of annotations is required to ensure consistency.

Each of the samples was also assessed by 'novice' raters. There was less agreement among these raters, and generally their ratings correlate more weakly with the fluency measures. Those which correlate best are nevertheless the same as for the 'expert' raters: speech rate and pause time. Combining all the measures does not however improve on the correlation obtained for speech rate alone. The differences between these 'novice' raters and the more experienced assessors should probably not be attributed to their being less sensitive to (dis)fluency features in L2 speech, but simply to their being less consistent in the way they relate their perceptions to a specific CEF descriptor.

11.5. Benchmarking oral samples

The measures described above are time-consuming to carry out. They are therefore not a practical option for day-to-day assessment of oral production, unless they can be automatised. To a certain extent automatisation is indeed possible. With an annotation tool such as ELAN,[4] unfilled pauses can be detected, marked and measured automatically, whether or not the recording has been transcribed. The search facility will then provide a table of these annotations, with the start-point, end-point and duration of each silence, which can be imported into a spreadsheet. A similar automatic measurement of silences can be carried out with Praat,[5] and de Jong and Wempe have also developed a Praat script for measuring speech rate through an automatic syllable count (see de Jong and Wempe 2009 for a description). These methods provide a less precise measure than transcription and annotation by hand, since they are not good at distinguishing filled pauses, laughs and other non-speech sounds; they therefore tend to include in the syllable count things that a human annotator would discard, and to underestimate the average duration of hesitation phenomena, as the most disfluent hesitations usually consist of pausal groups containing one or more silent pauses plus one or more filled pauses.

Despite these limitations, automatic measurements are a useful way of obtaining rough indicators of fluency without the need for painstaking transcription and annotation by hand. They can be complemented by, for example, a manual count of filled pauses, which can be done fairly rapidly. But all these measures, whether automatic or manual, are still more labour-intensive than is practical for everyday assessment. Their value therefore lies mainly in their potential use for benchmarking samples of L2 oral production, to provide empirically based evidence for fluency features at different CEF levels. One way of doing this is to define 'fluency bands', the ranges for certain measures within which speakers at each level will typically fall. An example of this is shown in Table 11.5, for the two quantitative measures that were found to correlate most strongly with CEF ratings for fluency. More evidence is needed to verify these bands, and to see to what extent they vary according to task type – notably between monologue and interactive tasks – but they could serve to specify fluency thresholds of

Table 11.5 'Fluency bands' for speech rate and hesitation time

bands		A1	A2	B1	B2	C1	NS
words per minute	min	34,13	61,67	72,14	93,62	136,66	134,53
	max	88,98	99,44	135,73	162,73	149,39	222,71
% hesitation time	max	64.04	56.12	49.32	41.70	30.40	34.67
	min	52.09	34.09	28.04	23.47	24.55	12.33

the type: *a speaker with a speech rate of less than 90 wpm or a pause rate of more than 40% on this type of task is unlikely to be above B1 level.*

A parallel application is in benchmarking samples of oral L2 production for the purposes of illustrating CEF levels and/or training assessors. For this purpose both central and borderline cases can be useful. One final example will serve to illustrate this. During the selection of representative samples for the *WebCEF* project, one speaker was unanimously rated B1 for fluency by nine different assessors, despite the fact that his speech rate is only just within the range identified here for B1 speakers and is considerably lower than the speech rate of other speakers rated A2. But his pauses are regularly spaced, with an average duration of just over 500ms. and no pause exceeds 1 second, so that the overall impression is not one of disfluency. He just happens to be a slow speaker.

Notes

[1] Information about *WebCEF* is available on the project website: http://www.webcef.eu
[2] *PAROLE* recordings and transcriptions are partly available on *TalkBank*: http://talkbank.org/BilingBank/
[3] http://www.dialang.org (Not accessible at the time of writing).
[4] http://www.mpi.nl/tools/
[5] http://www.fon.hum.uva.nl/praat/

References

Allwood, J., Nivre, J. and Ahlsén, E. (1990), 'Speech management: on the non-written life of speech'. *Nordic Journal of Linguistics* 13, (1), 3–48.

Berman, R. and Slobin, D. (1994), *Relating Events in Narrative: A Crosslinguistic Developmental Study.* Hillsdale NJ: Lawrence Erlbaum.

Clark, H. and Fox Tree, J. (2002), 'Using uh and um in spontaneous speaking'. *Cognition* 84, 73–111.

Council of Europe (2001), *Common European Framework of Reference for Languages: Learning, Teaching, Assessment.* Cambridge: Cambridge University Press.

Davies, A. (1991), *The Native Speaker in Applied Linguistics.* Edinburgh: Edinburgh University Press.

Dechert, H. (1980), 'Pauses and intonation as indicators of verbal planning in second language speech productions: two examples from a case study', in H. Dechert and M. Raupach (eds), pp. 271–285.

Dechert, H. and Raupach, M. (eds) (1980), *Temporal Variables in Speech.* The Hague: Mouton.

de Jong, N. and Wempe, T. (2009), 'Praat script to detect syllable nuclei and measure speech rate automatically'. *Behavior Research Methods*, 41, (2), 385–390.

Fillmore, C. (2000), 'On fluency', in H. Riggenbach (ed.), pp. 43–60. First published in C. Fillmore, D. Kempler and W. Wang (eds) (1979), *Individual Differences in Language Ability and Language Behavior.* New York: Academic Press, pp. 85–101.

Freed, B. (2000), 'Is fluency in the eyes (and ears) of the beholder?', in H. Riggenbach (ed.), pp. 243–265.

Freed, B., Segalowitz, N. and Dewey, D. (2004), 'Context of learning and second language fluency in French: comparing regular classroom, study abroad and intensive domestic immersion programs'. *Studies in Second Language Acquisition,* 26, (2), 275–301.

Fulcher, G. (1996), 'Does thick description lead to smart tests? A data-based approach to rating scales construction'. *Language Testing,* 13, 208–238.

Good, D. and Butterworth, B. (1980), 'Hesitancy as a conversational resource: some methodological implications', in H. Dechert and M. Raupach (eds), pp. 148–152.

Grosjean, F. (1980), 'Linguistic structures and performance structures: studies in pause distribution', in H. Dechert and M. Raupach (eds), pp. 91–106.

Hilton, H. (2008), 'Corpus Parole: architecture du corpus et conventions de transcription'. [Online] http://talkbank.org/BilingBank/PAROLE/PAROLE_manual.pdf (accessed May 15, 2009).

Hulstijn, J. (2007), 'The shaky ground beneath the CEFR: quantitative and qualitative dimensions of language proficiency'. *Modern Language Journal,* 91, (4), 663–667.

Iwashita, N., Brown, A., McNamara, T., and O'Hagan, S. (2008), 'Assessed levels of second language speaking proficiency: how distinct?' *Applied Linguistics,* 29, (1), 24–49.

Kormos, J. (2000), 'The role of attention in monitoring second language speech production'. *Language Learning,* 50, (2), 343–384.

Kormos, J., and Dénes, M. (2004), 'Exploring measures and perceptions of fluency in the speech of second language learners'. *System,* 32, 145–164.

Lennon, P. (1990), 'Investigating fluency in EFL: a quantitative approach'. *Language Learning,* 40, (3), 387–417.

Levelt, W. (1989), *Speaking: From Intention to Articulation.* Cambridge MA: MIT Press.

MacWhinney B. (2000), *The CHILDES Project: Tools for Analyzing Talk.* Mahwaw NJ: Lawrence Erlbaum.

Malvern, D. and Richards, B. (1997), 'A new measure of lexical diversity', in A. Ryan and A. Wray (eds), *Evolving Models of Language.* Clevedon: Multilingual Matters, pp. 58–71.

Mizera, J. (2006), *Working Memory and L2 Oral Fluency.* Unpublished PhD thesis, University of Pittsburgh. [online] http://etd.library.pitt.edu/ETD/available/etd-04262006-24945/unrestricted/Mizera.Dissertation.pdf (accessed May 15, 2009).

Molholt, G., Cabrera, M.J., Kumar, V.K. and Thompson, P. (2009), 'Correlating quantitative measures of speech with perceptions of fluency'. *CALICO 2009.* [Online]. https://calico.org/podcasts/fr-rm10/WS110015.mp3 (accessed May 20, 2009).

North, B. (2007), 'The CEFR illustrative descriptor scales'. *Modern Language Journal*, 91, (4), 656–659.

Noyau, C., de Lorenzo, C., Kihlstedt, M., Paprocka, U., Sanz Espinar, G., and Schneider, R. (2005), 'Two dimensions of the representation of complex events structures : granularity and condensation. Towards a typology of textual production in L1 and L2', in H. Hendriks (ed.), *The Structure of Learner Varieties*. Berlin: Mouton de Gruyter, pp. 157–201.

Osborne, J. (2007), 'Investigating L2 fluency through oral learner corpora', in M. C. Campoy and M. J. Luzón (eds), *Spoken Corpora in Applied Linguistics*, Frankfurt: Peter Lang, pp. 181–197.

Osborne, J. and Rutigliano, S. (2007), 'Constitution d'un corpus multilingue d'apprenants d'une L2: recueil et exploitation des données', in H. Hilton (ed.), *Acquisition et didactique, Actes de l'atelier didactique, AFLS 2005*. Chambéry: LLS, Collection Langages, pp. 141–156.

Raupach, M. (1980), 'Temporal variables in first and second language speech production', in H. Dechert and M. Raupach (eds), pp. 263–270.

Riggenbach, H. (ed.) (2000), *Perspectives on Fluency*. Ann Arbor, MI: University of Michigan Press.

Rossiter, M. (2009), 'Perceptions of L2 fluency by native and non-native speakers of English'. *The Canadian Modern Language Review*, 65, (3), 395–412.

Rühlemann, C. (2006), 'Coming to terms with conversational grammar: "Dislocation" and "dysfluency"'. *International Journal of Corpus Linguistics* 11, (4), 385–409.

Towell, R., Hawkins, R. and N. Bazergui, N. (1996), 'The development of fluency in advanced learners of French'. *Applied Linguistics*, 17, (1), 84–119.

Chapter 12

Preferred patterns of use of positive and negative evaluative adjectives in native and learner speech: an ELT perspective

Sylvie De Cock

This chapter reports on an investigation of attitudinal stance (Biber et al. 1999; Conrad and Biber 1999) in native and learner speech. Attitudinal stance conveys speakers' attitudes, likes or dislikes, or evaluations of events or personal experiences, for example. The focus of the study is on the adjectives that native speakers and advanced EFL learners use recurrently to express both positive and negative evaluation (Hunston and Sinclair 1999). The adjectives under investigation (e.g. *good, great, nice, wonderful, bad, awful, terrible*) fit into Biber et al.'s (1999) evaluative/emotive sub-category of descriptors. Native speakers' and learners' use of evaluative adjectives are analysed using the Louvain Corpus of Native English Conversation and the French, German and Chinese components of the Louvain International Database of Spoken English Interlanguage. This report concentrates on findings from an analysis of the preferred syntactic and collocational patterns in which these adjectives tend to be used, that can be regarded as useful targets for treatment in English language teaching (ELT).

12.1. Introduction

Conrad and Biber (1999: 57) identify the following three types of 'stance', a term they use to refer to 'the expression of personal feelings and assessments': epistemic stance, which comments on 'the certainty (or doubt), reliability, or limitations of a proposition', style stance, which describes 'the manner in which the information is being presented', and attitudinal stance, which 'conveys speakers' attitudes, feelings, or value judgements'.

This paper reports on selected findings from an investigation of attitudinal stance in native and learner speech. Attitudinal stance can be regarded as an important component of involvement (Chafe 1982) and socialisation (Mauranen 2002) in spoken interactions, as it expresses speakers' involvement with themselves and with the concrete reality of what they are talking about. Attitudinal stance can be conveyed using a variety of linguistic devices and patterns (see Hunston 2004; Hunston and Sinclair 1999). The focus of this study is on one aspect of attitudinal stance, namely the adjectives that native speakers and advanced EFL learners recurrently use to express positive and negative evaluation in informal speech.

The aim of this paper is to uncover the preferred patterns of use of positive and negative evaluative adjectives in native and learner speech and to shed light on the possible contribution of such a study for English language teaching. After describing the corpora used in the study and the selection of the evaluative adjectives under investigation, the paper first seeks to paint an overall picture of the use of frequently recurring positive and negative evaluative adjectives in native speaker speech and in the spoken productions of advanced EFL learners from Chinese, French and German mother-tongue backgrounds. The paper then concentrates on a series of findings from a contrastive analysis perspective of the preferred syntactic and collocational patterns in which the adjectives are used in the four varieties, and highlights some practical implications for English Language Teaching (ELT). The paper is rounded off by a number of concluding remarks.

12.2. Data and method

In this study learners' and native speakers' use of evaluative adjectives are analysed using the Chinese, French and German components of the Louvain International Database of Spoken English Interlanguage (henceforth LINDSEI_CH, LINDSEI_FR and LINDSEI_GER) and a comparable native speaker corpus, the Louvain Corpus of Native English Conversation (henceforth LOCNEC). The LINDSEI project was launched in 1995 at the Centre for English Corpus Linguistics, Université Catholique de Louvain, as the spoken counterpart of the International Corpus of Learner English (Granger 1998a). LINDSEI is made up of informal interviews with advanced EFL learners and currently contains data from learners from eleven different mother tongues (Bulgarian, Chinese, Dutch, French, German, Greek, Italian, Japanese, Polish, Spanish and Swedish). A LINDSEI CD-ROM containing these eleven learner varieties was released in October 2010 (see http://www.uclouvain.be/en-cecl.html). The learners who contributed data to LINDSEI (fifty learners per variety) are labelled as advanced on the basis of an external criterion: they are third and fourth year students of English at university. The Louvain Corpus of Native English Conversation (LOCNEC) is actually something of a misnomer as it contains informal interviews with fifty British university students. The corpora used in the study each total between approximately 70,000 and 110,000 words of interviewee speech.

The informal interviews in LINDSEI and LOCNEC are of similar length and follow the same set pattern: the main body of the interviews takes the form of an informal and open discussion mainly centred around topics such as university life, hobbies, foreign travel, or plans for the future. Each interview starts with one of three topics (topic 1: an experience that taught them a lesson, topic 2: a country that impressed them, topic 3: a film or play they liked/disliked), which the students were given a few minutes to choose and think about. This was designed to make the interviewees, and especially the learners, feel at ease. They were, however, specifically asked not to make any notes as it was intended that their spoken productions should be as spontaneous as possible. Each interview concludes with a short picture-based storytelling activity. This more controlled activity was included in the interview format to allow for targeted comparisons of lexis between various learner varieties and/or between the learner and the native speaker varieties.

Results from an analysis of recurrent sequences of words conveying attitudinal stance in the BNC spoken component and in the corpora used in this study suggest that LINDSEI and LOCNEC lend themselves particularly well to the study of a group of speakers' shared repertoire of preferred ways of expressing evaluation (De Cock 2007). The informal interviews are packed with expressions of personal attitudes and feelings (e.g. *I love, I really like, I really enjoy(ed), I enjoy(ed) it, (yes) I like it*), which can be closely related to the types of topics discussed and the informal character of the interviews.

The positive and negative evaluative adjectives under investigation in this study were identified on the basis of frequency lists of word forms from the corpora using WordSmith Tools 4.0 (Scott 2004). Two main criteria were used in the selection process: the first relates to frequency and the second to meaning. Because the focus of this analysis is on the preferred (syntactic and collocational) patterns in which positive and negative evaluative adjectives are used, only frequently recurring adjectives were taken into consideration. The frequency threshold was set to a minimum of

10 occurrences per 70,000 words in either LOCNEC and/or in any of the LINDSEI components. With respect to meaning, the adjectives selected for inclusion in the analysis had to be considered as prototypically evaluative, that is, their overt and only purpose is to evaluate (Channel 1999), and to fit into Biber et al.'s (1999: 509) evaluative/emotive subcategory of descriptors (i.e. adjectives denoting judgements, affect or emphasis). Examples of such prototypically evaluative/emotive adjectives include *good, great, nice, wonderful, bad, awful,* or *terrible.* Adjectives such as *big* and *little* were excluded because, although they can be used to express positive or negative evaluations of things or events (as in *a nice little house, poor little thing* or *a big mistake*), they are used prototypically to indicate size. The selection process was followed by a disambiguation phase in which any instances of the word forms not used as evaluative adjectives were removed from the working data after careful examination of the concordances of the items. The instances of *good, best* and *great* in (1), (2) and (3) were, for example, discarded:

(1) they . just er . try their **best** to help help us (LINDSEI_CH)
(2) I didn't think of that . erm . yeah for a while . but not for **good** because erm . I love my . country (LINDSEI_GER)
(3) and erm well I I don't read a **great** deal of plays (LOCNEC)

In some cases the disambiguation phase led to items being excluded altogether, where fewer than ten of their occurrences (per 70,000 words) were actually used as positive or negative evaluative adjectives.

12.3. Looking on the 'positive' side

Tables 12.1 and 12.2 include the positive and negative evaluative adjectives that meet the selection criteria just outlined. The adjectives *good* and *bad,* which can be regarded as the prototypical positive and negative evaluative adjectives, are ranked respectively among the top 2 and the top 4 frequently recurring adjectives in the tables. As the frequency counts indicate, the positive evaluative adjectives under scrutiny tend to occur with much higher frequencies than the negative evaluative adjectives. This trend can be observed in all four varieties. The preference for positive evaluation is also reflected in the number of types used: there are two to three times as many positive evaluative adjective types as negative ones in the corpora. It is interesting that the positive picture that emerges from our limited study of only one aspect of evaluation is in line with the 'bias towards positive items' observed by Mauranen (2002: 123) in her large-scale analysis of evaluation in academic speech using the MICASE corpus. It should be noted that a separate study on a number of verbs used to express positive and negative evaluation in LINDSEI and LOCNEC (Belin 2006) also reveals a general preference for the use of positive verbs like *love, like* or *enjoy*. Mauranen (2002) sees the positive bias in her corpus as evidence of the orientation of academic speech towards consensus rather than conflict. In our corpora of informal interviews this tendency towards positive items could be connected with interviewees' desire to make a positive impression on the interviewer and to establish rapport. The interviewers' attempts to put the students at ease during the interviews may also have had an impact. Another possible explanation could be that the interviewees were influenced by the topics discussed at the beginning of the interview: the first two topics could be regarded as rather positive and the students who chose to talk about the third topic overwhelmingly went for a film they liked. A number of the other topics discussed during the interview (e.g. hobbies, foreign travel or plans for the future) also had a fairly positive flavour.

An examination of the items in Tables 12.1 and 12.2 in context highlights the fact that focusing on positive and negative items alone hides a complex

Table 12.1 Frequently recurring positive evaluative adjectives

	LINDSEI_CH		LINDSEI_FR		LINDSEI_GER		LOCNEC (NS)	
1	good	231	good	85	nice	152	good	219
2	beautiful	228	beautiful	80	good	146	nice	122
3	satisfied	63	interesting	71	beautiful	57	interesting	39
4	happy	53	nice	61	interesting	48	interested	36
5	important	50	great	39	impressive	40	happy	30
6	better	32	happy	31	great	37	beautiful	28
7	successful	22	better	28	friendly	36	great	26
8	interesting	19	interested	22	happy	30	brilliant	24
9	pretty	17	funny	21	easy	28	amazing	23
10	impressive	16	important	19	better	26	better	23
11	favo(u)rite	16	wonderful	19	funny	24	best	17
12	interested	14	easy	15	right	19	easy	14
13	wonderful	10	impressive	14	satisfied	19	funny	14
14			lovely	14	interested	18	impressive	13
15			pretty	13	pretty	18	friendly	12
16			pleased	11	fine	17	lovely	12
17			amazing	10	easier	13	right	12
18			best	10	best	10	impressed	11
19							easier	10

Table 12.2   Frequently recurring negative evaluative adjectives

	LINDSEI_CH		LINDSEI_FR		LINDSEI_GER		LOCNEC (NS)	
1	ugly	50	difficult	46	difficult	48	difficult	40
2	angry	37	awful	31	hard	39	bad	38
3	difficult	26	bad	19	bad	36	weird	12
4	bad	24	ugly	15	angry	15	horrible	11
5	wrong	19	disappointed	11	ugly	15	hard	10
6	hard	19	sad	11	strange	13	awful	10
7	sad	16	angry	10	horrible	10		
8			strange	10				
9			boring	10				

situation, as both positive and negative evaluative adjectives can occur in non-assertive contexts. For example, while the adjectives *nice, great, interesting, awful* and *hard* tend to be mainly used in assertive contexts, the adjective *bad* is often used in the pattern *BE not (too/that/so/as) bad* in LOCNEC and LINDSEI_GER (see example 4), and the adjective *good* in the pattern *BE not (so/as) good* or *BE not (very/particularly) good* in the four non-native varieties (see example 5). The adjective *satisfied* (hardly ever used in LINDSEI_FR and never in LOCNEC) is frequently found in the pattern *BE not (really/very) satisfied* in LINDSEI_GER and LINDSEI_CH (see example 6).

That said, the overall picture that emerges when also considering the contexts of use of the frequently recurring positive and negative evaluative adjectives is still overwhelmingly positive.

(4) the next day we erm had a trip erm outside to the Reef so it was . *was not so **bad*** it was on a our sailing boat (LINDSEI_GER)
(5) I went back to my hometown to be a teacher but the[i:] experiment *is not so good* . so I I just want to (LINDSEI_CH)
(6) so she is telling him what to improve for example she *is **not** satisfied* . with . the way she is looking in that picture (LINDSEI_GER)

Example (6) also illustrates the fact that some of the most frequently recurring evaluative adjectives in the corpora can be traced to one specific part of the interview format in LINDSEI and LOCNEC, namely the short picture-based, storytelling activity. Table 12.3 lists the frequently recurring evaluative adjectives for which over 50% of their instances occur in this part of the interview (this percentage is given in brackets). Some adjectives (e.g. *satisfied* in LINDSEI_CH and LINDSEI_GER and *ugly*[1] in LINDSEI_CH, LINDSEI_GER and LINDSEI_FR) are only used in this task.

Table 12.3 Frequently recurring evaluative adjectives of which over 50% of instances occur in the picture-based storytelling activity

LINDSEI_CH	beautiful (77%), satisfied (93%), happy (64.5%), ugly (100%), angry (88%)
LINDSEI_FR	beautiful (62%), happy (52.5%), pretty (81%), ugly (80%), angry (77%)
LINDSEI_GER	beautiful (65%), happy (70%), satisfied (100%), pretty (90%), ugly (95%), angry (89%)
LOCNEC (NS)	happy (58%), beautiful (52%), pretty (60%)

The following three passages illustrate the close connection between some of these adjectives and the picture-based storytelling task.

mhm ... well so eh a painter .. is painting the portrait of a young lady .. sitting on a chair but . she doesn't seem to be: very **beautiful** <laughs> and erm .. the the painting is quite realistic so when it's . finished she looks at it (LINDSEI_FR)

but she wasn't **satisfied** with the picture because it's she thought it's very **ugly** and so the the[i:] artist changed the picture (LINDSEI_CH)

he changes the picture and now she's looking really really **beautiful** . and: erm . in the[i:] end she: shows it to her .. friends . her female friends .. and: seems to be very **happy** (LINDSEI_GER)

Because of the specific character of this task it was decided that the design of the LINDSEI CD-ROM should make it possible for researchers to either keep, discard, or work exclusively on the picture-based storytelling activity when analysing learner speech. This part of the interview would arguably be particularly well-suited to a detailed study of the range of adjectives or other items used by learners (and native speakers) to refer to how beautiful/ugly and happy/angry the female lead in the story is or appears to be.

12.4. Preferred patterns of use

As rightly pointed out by Granger (2009: 22), 'features of learner language uncovered by LC [learner corpus] research need not necessarily lead to targeted action in the classroom', or in textbooks or grammar books.

A number of factors such as learner needs, teaching objectives and teach-ability should guide linguists and ELT practitioners when attempting to determine which features should or should not be focused on in ELT. This section zooms in on a series of findings from an investigation of the preferred patterns of use of positive and negative evaluative adjectives in native and learner speech that can be regarded as possible targets for treatment in ELT materials aimed at learners who want to achieve near-native proficiency. Four major patterns of use will be discussed: predicative vs. attributive use, evaluative (sentential) relative clauses, adjective comple-mentation, and collocational patterns.

A comparison of the preferred syntactic environments of the evaluative adjective *good* in the native speaker corpus and in the learner varieties (Table 12.4) shows that it tends to be used more frequently in predicative position (see examples 7 and 8) in LOCNEC than in LINDSEI (both in relative and absolute terms). The preferred position (in relative terms) in LINDSEI_FR and especially in LINDSEI_CH is inside an NP before the head noun, as in (example 9).

(7) (...) wrote a script for a play at college . and I got to see that acted out *and it was really **good*** (...) (LOCNEC)

(8) and it's absolutely amazing fun and everyone's just . soaking wet and they don't care and *it's really **good*** (LOCNEC)

(9) it was a very **good** experience for me . yes because they . made a lot of critics (...) (LINDSEI_FR)

The adjective *good* is in fact used predicatively in a number of frequently recurring syntactically complete clausal sequences which are not recurrent in the learner corpora. These sequences, which include *it's good, it was good, (and / yeah) it was really good, it was quite good, that was good, it's really good* and *which is good*, appear to be typically used as a type of summarising evaluative comment on a situation, event or experience considered as enjoyable by the interviewee (see examples 7 and 8).

Table 12.4 Proportion of attributive and predicative uses of *good*

	Attributive use	Predicative use
LOCNEC (NS)	42%	58%
LINDSEI_GER	49%	51%
LINDSEI_FR	52%	48%
LINDSEI_CH	62%	38%

Table 12.5 Proportion of attributive and predicative uses of *bad*

	Attributive use	Predicative use
LOCNEC (NS)	25%	75%
LINDSEI_GER	35.5%	64.5%
LINDSEI_FR	48%	52%
LINDSEI_CH	52.5%	47.5%

The use of the evaluative adjective *bad* follows a similar trend to that of *good* in the native and learner corpora (Table 12.5): it is mainly used in predicative position, and the sequence *it's not too bad* emerges as frequently recurring in the NS data (see example 10).

(10) yeah you've got like a bit of countryside around and so *it's not too bad* yeah (LOCNEC)

Another preferred syntactic environment for a number of evaluative adjectives in the native speaker corpus is the evaluative relative clause introduced by *which*, as in examples (11) to (16). Many of these are sentential relative clauses (12 to 16), which comment on the whole previous sentence, series of clauses or utterance (Carter and McCarthy 2006). While a number of frequently recurring evaluative adjectives can be seen to occur in these clauses (e.g. *brilliant, excellent, amazing, interesting, impressive, bad*), the adjectives *good, nice* and *great* appear to be particularly frequent in such an environment: all of them have *which* amongst their most frequent collocates.

(11) and we've seen: Havana . *which is an amazing town* . very old and (LOCNEC)
(12) first of all the way that they speak English *which is great for me* cos I speak no Dutch at all (LOCNEC)
(13) you know you've always .. I've got other people to hitch with *which is good* (LOCNEC)
(14) we run them up and down our little railway and children come and ride on it *which is really good* <laughs> (LOCNEC)
(15) and again it's only five minutes' walk from my house *which is nice* and there's a bar (LOCNEC)
(16) they all come and visit me cos they think it's great having a student life so close to <X> so a lot of them travel up at weekends and that [*which is quite nice* (LOCNEC)

Table 12.6 Frequency of evaluative relative clauses and proportion of evaluative sentential relative clauses

LOCNEC 39 srcl: ca. 75%	>	LINDSEI_GER 15 srcl: ca. 60%	>	LINDSEI_FR 10 srcl ca. 30%	>	LINDSEI_CH 2 srcl 0%

As Table 12.6 shows, evaluative (sentential) relative clauses are a far less preferred syntactic environment for recurrent evaluative adjectives in the three learner varieties. The table also sheds light on the marked differences that can be found between the various learner corpora, with the German speaking learners (see examples 17 and 18) using twice as many clauses of this type as the French speaking learners (see example 19) and the Chinese learners using only a handful.

(17) I went to school with my erm host sister for about two weeks . erm. *which was really* **interesting** *as well* because she erm the school system is very (LINDSEI_GER)
(18) erm you have to pass a bridge . to get to England and you have to pay a toll *which was quite funny* (LINDSEI_GER)
(19) (...) they don't ask me to pay so . this is sometimes for just one article for thirty pages of something er I don't have to pay *which is really eh* **interesting** (LINDSEI_FR)

Sentential relative clauses have been regarded by Chafe (1982) and Biber (1988) as typically associated with the involved, interactive and non-informational style of spontaneous speech, and have been shown by Tao and McCarthy (2001) to be especially used to display speakers' attitudes to the events and experiences they are relating. Evaluative sentential relative clauses would in fact be a particularly good candidate for inclusion in ELT reference materials such as a contextualised discourse-oriented grammar of speech (Meunier 2002; O'Keeffe et al. 2007). As well as providing learners with a wider range of ways of expressing attitudinal stance in interactions, giving more prominence to this type of clauses could also help learners cope with the pressures of online processing in unplanned spoken discourse. The use of sentential relative clauses is consistent with the 'clause chaining style' or clause 'add-on strategy' that appears to be particularly well-suited to the constraints of real-time planning (Biber et al. 1999). Focusing on the recurrent patterns of use of the highly frequent prototypically positive and negative evaluative adjectives *good* and *bad* (outlined above) in ELT materials could offer learners similar benefits.

Another possible useful target for treatment in ELT is the recurrent pattern of complementation of the adjective *nice* in LOCNEC. Cases where *nice* is followed by a to-infinitive clause (examples 20 and 21) represent almost 20% of the uses of the adjective in predicative position in the native corpus. By contrast, this pattern represents a mere 4% and 7% of the uses of the adjective in predicative position in LINDSEI_FR and LINDSEI_GER respectively, and is notably absent from LINDSEI_CH.

(20) I don't know it'd sort of be **nice** *to have our own house in a way* (LOCNEC)

(21) it's **nice** *to walk round and you know fancy something* (LOCNEC)

Fun is one of the most frequent collocates of *good* in the NS corpus (see example 22). This collocation may deserve attention in ELT as it is virtually nonexistent in the learner varieties: the only occurrence in learner speech is found in LINDSEI_FR, where its use can be directly traced to input from the interviewer (a native speaker of English), who steps in to help the learner who is struggling to express positive evaluation (see example 23).

(22) and then this year I dance with Helen again . oh Claire was **good fun** too (LOCNEC)

(23) <interviewee> no .. it's .. very pleaseful .. <XX> pleased to
<interviewer> oh you mean you oh you mean you like it . you mean good fun
<interviewee> yeah **good fun** yes really (LINDSEI_FR)

Example 23 highlights the importance of considering input from other participants when analysing learner speech. Failure to do so might well lead to over-hasty conclusions about the presence of certain items or patterns. The **LINDSEI CD-ROM** provides information about the interviewer(s) in each of the subcorpora, relating to (among others) native language, knowledge of foreign languages, gender and status (e.g. familiar or unfamiliar).

When used predicatively, the adjective *good* is not exclusively used with the link verb *BE* in LOCNEC, but also with *SOUND* (see example 24). This link verb is also used with other frequently recurring evaluative adjectives like *nice*, *interesting* and *bad*, and with a number of other less frequent ones (e.g. *stupid* and *strange*). Although a few instances of this collocation pattern can be found in LINDSEI_GER (see example 25), it is largely underused in the learner corpora.

(24) oh right er .. I might have to look into that that *sounds* really **good** (LOCNEC)

(25) you can sometimes compare them to the[i:] American mentality . <overlap/> it *sounds* **strange** (LINDSEI_GER)

Evaluative adjectives are typically gradable (Hunston and Sinclair 1999) and collocate with a series of premodifying intensifiers. While a full report of evaluative adjective intensification in native and learner speech lies outside the scope of this paper, it appears that the learners in our corpora are unaware of some of the preferences of the adjectives *great* and *wonderful.* The Chinese learners use the string *very wonderful* (see example 26) and the French learners repeatedly use *very great* (see example 27). These sequences echo one of the findings from Granger's study of amplifier + adjective collocations (1998b: 148). She found that the French-speaking learners in her investigation tended to use *very* as a 'general-purpose' item and a 'safe bet'. The use of *very* turns out to be far from 'safe' with *wonderful* and *great,* however. Interestingly, in most cases, the native speakers in our corpus chose not to intensify these two adjectives.

(26) so the first impression I got is wow it's very fantastic **very wonderful** very . really very beautiful the the night sight (LINDSEI_CH)

(27) it was **very great** for them to live that way . and in fact (LINDSEI_FR)

12.5. Concluding remarks

Having highlighted a number of possible candidates for treatment in ELT, the next step in this investigation of positive and negative evaluative adject-ives in native and learner speech would be to attempt to identify and develop the optimal form of treatment of the phenomena discussed in this report, such as data-driven activities based on native and learner data (Nesselhauf 2004). Another possible follow-up to this investigation would be to use a pedagogically annotated corpus of textbook materials like the *TeMa* corpus (Meunier and Gouverneur 2007) to examine the extent to which preferred patterns in NS speech are included in listening comprehension activities, and are the focus of discussions and/or exercises.

I would like to end this paper by focusing on one specific aspect of the LINDSEI corpus that should not be lost sight of when analysing learner varieties. As was mentioned in Section 2, the learners in LINDSEI (and in ICLE) are labelled as advanced on the basis of an external criterion. A recent study in Granger et al. (2009) shows that ICLE contains differences in proficiency level both across and within subcorpora. A random sample of 20 essays was submitted to a professional rater whose task was to grade them using the descriptors for writing in the Common European Framework of Reference for Languages. The results showed that the Chinese learners tend to be labelled as higher intermediate (B2), whereas the French-speaking and especially the German-speaking learners tended to be labelled as advanced (C1 and C2). It does not seem unreasonable to expect similar differences across and within the various LINDSEI components. Such differences may, for example, help explain why the patterns in LINDSEI_GER tend to be closer to those found in LOCNEC, and why the patterns in LINDSEI_CH differ more markedly from those in the NS corpus.

Note

[1] It is noteworthy that the adjective *ugly* occurs far more frequently in LINDSEI_CH than in the other varieties under study. Xiao Chen (personal communication) proposes the following possible explanations: (1) one of the Chinese equivalents of *ugly* is rather soft and not as strong as the English adjective; (2) *ugly* appears to be 'commonly taught as the antonym of *beautiful* without mentioning its taboo flavour', while other milder antonyms of *beautiful* are rather poorly represented in teaching materials; (3) when performing the picture-story task, the Chinese learners tended to be highly imaginative and may have resorted to an adjective like *ugly* for dramatic effect.

References

Belin, A. (2006), How do you Like it? : Likes and Dislikes in Native Speaker and Advanced Learner Spoken English. Unpublished MA dissertation. Université Catholique de Louvain.

Biber, D. (1988), *Variation across Speech and Writing*. Cambridge: Cambridge University Press.

Biber, D., Johansson, S., Leech, G., Conrad, S. and Finegan, E. (1999), *Longman Grammar of Spoken and Written English*. London: Longman.

Carter, R. and McCarthy, M. (2006), *Cambridge Grammar of English. A Comprehensive Guide. Spoken and Written English Grammar Usage.* Cambridge: Cambridge University Press.

Chafe, W.L. (1982), 'Integration and involvement in speaking, writing, and oral literature', in D. Tannen (ed.), *Spoken and Written Language: Exploring Orality and Literacy.* Norwood: Ablex, pp. 35–54.

Conrad, S. and Biber, D. (1999), 'Adverbial marking of stance in speech and writing', in S. Hunston and G. Thompson (eds), pp. 56–73.

Channel, J. (1999), 'Corpus-based analysis of evaluative lexis', in S. Hunston and G. Thompson (eds), pp. 38–55.

De Cock, S. (2007), 'Routinized building blocks in native speaker and learner speech: Clausal sequences in the spotlight', in M.C. Campoy and M.J. Luzón (eds), *Spoken Corpora in Applied Linguistics.* Bern: Peter Lang, pp. 217–233.

Granger, S. (1998a), 'The computerized learner corpus: a versatile new source of data for SLA research', in S. Granger (ed.), *Learner English on Computer.* London and New York: Addison Wesley Longman, pp. 3–18.

Granger, S. (1998b), 'Prefabricated patterns in advanced EFL writing: Collocations and formulae', in A.P. Cowie (ed.), *Phraseology: Theory, Analysis and Applications.* Oxford: Oxford University Press, pp. 145–160.

Granger, S. (2009), 'The contribution of learner corpora to second language acquisition and foreign language teaching: A critical evaluation', in K. Aijmer (ed.), *Corpora and Language Teaching.* Amsterdam and Philadelphia: John Benjamins, pp. 13–32.

Granger, S., Dagneaux, E., Meunier, F., Paquot, M. (2009), *The International Corpus of Learner English. Handbook and CD-ROM. Version 2.* Louvain-la-Neuve: Presses universitaires de Louvain.

Hunston, S. (2004), 'Counting the uncountable: Problems of identifying evaluation in a text and in a corpus', in A. Partington, J. Morley and L. Haarman (eds), *Corpora and Discourse.* Bern: Peter Lang, pp. 157–188.

Hunston, S. and Sinclair, J. (1999), 'A local grammar of evaluation', in S. Hunston and G. Thompson (eds), pp. 74–101.

Hunston, S. and Thompson, G. (eds) (1999), *Evaluation in Text. Authorial Stance and the Construction of Discourse.* Oxford: Oxford University Press.

Mauranen, A. (2002), '"A good question". Expressing evaluation in academic speech', in G. Cortese and P. Riley (eds), *Domain-specific English: Textual Practices across Communities and Classrooms.* Frankfurt: Peter Lang, pp. 115–140.

Meunier, F. (2002), 'The pedagogical value of native and learner corpora in EFL grammar teaching', in S. Granger, J. Hung and S. Petch-Tyson (eds), *Computer Learner Corpora, Second Language Acquisition and Foreign Language Teaching.* Amsterdam and Philadelphia: John Benjamins, pp. 119–141.

Meunier, F. and Gouverneur, C. (2007), 'The treatment of phraseology in ELT textbooks', in E. Hidalgo, L. Quereda and J. Santana (eds), *Corpora in the Foreign Language Classroom.* Amsterdam and New York: Rodopi, pp. 119–139.

Nesselhauf, N. (2004), 'Learner corpora and their potential in language teaching', in J. Sinclair (ed.), *How to Use Corpora in Language Teaching.* Amsterdam and Philadelphia: John Benjamins, pp. 125–152.

O'Keeffe, A., McCarthy, M. and Carter, R. (2007), *From Corpus to Classroom.* Cambridge: Cambridge University Press.

Scott, M. (2004), *WordSmith Tools 4.* Oxford: Oxford University Press.

Tao, H. and McCarthy, M. (2001), 'Understanding non-restrictive which-clauses in spoken English, which is not an easy thing'. *Language Sciences*, 23, 651–677.

Chapter 13

BAWE: an introduction to a new resource

Hilary Nesi

The British Academic Written English (BAWE) corpus was developed with ESRC funding as part of the project entitled 'An investigation of genres of assessed writing in British Higher Education' (2004–2007). The project aimed to characterise proficient student writing, and to compare writing across disciplines and levels of study. The corpus consists of just under 3000 student assignments of good standard (6,506,995 words), at four levels and in many disciplines. Information about discipline and level is provided in the header for each assignment file, alongside other types of contextual information which did not influence collection policy. We believe that BAWE is currently the only complete corpus of its kind in the public domain. It offers opportunities to investigate student writing which has been judged to conform to departmental requirements, but which differs markedly from expert and near-expert academic writing, such as textbooks and research article, in terms of its communicative intent.

13.1. Background to the project

The project 'An investigation of genres of assessed writing in British Higher Education' grew out of a concern that too little was known about the types of writing students produced in British universities, and a concern that students taking academic writing courses might be introduced to an inadequate or inappropriate range of academic writing genres.

Most course books for students at intermediate level seem to regard academic writing as more or less synonymous with essay writing. Thoreau (2006: 29), for example, tells students 'if you know about two essay genres [expository and argumentative], you will have a good foundation for tertiary study', while Bailey (2006) offers the 'comparison essay' and the 'discussion essay' as two of his three main models for written assignments (the third is the questionnaire survey). Course books for more advanced students, on the other hand, tend to shift their focus to research writing, interpreted narrowly as the 'research paper' with an Introduction, Methods, Results, Discussion (IMRD) structure (Hamp-Lyons and Heasley 2006), or more broadly to include 'research essays', book/article reviews, theses and research publications generally (Craswell 2005). Thus the course books include high status genres that some students may aspire to write, such as the research article, at the expense, perhaps understandably, of professional genres which occur in a restricted range of disciplines, such as those belonging to what we have called 'Design Specification' genre family. They also neglect commoner pedagogic genres, such as those belonging to the 'Critique' and 'Explanation' genre families, which remain occluded (Swales 1996) because they are not produced by professionals and are rarely written or read outside the academy. These types of genre tend to be neglected not only by course book writers, but also by discourse analysts and writing researchers.

Theses have been investigated fairly thoroughly from a genre/discourse perspective (e.g. Bunton 2002; Charles 2006; Thompson 2005), and the research article (RA) has long been the most popular academic genre for analysis, with seminal work on RA discourse dating from the 1980s (e.g. Swales 1981, 1984) and continuing to this day (e.g. Bruce 2008; Hyland 2008; Ozturk 2007). These genres are particularly attractive to applied linguists because expert texts are in themselves admirable and worthy of scrutiny, and because there are many novice academics who aspire to write RAs, and many novice supervisors who need to guide students through the thesis writing process. A further incentive for applied linguists is the fact that theses and published articles are available in the public domain, making corpus compilation relatively easy. However the enthusiasm for these research genres, leading to a situation where 'academic writing' risks being equated solely with RAs and theses, obscures the fact that they do not represent the bulk of what is written in academic contexts, that is, the assignments produced by students on taught degree programmes for assessment purposes. Assessed student writing is produced with the primary intention of demonstrating requisite academic knowledge and skills. It has a different social function and communicative intent, and therefore it is unlikely to display the same generic features as writing intended to present and promote original research.

Of course the university student assignment is not an entirely neglected genre, and there have been a number of excellent studies of small collections of such writing, usually within just one or two disciplines and with reference to one particular discourse feature (see, for example, North 2005a, 2005b; Woodward-Kron, 2002). Before the development of the BAWE corpus, however, no fully documented collection existed which might enable large scale comparisons of assignments across disciplines and levels of study. The only comparable collections are two smaller corpora which are currently under development in the United States: the Michigan Corpus of Upper-level Student Papers (MICUSP) (Römer and Wulff 2010), and the Portland State University Corpus of Student Academic Writing (Conrad and Albers 2008). These, however, do not cover the same range of levels or disciplines as BAWE.

Our first attempt to create a corpus of student assignments was not entirely successful, and provided some insight into why such a corpus did not yet exist. A pilot project was run from May 2001 to November 2002, during which time 499 assignments from 70 student writers were collected. The project did not adopt any particular collection policy, and simply accepted any high-grade assignment offered by any willing student. We found that writers tended to come from a limited range of disciplines (largely from the humanities, with very few from the hard sciences), and there was a disproportionate number of assignments from the first year of study (44%) (see Nesi et al. 2004). Fewer science students seemed interested in contributing, and in any case they produced less written work, while the fact that students could contribute work written in preceding years but could not contribute work that had not yet been assessed probably accounted for the diminishing availability of assignments in the upper levels. To fulfil the aims of the main project, which received funding from the UK Economic and Social Research Council (ESRC) in 2004, it was evident that it would be necessary to devise a more systematic approach to data collection

For this project we proposed to integrate ethnographic, multidimensional and functional linguistic approaches to text description, each of which suggested a different method of sampling, as discussed in Gardner (2008). Ethnographic aspects of the study favoured cluster sampling and the targeting of specific university discourse communities, whereas random sampling seemed an appropriately objective way of collecting data for computational analysis. Purposive sampling involving the targeting of specific text types, on the other hand, seemed best as a means of obtaining a rich array of data for genre analysis.

We finally arrived at a collection policy which involved stratified sampling, a compromise which took into account these conflicting approaches to corpus analysis, together with the practical constraints on policy implementation. We did conduct interviews with staff and students (see Nesi and Gardner 2006; Gardner and Powell 2006), but we rejected the idea of sampling selected clusters of contributors because we did not have the resources (or the persuasive power) to guarantee contributions from sufficient numbers of individuals within specified departmental communities. We considered random sampling, but even if it had been possible to identify a random sample of potential student contributors, our experience with the pilot corpus had taught us that it would be impossible to force contributions from them. We abandoned more purposive sampling, although we wanted to gather several instances of each assignment type we encountered, because it soon became clear that it would be impossible to create a multimillion word corpus if we set restrictions on the genre of contributions, as well as on their grade, discipline and year of study. In any case, at the collection stage we had not yet identified and described the types of assignments students write, and we had little idea of the distribution patterns of these types across disciplines and levels.

13.2. The design matrix

We used a 4-by-4 matrix to guide the data collection. This combined four levels of study with four broad disciplinary groupings, and we hoped to fill each of the 16 cells with a roughly equal quantity of assignments, rejecting all but a few contributions which were superfluous to these requirements (we retained an 'other' category, to round up numbers). Table 13.1 represents our ideal corpus structure in more detail, and our plan to collect 3,500 assignments across 28 disciplinary fields.

Table 13.1   The plan for BAWE corpus collection

Disciplinary Group	Subject	Per level (1, 2, final, and Masters)	Total
Arts & Humanities (AH)	Applied Linguistics/Applied English Language Studies	32	128
	Classics	32	128
	Comparative American Studies	32	128
	English Studies	32	128
	History	32	128
	Philosophy	32	128
	(Archaeology)	16	64

Life Sciences (LS)	Agriculture	32	128
	Biological Sciences/ Biochemistry	32	128
	Food Science and Technology	32	128
	Health and Social Care	32	128
	Plant Biosciences	32	128
	Psychology	32	128
	(Medical Science)	16:48[1]	64
Physical Sciences	Architecture	32	128
(PS)	Chemistry	32	128
	Computer Science	32	128
	Cybernetics & Electronic Engineering	32	128
	Engineering	64	256
	Physics	32	128
	(Mathematics)	16	128
Social Sciences (SS)	Anthropology	32	128
	Business	32	128
	Economics	32	128
	Hospitality, Leisure and Tourism Management	32	128
	Law	32	128
	Sociology	32	128
	(Publishing)	16	64
Other	Other	43	172
Total			**3500**

[1] The Medical School ran a graduate-entry two-phase course.

Our matrix was not designed to represent proportionally the quantity of writing produced in each discipline and at each level, or to ensure perfect representation of all the genres produced in the target disciplines. Students usually write more in their final year(s), and some disciplines are understood to be more discursive than others (as indicated in British university rules concerning PhD thesis length – usually a maximum of 80,000 words in the Humanities and Social Sciences, but only 50,000 words in the Sciences). Also we knew we could not collect assignments for every module in every discipline, and that module tutors were liable at any time to introduce new tasks with different generic expectations. We realised we might miss some unusual genres, especially if only a few students selected particular writing tasks, or if the assignments written for particular tasks only received low grades (we did not accept assignments graded below 60%). Nevertheless steps were taken to encourage variety in the corpus in terms of both assignment type and authorship by prompting contributors to submit additional work of a different type, if possible, while preventing individuals from contributing more than three assignments from any single module.

13.3. The corpus contents

Assignments were collected at Oxford Brookes, Reading and Warwick, and, in the final year of the project, Coventry University, to make up numbers in disciplines which still lacked sufficient contributions. Most cells of our matrix were not quite filled, as can be seen from Table 13.2.

It will be noted that the number of texts exceeds the number of assignments. This is because some assignments consisted of more than one independent text, submitted together to receive a single grade. It will also be noted that the total number of contributors (627) is not the sum of all the contributors at each level. This is because most students contributed assignments at more than one level.

Table 13.2 Numbers of students, assignments, texts and words by grouping and level

Disciplinary Grouping		Level 1	Level 2	Level 3	Masters	Total
Arts and Humanities (AH)	students	101	83	61	23	
	assignments	239	228	160	78	705
	texts	254	232	160	82	728
	words	468,353	583,617	427,942	234,206	1,714,118
Life Sciences (LS)	students	74	71	42	46	
	assignments	180	193	113	197	683
	texts	186	203	92	246	727
	words	299,370	408,070	263,668	441,283	1,412,391
Physical Sciences (PS)	students	73	60	56	36	
	assignments	181	149	156	110	596
	texts	201	156	159	121	637
	words	300,989	314,331	426,431	339,605	1,381,356
Social Sciences (SS)	students	85	88	75	62	
	assignments	207	197	162	202	777[1]
	texts	215	205	165	210	804[2]
	words	371,473	475,668	440,674	688,921	1,999,130[3]
Total students		333	302	234	167	627
Total assignments		807	767	591	6587	2761[1]
Total texts		856	796	576	659	2896[2]
Total words		1,440,185	1,781,686	1,558,715	1,704,015	6,506,995[3]

[1] Includes 9 assignments of unknown level.
[2] Includes 9 texts of unknown level.
[3] Includes 22,394 words of unknown level.

Table 13.3 provides a more complete picture of the disciplines represented in the corpus. 'Discipline' is not synonymous with 'Department', because some assignments in the same field came from more than one university, and departments with slightly different names have been conflated ('Computer Science' and 'Computing', for example). We recognise that

Table 13.3 Number of assignments by discipline and year

Disciplinary Grouping	Discipline	Level 1	Level 2	Level 3	Masters	Total
Arts and Humanities (AH)	Archaeology	23	21	15	17	76
	Classics	33	27	15	7	82
	Comparative American Studies	29	26	13	6	74
	English	35	35	28	8	106
	History	30	32	31	3	96
	Linguistics	27	31	24	33	115
	Other	19	22	9	0	50
	Philosophy	43	34	25	4	106
	Total	**239**	**228**	**160**	**78**	**705**
Life Sciences (LS)	Agriculture	35	35	30	34	134
	Biological Sciences	52	50	26	41	169
	Food Sciences	26	36	32	30	124
	Health	35	33	12	1	81
	Medicine	0	0	0	80	80
	Psychology	32	39	13	11	95
	Total	180	193	113	197	683
	Total	**180**	**193**	**82**	**228**	**683**
Physical Sciences (PS)	Architecture	2	4	2	1	9
	Chemistry	23	24	29	13	89
	Computer Science	34	13	30	10	87
	Cybernetics & Electronics	4	4	13	7	28
	Engineering	59	71	54	54	238
	Mathematics	8	5	12	8	33
	Meteorology	6	9	0	14	29
	Other	0	1	0	0	1
	Physics	37	14	14	3	68
	Planning	8	4	2	0	14
	Total	181	149	156	110	596
	Total	**181**	**149**	**155**	**111**	**596**

(Continued)

Table 13.3 (Cont'd)

Disciplinary Grouping	Discipline	Level 1	Level 2	Level 3	Masters	Total
Social Sciences (SS)	Anthropology	14	12	6	17	49
	Business	32	33	31	50	146
	Economics	30	30	23	13	96
	HLTM	14	21	29	29	93
	Law	37	37	31	28	134[1]
	Other	0	2	3	4	9
	Politics	37	33	15	25	110
	Publishing	11	4	0	15	30
	Sociology	32	25	24	21	110[2]
	Total	**207**	**197**	**162**	**202**	**777[3]**
Total		**807**	**767**	**591**	**587**	**2761[3]**

[1] 1 of unknown year.
[2] 8 of unknown year.
[3] 9 of unknown year.

'discipline' is a difficult concept to define, however, and that 'variation in epistemology and discourse occurs not only across disciplines, but also within disciplines' (Nesi and Gardner 2006: 101). Assignments produced for modules referring to more than one discipline were counted as belonging within the discipline of the department that taught the module, although this was not always apparent from their titles; for example while Psychology was the home department for the module 'Psychology and the Law', Law was the home department for the module 'Medicine and the Law'.

The assignments are distributed almost equally between 'distinction' grade (1,251) and 'merit' grade (1,402). The majority were written by students who identified themselves as 'native' or 'near-native' speakers of English: 1,953 were written by students who reported that English was their mother tongue, and an additional 42 were written by students who claimed another language as their L1, but who had received all their secondary education in the United Kingdom. Such students included bilingual speakers of English and a UK minority language such as Punjabi, Urdu or Welsh, who might be considered native speakers of English for all practical purposes.

13.4. Markup conventions

The corpus was marked up according to the guidelines of TEI P4 (Sperberg-McQueen and Burnard 2004). A DTD containing only a subset of all

TEI elements and attributes was created for BAWE (see Ebeling and Heuboeck 2007; Heuboeck et al. 2009). Information of the following types was encoded:

- header information
- document structure and hierarchy
- types of front and back matter
- functional features within running text
- character formatting

All personal information relating to the writer or any third parties was anonymised. Information about the discipline and level of each assignment was placed in the header, alongside other types of contextual information which had not affected the planning of the design matrix and which did not influence collection policy. The gender and the first language of the contributor was recorded, for example, but gender proportions necessarily varied from cell to cell of the design matrix, and the proportion of non-native speakers was much greater in some disciplines than in others, and at Masters as opposed to undergraduate levels. We also recorded the number of years of UK secondary education each contributor had received, in view of the fact that in the British university context a contributor's choice of first language may reflect affiliation rather than proficiency, and that experience of the British educational system implied knowledge of British academic linguistic and generic conventions. A 'merit' or 'distinction' grade was recorded for each assignment, corresponding to upper second or first class degree level.

Because it is encoded in the header, the information concerning discipline, level, gender, first language, secondary education and assignment grade can be used to filter assignments according to individual requirements when searching the BAWE corpus with a concordancing program such as Wordsmith Tools, or via the corpus query interface Sketch Engine. Some researchers may want to interrogate a sub-corpus of native speaker assignments, for example, or a sub-corpus of assignments at distinction level, if they view these as representing greater conformity to the norms of the British academic discourse community. By so doing, however, they will inevitably lose some of the benefits of the design matrix in terms of balance across levels and disciplines.

13.5. Findings relating to genre families

Information regarding the broad 'genre family' to which each assignment belongs is also included in the header. A list of these genre families was developed through an iterative process involving multiple readings of the 2896 texts, paying particular attention to headings and sub-headings, the first sentence of each paragraph and any statements of purpose in abstracts, introductions and conclusions. As the final list of thirteen families was not governed by any prior categorisation systems, however, our genre family names do not necessarily match those used by other researchers, and our nomenclature risks being a source of confusion. For example our *explanation* seems to approximate to *exposition* as used by Hale et al. (1996), and to *report genres* in the schools literature (e.g. Martin 1989; Veel 1997), while explanation in secondary school history (Coffin 2006) may be closer to our *essay* genre family.

While informed by data from staff and student interviews, our genre family list also ignored the nomenclature used by contributors. The latter proved inconsistent, and often obscured generic similarities and differences between assignments produced in different departments. Thus the genre family assigned to a text does not necessarily match the student writer's own metatextual description, or the assignment type they named when submitting their work. The thirteen genre families used for the text headers were as follows:

Case Study: A description of a particular case with recommendations or suggestions for future action, written to gain an understanding of professional practice (e.g. in business, medicine or engineering). Examples include patient case notes and company reports.

Critique: A text including a descriptive account, explanation and evaluation, often involving tests, written to demonstrate understanding of the object of study and to demonstrate the ability to evaluate and/or assess the significance of the object of study. Examples include reviews of academic articles, books, films, plays or websites and evaluations of legislation or policy.

Design Specification: A text typically including an expression of purpose, an account of component selection and a proposal, possibly including an account of the development and testing of the design. Examples include specifications of the design of buildings, databases, products and systems.

Empathy writing: A letter, newspaper article or similar non-academic genre, written to demonstrate understanding and appreciation of the relevance of academic ideas by translating them into a non-academic register for a non-specialist readership. Examples include newspaper articles, letters and information leaflets.

Essay: A text written to develop the ability to construct a coherent argument and develop critical thinking skills. The essay may take the form of a discussion (issue, pros/cons, final position); exposition (thesis, evidence, restate thesis); factorial (outcome, conditioning factors); challenge (opposition to existing theory); consequential (input, consequences, restatement) or commentary (series of comments on a text).

Exercise: Data analysis or a series of responses to questions, written to provide practice in key skills and to consolidate knowledge of key concepts.

Explanation: A descriptive account and explanation, written to demonstrate understanding of the object of study and the ability to describe and/or assess its significance. Examples include overviews of instruments, methods, species and substances.

Literature Survey: A summary including varying degrees of critical evaluation, written to demonstrate familiarity with the literature relevant to the focus of study. Examples include annotated bibliographies, anthologies, notes taken from multiple sources and summaries of book chapters.

Methodology Recount: A description of procedures undertaken by the writer, possibly including Introduction, Methods, Results and Discussion sections, written to develop familiarity with disciplinary procedures and methods, and additionally to record experimental findings. Examples include lab reports, field reports and program development reports.

Narrative Recount: A fictional or factual recount of events, written to develop awareness of motives and/or the behaviour of organisations or individuals (including oneself). Examples include biographies, plot synopses and reflective recounts.

Problem question: A text presenting relevant arguments or possible solution(s) to a problem, written to practise the application of specific methods in response to simulated professional scenarios. Examples include law problem questions, and responses to medical problems.

Proposal: A text including an expression of purpose, a detailed plan and persuasive argumentation, written to demonstrate the ability to make a case for future action. Examples include business, marketing and catering plans and research proposals.

Research Report: A text typically including a Literature Review, Methods, Findings and Discussion, or several 'chapters' relating to the same theme, written to demonstrate the ability to undertake a complete piece of research, including research design, and to appreciate its significance in the field.

One obvious conclusion that can be drawn from this categorisation scheme is that university students write for a range of purposes, not all of them identical to the purposes of professional academics. Some assignment types, such as the Case Study or Design Specification, are generically similar to texts produced in the professions, but only the Research Report bears much generic resemblance to the thesis or research article.

The distribution of the genre families in the corpus is presented in Table 13.4. The essay is the best represented category, although in the Physical Sciences (PS) and Life Sciences (LS) it is outnumbered by submissions belonging to other families (Methodology Recounts, Design Specifications and Critiques). Also, some genre families are rare or totally absent from some disciplinary groupings, particularly the Arts and Humanities (AH).

Multidimensional analysis was conducted by Doug Biber and his team at Northern Arizona University, using factor analysis to calculate variation between disciplines, genres and levels of study on the basis of the co-occurrence of linguistic patterns (see Biber 1988; Conrad and Biber 2001). Overall the corpus was shown to be carefully written and information-rich, but there were also significant differences among genre families, as can be seen from Table 13.5. The entirely negative scores on the 'involved' and 'narrative' dimensions indicate a high informational focus and a low level of narration, while the entirely positive scores for 'explicit' and 'abstract' qualities indicate lexically dense text containing passives, past participial

Table 13.4 Distribution of genre families by disciplinary group

	AH	LS	PS	SS	Total
Case Study	0	91	37	66	194
Critique	48	84	76	114	322
Design Specification	1	2	87	3	93
Empathy Writing	4	19	9	3	35
Essay	602	127	65	444	1238
Exercise	14	33	49	18	114
Explanation	9	117	65	23	214
Literature Survey	7	14	4	10	35
Methodology Recount	18	158	170	16	362
Narrative Recount	10	25	21	19	75
Problem Question	0	2	6	32	40
Proposal	2	26	19	29	76
Research Report	9	22	16	14	61
Total	724	720	624	791	2859

Table 13.5 Multiple range test scores for genre families

	Involved	Narrative	Explicit	Abstract	Persuasive
Essay	-14.327	-2.4788	6.234	5.920	-1.8345
Methodology Recount	-15.856	-3.6533	4.506	7.304	-2.5011
Critique	-14.833	-3.0714	5.988	6.381	-1.6127
Explanation	-15.411	-3.5878	5.042	5.848	-2.2744
Case Study	-16.402	-2.8617	5.772	4.450	-0.4519
Exercise	-12.098	-3.8543	4.628	5.678	-1.3301
Design Specification	-13.090	-4.0223	4.079	6.750	0.6702
Proposal	-16.421	-3.7855	6.326	4.793	1.2799
Narrative Recount	-4.818	-1.1128	3.814	3.957	-0.7439
Research Report	-16.186	-3.1156	5.524	7.198	-2.4064
Problem Question	-11.950	-2.7730	5.222	6.429	1.6295
Literature Survey	-17.907	-2.6214	6.311	5.047	-3.4343
Empathy Writing	-11.500	-2.7369	4.533	4.472	0.7713

clauses and other features typical of academic prose. Mixed scores on the 'persuasive' dimension, however, indicate variation in the degree of argumentation (Problem Questions and Proposals being the most persuasive, and Literature Surveys the least). Most student writing simply does not need to 'create a research space' in the manner of research article introductions, because the centrality of the topic is not usually in question, and the tutor is duty-bound to read the text.

13.6. Conclusion

Clearly the BAWE corpus is a very rich resource, offering a currently unique opportunity to investigate academic texts which have been judged to conform to departmental requirements (on the evidence of the grade awarded), but which differ markedly from professional academic writing in terms of their communicative intent. A certain amount of research has already been conducted with reference to the corpus, for example Gardezi and Nesi (2009), Gardner (2008), Gardner and Holmes (2009) and Holmes and Nesi (2009). Future researchers might seek to trace not only the development of novice academic writers, and their gradual approximation to the norms of professional writing as evidenced in published academic texts, but also the development of novice writers preparing for careers in the professions, and developing the skills to write (for example) civil engineering site reports, or location reports for the tourism industry. Other potential lines of enquiry might include investigations of specific genre families, and the writing demands of specific disciplines across years of study. The corpus compilers encourage research of this sort, and have made BAWE freely available to all those who register with the Oxford Text Archive. It is listed as resource number 2539.

Acknowledgement

The project *An Investigation of Genres of Assessed Writing in British Higher Education,* including the development of the British Academic Written English corpus, was conducted at the Universities of Warwick, Reading and Oxford Brookes under the directorship of Hilary Nesi and Sheena Gardner (formerly of the Centre for Applied Linguistics [previously called CELTE], Warwick), Paul Thompson (formerly of the Department of Applied Linguistics, Reading) and Paul Wickens (Westminster Institute of Education, Oxford Brookes), with funding from the ESRC (RES-000-23-0800).

References

Bailey, S. (2006), *Academic Writing: a Handbook for International Students* (2nd edn.). London: Routledge.

Biber, D. (1988), *Variation across Speech and Writing.* Cambridge: Cambridge University Press.

Bruce, I. (2008), 'Cognitive genre structures in Methods sections of research articles: a corpus study'. *Journal of English for Academic Purposes,* 7, (1), 38–54.

Bunton. D. (2002), 'Generic moves in PhD theses introductions', in J. Flowerdew (ed.), *Academic Discourse.* London: Longman, pp. 57–75.

Charles, M. (2006), 'Phraseological patterns in reporting clauses used in citation: a corpus-based study of theses in two disciplines'. *English for Specific Purposes,* 25, (3), 310–331.

Charles, M., Pecorari, D., and Hunston, S. (eds) (2009), *Academic Writing: at the Interface of Corpus and Discourse.* London: Continuum.

Coffin, C. (2006), *Historical Discourse: the Language of Time, Cause and Evaluation.* London: Continuum.

Conrad, S. and Biber, D. (eds) (2001), *Variation in English: Multidimensional Studies.* Essex: Pearson Education.

Conrad, S. and Albers, S. (2008), 'A new corpus of student academic writing'. Paper presented at the American Association for Corpus Linguistics Conference, March 13–15, 2008. Brigham Young University, Utah. [Online] http://corpus. byu.edu/aacl2008/ppt/29.ppt (accessed September 16, 2009).

Craswell, G. (2005), *Writing for Academic Success: a Postgraduate Guide.* London: Sage Publications.

Ebeling, S. and Heuboeck, A. (2007), 'Encoding document information in a corpus of student writing: the experience of the British Academic Written English (BAWE) corpus'. *Corpora*, 2, (2), 241–256.

Gardezi, S.A. and Nesi, H. (2009), 'Variation in the writing of economics students in Britain and Pakistan: the case of conjunctive ties', in M. Charles, S. Hunston. and D. Pecorari (eds), pp. 236–250.

Gardner, S. (2008), 'Integrating ethnographic, multidimensional, corpus linguistic and systemic functional approaches to genre description: an illustration through university history and engineering assignments', in E. Steiner and S. Neumann (eds), *Proceedings of the 19th European Systemic Functional Linguistics Conference and Workshop*. 23- 25 July 2007, Universität des Saarlandes, Saarbrücken, Germany, pp 1–34. Available [Online] http://scidok.sulb.uni-saarland.de/volltexte/2008/1688/ (accessed September 16, 2009).

Gardner, S. and Holmes, J. (2009), 'Can I use headings in my essay? Section headings, macrostructures and genre families in the BAWE corpus of student writing', in M. Charles, S. Hunston. and D. Pecorari (eds), pp. 251–271.

Gardner, S. and Powell, L. (2006), 'An investigation of genres of assessed writing in British Higher Education'. Paper presented at the annual seminar Research, Scholarship and Practice in the area of Academic Literacies. University of Westminster, June 30, 2006. [Online] http://www.coventry.ac.uk/researchnet/external/content/1/c4/33/84/v1193312407/user/genresbhe_handout.pdf (accessed September 16, 2009).

Hale, G.A., Taylor, C., Bridgeman, B., Carson, J., Kroll, B. and Kantor, R. (1996), A Study of Writing Tasks Assigned in Academic Degree Programs (TOEFL Research Report No. RR 54). Princeton, NJ: Educational Testing Service.

Hamp-Lyons, L. and Heasley, B. (2006), *Study Writing* (2nd edn.). Cambridge: Cambridge University Press.

Heuboeck, A., Holmes, J. and Nesi, H. (2009), *The BAWE Corpus Manual*, Version II. [Online] http://www.coventry.ac.uk/bawe (accessed September 16, 2009).

Holmes, J. and Nesi H. (2009), 'Verbal and mental processes in academic disciplines', in M. Charles, S. Hunston. and D. Pecorari (eds), pp. 58–72.

Hyland, K. (2008), 'Disciplinary voices: interactions in research writing'. *English Text Construction*, 1, (1), 5–22.

Martin, J. (1989), *Factual writing: Exploring and Challenging Social Reality*. Oxford: Oxford University Press.

Nesi, H. and Gardner, S. (2006), 'Variation in disciplinary culture: University tutors' views on assessed writing tasks', in R. Kiely, P. Rea-Dickins, H. Woodfield and G. Clibbon (eds), *Language, Culture and Identity in Applied Linguistics, British Studies in Applied Linguistics*, Vol. 21. London: Equinox Publishing, pp. 99–117.

Nesi, H., Sharpling, G. and Ganobcsik-Williams, L. (2004), 'The design, development and purpose of a corpus of British student writing'. *Computers and Composition*, 21, (4), 439–450.

North, S. (2005a), 'Different values, different skills? A comparison of essay writing by students from arts and science backgrounds'. *Studies in Higher Education*, 30, (5), 517–533.

North, S. (2005b), 'Disciplinary variation in the use of theme in undergraduate essays'. *Applied Linguistics*, 26, (3), 431–452.

Ozturk, I. (2007), 'The textual organisation of research article introductions in applied linguistics: Variability within a single discipline'. *English for Specific Purposes*, 26, (1), 25–38.

Römer, U. and Wulff, S. (2010), 'Applying corpus methods to writing research: explorations of MICUSP'. *Journal of Writing Research*, 2, (2), 99–127.

Sperberg-McQueen, C.M. and Burnard, L. (eds) (2004), *TEI P4 – Guidelines for Electronic Text Encoding and Interchange, XML-compatible Edition*. [Online] http://www.tei-c.org/P4X/ (accessed September 16, 2009).

Swales, J. (1981), *Aspects of Article Introductions*. Birmingham: Language Studies Unit, University of Aston.

Swales, J. (1984), 'Research into the structure of introductions to journal articles and its application to the teaching of academic writing', in R. Williams, J. Swales and J. Kirkman (eds), *Common Ground: Shared Interests in ESP and Communication Studies*. Oxford: Pergamon Press, pp. 77–86.

Swales, J. (1996), 'Occluded genres in the academy: the case of the submission letter', in E. Ventola and A. Mauranen (eds), *Academic Writing: Intercultural and Textual Issues*. Amsterdam and Philadelphia: John Benjamins, pp. 45–58.

Thompson, P. (2005), 'Points of focus and position: intertextual reference in PhD theses'. *Journal of English for Academic Purposes*, 4, (4), 307–323.

Thoreau, M. (2006), *Write on Track: a Guide to Academic Writing*. Auckland, New Zealand: Pearson Education.

Veel, R. (1997), 'Learning how to mean – scientifically speaking: apprenticeship into scientific discourse in the secondary school', in F. Christie and J.R. Martin (eds), *Genre and Institutions: Apprenticeship into Scientific Discourse*. Cassell: London, pp. 161–195.

Woodward-Kron, R. (2002), 'Critical analysis versus description? Examining the relationship in successful student writing'. *Journal of English for Academic Purposes*, 1, (2), 121–143.

Chapter 14

The impact of culture on the use of stance exponents as persuasive devices: the case of GRICLE and English native speaker corpora

Anna-Maria Hatzitheodorou and Marina Mattheoudakis

This chapter examines the projection of stance in learner corpora containing essays in English written by Greek and American university students. In particular, it discusses how stance exponents (boosters, hedges and attitude markers) are used to achieve persuasion. The findings reveal that Greek university students deploy different rhetorical techniques from their American counterparts and prefer boosters (*of course, undoubtedly*) and attitude markers (*unfortunately*) to hedges (*perhaps*); hence their more emphatic writing. The paper argues that a major factor to influence the ways in which Greek learners structure their arguments is transfer of linguistic and cultural patterns from L1 to L2, and that a cross-cultural framework of teaching should be adopted, aiming to sensitise L2 learners to the L2 style of writing.

14.1. Introduction

In argumentative essays, writers aim to persuade readers by presenting ideas and attitudes (see Halliday's 1994 ideational and interpersonal meta-functions of language). To achieve persuasion, writers need to create a credible persona (Hyland 2005); this refers to *ethos*, the first of the three modes of persuasion according to Aristotle, the other two being *pathos* (an appeal to the emotions or values of the audience) and *logos* (an appeal to reason) (Barnes 1984). Persuasion can be effected through stance exponents such as hedges, boosters and attitude markers. In this chapter, we examine how advanced Greek learners of English at tertiary level and American university students employ stance markers, looking at the adverbials used by each group. Since the premise of our argument is that all written production is situated in a cultural context, our discussion of students' writing will be informed by tenets of cross-cultural research and contrastive rhetoric.

Insofar as cultural features are reflected in writing, it seems necessary to consider students' writing through the lens of cross-cultural research. To this aim, we will make use of Hofstede's (1980) model, with its four dimensions on which cultures may differ: (a) power-distance, (b) uncertainty avoidance, (c) individualism-collectivism, and (d) masculinity-femininity. Power-distance refers to the extent to which a culture accepts unequal distribution of power and either challenges or accepts the decisions of power holders (Hofstede 1986). Uncertainty avoidance indicates the degree of (in)tolerance that a culture is willing to exhibit towards unpredictability, lack of structure and uncertainty (*ibid*). Individualism-collectivism refers to the degree of importance attached to the self or the group (Hofstede 1994). Hofstede (1980) maintains that power distance, uncertainty avoidance and collectivism can all be expected to affect written production, and it is precisely these three dimensions which will inform our comparison of American and Greek students' writings. The fourth dimension, masculinity-femininity, which relates to cultural attitudes towards masculine assertiveness and feminine nurturance (*ibid*), will not be considered.

14.2. Categories of stance

According to Hyland (2005: 176–177), stance comprises four main elements: (a) hedges, (b) boosters, (c) attitude markers and (d) self-mention (Figure 14.1). Hyland and Tse (2004) and Hyland (2005) argue that writers employ hedges to withhold full commitment to a proposition (e.g. *might, perhaps*), and boosters to emphasise the writer's certainty with

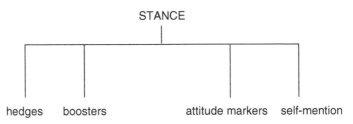

FIGURE 14.1   Categorisation of stance features according to Hyland (2005)

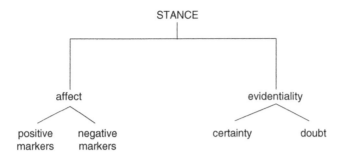

FIGURE 14.2   Categorisation of stance features according to Biber and Finegan (1989)

respect to the proposition (e.g. *definitely*). Attitude markers are used to pull readers into agreement (e.g. *unfortunately, surprisingly*). Finally, self-mention makes explicit reference to author(s), e.g. *I, we.*

To account for instances of attitudinal stance which are not normally included in studies of academic discourse, we will enrich Hyland's framework with elements taken from Biber and Finegan's model (1989). In the latter, stance features are divided between two pragmatic functions, affect and evidentiality. Affect includes both positive and negative markers expressing the author's personal feelings and attitude (e.g. *happily, sadly*: see Ochs, 1989). Evidentiality covers grammatical categories that express the author's certainty (e.g. *impossible, obvious*) or doubt (e.g. *perhaps*) (Figure 14.2).

14.3. An adapted model of stance

For our analysis, we adapt the two frameworks of stance presented above to provide an alternative categorisation of stance features. This follows Hyland's categorisation (i.e., hedges, boosters, attitude markers, self-mention), but further divides attitude markers into affect and opinion. Adopting Biber and Finegan's affect category allows us to account for expressions that are normally found in argumentation in general, but not in academic discourse, which is the focus of Hyland's model. Thus the affect sub-category includes items which express the writer's emotional attitude and personal feelings (e.g. *happily, luckily*: cf. Biber and Finegan 1989: 94), while the opinion sub-category includes items which introduce the writer's cognitive attitude to the proposition stated (e.g. *I think, I agree*) (Figure 14.3). While Hunston and Thompson (2000: 6) view opinion as referring to both epistemic and affective stance, in our model we see opinion as having a more

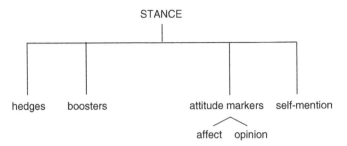

FIGURE 14.3 Categorisation of stance features proposed in this study

pronounced cognitive orientation. Biber and Finegan's evidentiality does not need to be incorporated as a category in our model, as its features are already covered by Hyland's hedges and boosters (Hyland 2005). And while there is an obvious overlap between their 'attitude markers' and Hyland's 'self-mention', which indicates the degree of explicit authorial presence as expressed by personal pronouns and possessive adjectives (e.g. *I, my*), the latter also includes various expressions which do not fall into the 'attitude markers' category, e.g. *I would point out that, I divided the groups into,* etc.

The following are examples of stance features as presented in our model:

> Hedges: possibly, probably, may, might, maybe, presumably, relatively, etc.
>
> Boosters: it is evident that, it is clear that, it is a fact that, it is true that, it is obvious that, clearly, evidently, obviously, definitely, certainly, truly, etc.
>
> Attitude markers – affect: I feel, I hope, it amazes me, it surprises me, it is shocking, it is (un)fortunate, (un)fortunately, happily, luckily, conveniently, hopefully, etc.
>
> Attitude markers – opinion: I think, I agree, I believe, I consider, I gather, I conclude, in my opinion, in my view, according to me, interestingly, etc.
>
> Self-mention: I, we, my, our.

14.4. Research on stance in learner corpora

Recently there has been growing interest in examining learners' writing from a stance-oriented perspective. Neff et al. (2004) investigated how native speakers of English and Spanish learners of English use modal verbs in order to indicate stance, comparing SPICLE, the Spanish subcorpus of the International Corpus of Learner English (ICLE), with the American component of the Louvain Corpus of Native English Essays (LOCNESS). They found important differences between the two corpora and suggested that factors in these differences may include lack of specific writing instruction in L1, typological differences between the two languages, and transfer of L1 discourse conventions. In a later study, Neff (2008) examined interpersonal expressions that encode certainty, attitude and impersonal presentation of arguments in SPICLE and LOCNESS. She attributed the differences between the two corpora to (a) incomplete mastery of the English modal system, (b) the novice writer factor, and (c) L1 transfer. Ädel (2006) compared the use of personal and impersonal metadiscourse (i.e. features the writer uses to comment on the ongoing text and to relate to the reader) by Swedish learners of English and British and American native speakers. For this purpose, she used the Swedish subcorpus of ICLE (SWICLE) and the British and American subcorpora of LOCNESS. She suggested that differences between native and non-native corpora can be attributed to four factors: (a) differences in genre, (b) learners' register awareness, (c) cultural conventions, and (d) general learner strategies. Her conclusions are partly matched by Gilquin and Paquot (2008), who compared learners' writings drawn from various subcorpora of ICLE (corresponding to 16 mother tongue backgrounds) with the British National Corpus (BNC). They found that EFL learners tend to use features that are typical of speech in their writing, and concluded that learners are not aware of register differences. Their lack of register awareness was attributed to (a) the influence of speech, (b) L1 transfer, (c) teaching-induced factors, and (d) developmental factors.

14.5. Aims of the study

This paper examines the projection of stance in the essays of Greek advanced learners of English and of American students, and the extent to which their written production is influenced by cultural factors. To this aim, data from three corpora will be discussed within the framework for stance analysis presented above. The following questions will be addressed:

- How do Greek and American students structure their arguments to indicate stance and achieve persuasion?
- To what extent (if any) do cultural factors influence their use of rhetorical techniques?

14.6. L1 and L2 instruction in Greece

Before presenting our study, we provide some information about L1 and L2 instruction in Greece, so as to facilitate the interpretation of our findings within a broader context. State English language instruction in Greece spans seven to nine years, and may be further intensified by private language courses aiming to enable learners to obtain language certificates, which are highly valued. Learners are extensively exposed to and required to produce various written text types. However, insofar as the ultimate goal of learning the language is to obtain a language certificate at an early age, there is little time for learners to master an L2 style of writing, and their young age does not help them in this respect. For ease of instruction, models of essays in English are typically presented in a prescriptive manner, a procedure that neither promotes critical thinking nor helps learners to assimilate the L2 style. Thus, when left to their own devices, students tend to fall back on badly learnt structures or literal translations from the equivalent Greek.

Alongside EFL instruction, the high school curriculum includes rigorous instruction in argumentation in Greek, and the writing of a Greek argumentative essay is a required component of university entrance exams. Greek high school students are typically exposed to essays written by skilled Greek writers, which are considered to be exemplary written discourse, and are encouraged to produce argumentation of their own based on these models. Therefore, when entering a university department of English, Greek students have a repository of knowledge on how to write argumentation based on their exposure to the genre in their native language in over six years of schooling. Intensive instruction in writing in English is not feasible at the university level due to class sizes, and students' written production is thus a combined result of their exposure to L2 during both secondary and tertiary education, and of their knowledge of L1 writing acquired during their high school years.

14.7. Methodology

14.7.1. Participants and materials

The participants in this study were 176 Greek native speakers in the third and fourth year of university studies at the School of English, Aristotle University of Thessaloniki in Greece, aged from 20 to 22 years. The data used were drawn from the Greek Corpus of Learner English (GRICLE), which was compiled following the ICLE guidelines (Granger et al. 2002), totalling 177,490 words. Each student was required to produce two argumentative essays of at least 500 words each on a given set of topics (Appendix I). The procedure was timed and students had access to reference tools (dictionaries, grammars, etc.).

As an extended and representative sample of English native speaker writing, we used two corpora of student essays. The first was the American collection of LOCNESS, compiled at the University of Louvain (149,580 words). These essays were written by American third and fourth year university students, and the methodology followed in compiling the corpus was similar to that used for the other ICLE subcorpora. In particular, the number and size of essays produced by each student were similar in both GRICLE and LOCNESS, and the topics were selected from the same list (see Appendices I and II). The American students were also allowed access to other resources when writing; however, not all of their essays were timed. The second native speaker corpus was the American collection of the Polish and English Language Corpora for Research and Applications (PELCRA: Leńko-Szymańska 2006), which includes argumentative essays written by American first- and second-year students, timed and written in class on a particular topic, totalling 25,467 words (see Appendix II). The choice of PELCRA was made in order to increase the size of the native-speaker corpus while still maintaining comparability of data: the student population, the genre of texts and the conditions of data collection are similar in both subcorpora.

Although we acknowledge that American students' writing cannot be regarded as a prototype of effective writing, this choice allows us to compare essays by students of a similar age range (the American students were 19 to 22 years old) and with similar writing expertise (cf. Lorenz, 1999 for a similar claim). However, we also made use of the Hellenic National Corpus (HNC), a corpus of native Greek expert writing compiled by the Institute for Language and Speech Processing, in order to examine the extent to which Greek learners transfer rhetorical techniques from L1 to L2. We chose a corpus of Greek expert writing as representing the model that Greek learners are taught to aim at (Table 14.1).

Table 14.1   Corpora used in this study

Corpus	Words
GRICLE (Greek Corpus of Learner English)	177,490
LOCNESS (Louvain Corpus of Native English Speakers)	149,580
PELCRA (Polish and English Language Corpora for Research and Applications)	25,467
HNC (Hellenic National Corpus)	1,725,214

14.7.2. Procedure

We first read through GRICLE and the native corpora to establish how Greek learners and American university students respectively employ stance exponents to develop their arguments. This manual processing shed light on the writing tendencies of Greek learners in the production of argumentation in English. To express stance, the Greek learners choose a variety of grammatical categories (e.g. adverbials, nouns, etc.) and lexical chunks (e.g. *it is true that*); for the purpose of the present paper, we focus exclusively on their use of adverbials, where a noteworthy tendency was their preference for a wide range of boosters (e.g. *of course, undoubtedly*). We then made use of Hyland's (2005) list of metadiscourse items, and checked whether all the adverbials listed under the categories of hedges, boosters and attitude markers were to be found in GRICLE and the native corpora. We used MonoConc Pro (Barlow 2004) for running concordances and WordSmith Tools 5 (Scott 2009) for determining frequency.

14.8. Results

14.8.1. Quantitative analysis

As Table 14.2 shows, the use of boosters in GRICLE is much more extensive than that of hedges and attitude markers (334 occurrences of boosters, 112 of hedges, 95 of attitude markers). Boosters are also much more frequent in GRICLE than in the native corpora (334 vs. 163 occurrences respectively). Conversely, hedging is a more common rhetorical choice in the native speakers' writing (196 occurrences in the native corpora vs. 112 in GRICLE): *maybe* is the only hedging device that features more frequently in GRICLE than in the native corpora. Attitude markers indicating affect are twice as frequent in GRICLE as in the native corpora (95 vs. 46); in particular, *unfortunately* features extensively in GRICLE (83 occurrences vs. 26 in the native corpora), while other attitude markers (*luckily, happily*, etc.) are used rarely in both corpora. Figures 14.4 and 14.5 illustrate the results for specific boosters and hedges.

14.8.2. Qualitative analysis

Boosters

The analysis of stance exponents demonstrated that Greek learners, compared to native speakers, show a tendency to be more emphatic in their

Table 14.2 Comparative results regarding the frequency of stance indicators

Stance indicators	GRICLE (177,490)	LOCNESS & PELCRA (175,047)
Boosters		
Of course	*N=153; 8.62 per 10,000 words*	*N=34; 1.94 per 10,000 words*
No doubt/undoubtedly/ without any doubt	*N=63; 3.54*	*N=13; 0.74*
Indeed	*N=46; 2.59*	*N=15; 0.86*
Certainly	*N=37; 2.08*	*N=22; 1.26*
Definitely	*N=12; 0.66*	*N=28; 1.59*
Truly	*N=14; 0.78*	*N=24; 1.37*
Clearly	*N=9; 0.5*	*N=27; 1.54*
	Total: 334	**Total: 163**
Hedges		
Probably	*N=47; 2.64*	*N=52; 2.97*
Maybe	*N=44; 2.48*	*N=39; 2.22*
Perhaps	*N=8; 0.45*	*N=46; 2.63*
Possibly	*N=8; 0.45*	*N=22; 1.26*
Likely	*N=5; 0.28*	*N=37; 2.11*
	Total: 112	**Total: 196**
Attitude markers – affect		
Unfortunately	*N=83; 4.67*	*N=26; 1.49*
Hopefully	*N=4; 0.22*	*N=13; 0.74*
Fortunately	*N=4; 0.22*	*N=2; 0.11*
Happily	*N=3; 0.16*	*N=3; 0.17*
Luckily	*N=1; 0.05*	*N=2; 0.11*
	Total: 95	**Total: 46**

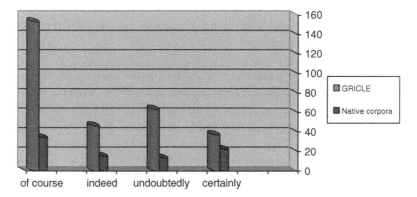

Figure 14.4 Specific boosters in GRICLE and the native corpora

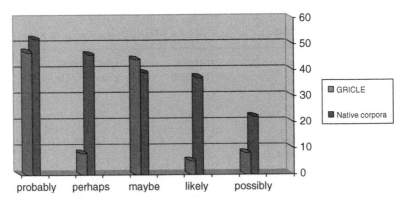

FIGURE 14.5 Specific hedges in GRICLE and the native corpora

argumentative writing by making extensive use of boosters and avoiding mitigation of claims (see Hinkel (2002) for similar findings regarding amplifiers and Lorenz (1998) for learner overuse of adjective intensification). Extract (1) below is indicative of this tendency [Appendix I, topic 1]:

(1) The church had more power than the state had and *of course* could contribute to changes as concerning the state. but now we see that the there are differences from the previous centuries. The phenomenon that has the dominant power nowadays is *undoubtedly* television or the 'magic box' as some people call it. Television has the power to change the ideas some people might have about some issues and *of course* it has a great influence in those people who do not have the critical mind to see in depth what the television gives to the people as facts. (GRICLE)

Greek learners' preference to boost their arguments is also reflected in the lexical choices they make in order to present an ethos that is confident and assured (see Hyland 2005); this is attested in the italicised parts of example (2) [Appendix I, topic 1]:

(2) Among the positive effects of television, some *things must be taken for granted, no leaving room for doubt* and further discussion. *Above all,* television informs people. *To a great extend,* informativeness of television has been used as an excuse, shadowing the drawbacks. (GRICLE)

Of course is the most frequently used booster in both corpora, performing similar functions: (a) it provides emphasis, and (b) it presents an argument, the scope of which will be later modified with the addition of a contrastive lexical item (e.g. *but, however,* etc.). However, the emphatic function features more frequently in GRICLE, while the second function seems more common in the native corpora:

(3) However, in a strange way nature has already started to take her revenge. Everyday, we become witnesses of terrible physical disasters that cause a lot of destroys and unfortunately kills a lot of people. We are talking *of course* about earthquakes, overflows or about the new-known to most of us tsounami. (GRICLE) [Appendix I, topic 4]

(4) No, *of course* it is not fair that millions of people in this country do not have the same advantages as the middle and upper classes. *However,* it is also not fair that some welfare recipients candidly admit that they could work more if they really wanted to work more. (LOCNESS) [Appendix II, topic 4]

(5) There are *of course* both upsides and downsides to mobile phones, *but* I feel the good out ways the bad. (PELCRA) [Appendix II, topic 12]

Hedges

Hedging features more often in the native corpora than GRICLE. This finding is in line with Anglo-American rhetorical conventions, where overstatements are generally discouraged so as to allow alternative arguments to be expressed (see Hyland 2005). In example (6) below, the writer acknowledges opposition and, by means of hedges, creates a space for readers to express their disagreement. This is a common Anglo-American technique that writers employ in the attempt to persuade their readers:

(6) Our society and the feminists that support this equality is so intent on creating this type of environment, that *perhaps* we have become obsessed with just that and ultimately losing a part of what should be a unique creation. We were created different and we are different. *Maybe* we are different for a reason and those differences should not necessarily be viewed as negative. *Maybe* we were made different to stay different and *perhaps* in trying to create this equality we *may* lose something very unique and special that can never be regained. What consequences *might* there be for us that we cannot undo? (LOCNESS) [Appendix II, topic 5]

Turning to the use of specific hedges, we notice native speakers' preference for sequences consisting of hedges such as *probably* and *possibly* accompanied by modal verbs (example 7):

(7) To sum it all up mobile phones are really a good thing for our world today. They can help save money for some people and make money for others. They *could possibly* save someone's life, very quickly, and they *may possibly* even teach some people how to manage money, time and maybe even themselves, a little better. (PELCRA) [Appendix II, topic 12]

The frequency of such sequences varies in the two corpora: *probably + would* features 19 times in the native corpora and 9 times in GRICLE (1.08 vs. 0.5 per 10,000 words); *modal verb + possibly* features 12 times in the native corpora and 3 times in GRICLE (0.68 vs. 0.16 per 10,000 words). While not particularly high, these frequencies point to the presence of phraseological patterns (cf. Groom, 2005), that is, pre-constructed set phrases which function as a single choice (Sinclair 1991), which are worth highlighting.

Attitude markers

The use of attitude markers is limited in both corpora, with the exception of the adverb *unfortunately*. This could lead us to disregard them were it not for the notably higher frequency of *unfortunately* in GRICLE than in the native corpora (83 vs. 26 occurrences). A closer look at the use of this adverb in GRICLE indicates that it collocates strongly with *but* (one in four occurrences), whereas the corresponding ratio in LOCNESS is only one in twenty-six. Concordance 1 from GRICLE illustrates this use.

Concordance 1. *but unfortunately* in GRICLE

```
. . . who acted and behaved like men,        but unfortunately  had the body of a woman.
. . . that try and give battles every day,   but unfortunately  that is not enough. Unless each . . .
. . . Of course we have some courses         but unfortunately  is really difficult to take part in them . . .
. . . We could easily recycle it,            but unfortunately  we do not have that kind of . . .
. . . course, improved much since then       but unfortunately, the above are still true in many . . .
. . . either sexually or psychologically.    But unfortunately  there are women who want to consider . . .
. . . nature is calling out for help         but unfortunately  people continue to exploit and . . .
. . . nature keeps calling for help          but unfortunately  it seems that nobody hears.
. . . society by offering their services.    But unfortunately, It's obvious that Greece like other . . .
. . . is calling out for help                but unfortunately  the modern man/woman tends to be . . .
. . . channels that are worth watching.      But unfortunately, there are low culture programmes . . .
. . . men would be wiser, more mature,       but unfortunately  the situation has only . . .
. . . before they get their degree.          But unfortunately  this does not happen for all the . . .
. . . to be a means of information           but unfortunately  and this is obvious nowadays has become
. . . supply many cities with current        but unfortunately  not so many countries use them.
. . . phrase not only is true nowadays       but unfortunately  It will be more true in the future
. . . to be a means of information           but unfortunately  and this is obvious nowadays has become
. . . has played a major part in this,       but unfortunately  this social change although it supplied
```

To help explain the frequency of this structure in GRICLE, we looked at argumentative writing by Greek skilled writers, particularly the frequency and use of *allá dystychós* ('but unfortunately') in the HNC. The results of our search indicated that the Greek translation equivalent is quite commonly used and that there is a tendency for the two lexical items, *allá* ('but') and *dystychós* ('unfortunately') to co-occur. We could refer to this tendency as a discourse-driven preference used to aid connectivity. According to Thompson and Zhou (2000: 131), *unfortunately* denies 'the positive expectations set up by the preceding text', and *dystychós* performs a similar function in Greek. However, whereas *unfortunately* is both a cohesive and evaluative indicator, and can therefore replace *but* (Thompson and Zhou 2000), *dystychós*, when it stands alone, functions mainly as an attitude marker rather than a cohesive device, and therefore cannot replace *allá* ('but'). In LOCNESS, *unfortunately* generally appears in initial position, while in GRICLE it more often appears in mid-sentence, possibly because it collocates so strongly with *but*.

14.9. Discussion

To account for the differences presented between GRICLE and the native corpora, we may first interpret our findings in relation to L1 linguistic and cultural influence. In order to assess the possible influence of the L1 on Greek learners' rhetorical choices, we looked at argumentative writing by Greek skilled writers in the HNC, examining the translation equivalents of some boosters to establish possible cases of transfer. Our analysis indicated that persuasion is primarily effected by means of boosting. Example (8) illustrates a Greek writer's unhedged certainty and commitment to the proposition:

(8) This plan will *undoubtedly* give banks an important competitive advantage and will lead *no doubt* to further collectivisation in banking with inevitable consequences for access to loans and the costs accompanying them. (HNC, our translation)

If these choices are culturally induced, it is possible that learners may be misled into believing that they can transfer these conventions to L2 writing. Greeks do not favour uncertainty, and this is reflected in their tendency to be emphatic and avoid hedging. This can be accounted for by the collectivism, high uncertainty avoidance and high power distance which are characteristic of Greek society (Hofstede 1980). Hofstede's claims have been corroborated by Koutsantoni (2003), who attributes uncertainty avoidance and high power distance to the fact that Greek intellectual style has been influenced by the Teutonic and Gallic rhetorical traditions. According to Galtung (1981), these traditions tend to be absolute and authoritarian, which is why they may sound more categorical than the Saxonic tradition, which is non-authoritarian and fosters negotiation (hence the Saxonic preference for indirect claims, that can be achieved through hedging). Hinkel (2002) found that in non Anglo-American traditions, overstatements and exaggerations are a common means of persuasion, and in her study of research articles, Koutsantoni (2005) found that Greek engineers are more emphatic than tentative in their writings. When Greek academic writers amplify their arguments, they adopt the presupposition that if something is obvious to them, it should also be obvious to their readers. In this sense, they aim to create in-group solidarity (*ibid*).

Such findings point towards the need to look at data in the light of contrastive rhetoric and to raise learners' awareness of differences between L1 and L2 rhetorical conventions. This need has similarly been underscored by Frankenberg-Garcia (1990) and McKenny and Bennet (this volume). Contrastive rhetoric has developed into intercultural rhetoric given the growing emphasis on the social aspects of writing (Connor 2004), and the latter become transparent if we look at both national or ethnic cultures and what Holliday (1999) has referred to as 'small cultures'.

National culture would explain the rhetorical choices made by particular national or ethnic groups. An example would be the tendency of Greek writers to boost their statements. Influenced by their national cultures, learners may employ different rhetorical strategies in their writings (cf. Granger and Petch-Tyson 1996; Hinkel 1997; Hyland and Milton 1997; Neff et al. 2004; Leńko-Szymańska 2006). Small cultures instead refer to 'small social groupings or activities wherever there is cohesive behaviour' (Holliday 1999: 237). An example would be English language learner culture. Unlike national culture, a small culture may extend beyond national divisions: English language learner culture may include groups of people in various national cultures. National and small cultures, as Holliday (1999) and Atkinson (2004) have claimed, interact and overlap in their manifestations. This means that language learners' choices when they use the L2 will be influenced both by their national or ethnic culture and by the various small cultures to which they belong, e.g. classroom culture, youth culture, etc.

The small culture we consider here is that of advanced learners of English who have been exposed to systematic instruction in argumentative writing for a substantial number of years, and are now in the final years of their university studies attempting to become members of the academic community. The specific characteristics found in the writings of this social group are not only a result of their respective national culture but also of their development as what we might call 'developing writers' (Granger 2004). Their skills in academic writing are in a continuous process of development in both English and their L1, and thus the choices they make, as witnessed in our corpus, may represent necessary stages they have to pass through to reach writing expertise. Thus Greek learners' preference for boosters may be a discourse strategy adopted to enable them to organise their thinking and enhance the force of their arguments: Neff (2008) proposes a similar explanation of Spanish learners' tendency to intensify rather than mitigate their claims.

A final point that needs to be made is that while hedging is limited in GRICLE, there is a profound preference for *maybe*. This is in line with Gilquin and Paquot's (2008) findings, which indicated that learners from various L1 backgrounds use discourse features which are more typical of speech rather than writing.

14.10. Conclusion

Greek advanced learners of English and English native speakers deploy different rhetorical techniques when they aim to persuade their readers. Compared to native speakers, Greeks wish to project a confident attitude, and believe that in order to achieve this, they should make frequent use of boosters (undoubtedly, of course, etc.); hence, their writing is more emphatic. We have argued that such tendencies may be attributed to a combination of factors relating to (a) L1 and L2 instruction materials and techniques during secondary and tertiary education, (b) transfer of L1 writing style and cultural features, and (c) development as L2 writers.

We would not wish to espouse a writing curriculum in which the rhetorical conventions of L2 are taught in a prescriptive manner, and native speaker norms followed blindly. We believe, however, that L2 learners need to become more consciously attuned to the fact that culture affects thinking and writing practices. If this idea informs our instruction, we may help students become aware of how propositional content is organised and presented in the writing practices of another language. This in turn may help them to internalise L2 patterns of reasoning and presentation, and thus to become more effective writers in the L2.

References

Ädel, A. (2006), *Metadiscourse in L1 and L2 English*. Amsterdam: John Benjamins.

Atkinson, D. (2004), 'Contrasting rhetorics/contrasting cultures: why contrastive rhetoric needs a better conceptualization of culture'. *Journal of English for Academic Purposes*, 3, (4), 277–289.

Barlow, M. (2004), *MonoConc Pro*. Houston: Athelstan.

Barnes, J. (ed.), (1984), *The Complete Works of Aristotle. The Revised Oxford Translation*, vol.2. New Jersey: Princeton University Press.

Biber, D. and Finegan, E. (1989), 'Styles of stance in English: lexical and grammatical marking of evidentiality and affect'. *Text*, 9, (1), 93–124.

Connor, U. (2004), 'Intercultural rhetoric research: beyond texts'. *Journal of English for Academic Purposes*, 3, (4), 291–304.

Frankenberg-Garcia, A. (1990), 'Do the similarities between L1 and L2 writing processes conceal important differences?' *Edinburgh Working Papers in Applied Linguistics*, 1, 91–102.

Galtung, J. (1981), 'Structure, culture and intellectual style: an essay comparing Saxonic, Teutonic, Gallic and Nipponic approaches'. *Social Science Information*, 20, (6), 817–856.

Gilquin, G. and Paquot, M. (2008), 'Too chatty: learner academic writing and register variation'. *English Text Construction*, 1, (1), 41–61.

Granger, S. (2004), 'Computer learner corpus research: current status and future prospects', in U. Connor and T.A. Upton (eds), *Applied Corpus Linguistics: A Multidimensional Perspective*. Amsterdam and New York: Rodopi, pp. 123–145.

Granger, S. and Petch-Tyson, S. (1996), 'Connector usage in the English essay writing of native and non-native EFL speakers of English'. *World Englishes*, 15, (1), 17–27.

Granger, S., Dagneaux, E. and Meunier, F. (2002), *The International Corpus of Learner English/Handbook and CD-ROM*. Louvain-la-Neuve: Presses Universitaires de Louvain.

Groom, N. (2005), 'Pattern and meaning across genres and disciplines: an exploratory study'. *Journal of English for Academic Purposes*, 4, 257–277.

Halliday, M.A.K. (1994), *An Introduction to Functional Grammar*. London: Arnold.

Hinkel, E. (1997), 'Indirectness in L1 and L2 academic writing'. *Journal of Pragmatics*, 27, 361–386.

Hinkel, E. (2002), *Second Language Writers' Text*. Mahwah, NJ: Lawrence Erlbaum.

Hofstede, G. (1980), *Culture's Consequences: International Differences in Work-related Values*. London: Sage.

Hofstede, G. (1986), 'Cultural differences in teaching and learning'. *International Journal of Intercultural Relations*, 10, 301–320.

Hofstede, G. (1994), *Cultures and Organizations*. London: McGraw-Hill.

Holliday, A. (1999), 'Small cultures'. *Applied Linguistics*, 20, (2), 237–264.

Hyland, K. (2005), *Metadiscourse: Exploring Interaction in Writing*. London: Continuum.

Hyland, K. and Milton, J. (1997), 'Hedging in L1 and L2 student writing'. *Journal of Second Language Writing*, 6, (2), 183–206.

Hyland, K. and Tse, P. (2004), 'Metadiscourse in academic discourse: a reappraisal'. *Applied Linguistics*, 25, (2), 156–177.

Koutsantoni, D. (2003), *Rhetoric and Culture in Published and Unpublished Scientific Communication: A Comparative Study of Texts Produced by Greek and Native English Speaking Engineers*. Unpublished Ph.D Thesis, University of Birmingham.

Koutsantoni, D. (2005), 'Greek cultural characteristics and academic writing'. *Journal of Modern Greek Studies*, 23, 97–138.

Leńko-Szymańska, A. (2006), 'The curse and the blessing of mobile phones – a corpus-based study into American and Polish rhetorical conventions', in A. Wilson, D. Archer and P. Rayson (eds), *Corpus Linguistics Around the World*. Amsterdam and New York: Rodopi, pp. 141–154.

Lorenz, G. (1998), 'Overstatement in advanced learners' writing: stylistic aspects of adjective intensification', in S. Granger (ed.), *Learner English on Computer*. London and New York: Addison Wesley Longman, pp. 53–66.

Lorenz, G. (1999), *Adjective Intensification—Learners versus Native Speakers. A Corpus Study of Argumentative Writing*. Amsterdam and New York: Rodopi.

Neff, J. (2008), 'Contrasting English-Spanish interpersonal discourse phrases', in F. Meunier and S. Granger (eds), *Phraseology in Foreign Language Learning and Teaching*. Amsterdam and Philadelphia: John Benjamins, pp. 85–99.

Neff, J., Ballesteros, F., Dafouz, E., Martinez, F., Rica, J.P., Diez, M. and Prieto, R. (2004), 'Formulating writer stance: a contrastive study of EFL learner corpora', in U. Connor and T.A. Upton (eds), *Applied Corpus Linguistics: A Multidimensional Perspective*. Amsterdam and New York: Rodopi, pp. 73–89.

Ochs, E. (1989), 'Introduction'. *Text*, 9, (1), 1–5.

Scott, M. (2009), *WordSmith Tools 5 manual*. [Online] http://www.lexically.net/downloads/version5/HTML/index.html (accessed May 2009).

Sinclair, J. (1991), *Corpus, Concordance, Collocation*. Oxford: Oxford University Press.

Thompson, G. and Zhou, J. (2000), 'Evaluation and organization in text: the structuring role of evaluative disjuncts', in S. Hunston and G. Thompson (eds), *Evaluation in Text*. Oxford: Oxford University Press, pp. 121–141.

Appendix I: Topics for GRICLE

1. Marx once said that religion was the opium of the masses. If he was alive at the beginning of the 21st century, he would replace religion with television.

2. Most university degrees are theoretical and do not prepare students for the real world. They are therefore of very little value.

3. Feminists have done more harm to the cause of women than good.

4. In the 19th century, Victor Hugo said: 'How sad it is to think that nature is calling out but humanity refuses to pay heed.' Do you think it is still true nowadays?

5. Some people say that in our modern world, dominated by science, technology and industrialization, there is no longer a place for dreaming and imagination. What is your opinion?

Appendix II: Topics for native corpora

LOCNESS [sample list of topics]

1. Great inventions and discoveries of 20th century and their impact on people's lives.
2. Money is the root of all evil
3. Crime does not pay
4. The welfare system
5. Feminists have done more harm to the cause of women than good
6. Adolescent suicide
7. AIDS
8. Pre-marital sex
9. Homelessness
10. Orphanages
11. Abortion

PELCRA

12. The mobile phone – the curse or the blessing of the end of the twentieth century.

Chapter 15

Polishing papers for publication: palimpsests or procrustean beds?

John McKenny and Karen Bennett

This chapter analyses a corpus of academic papers written in English by established Portuguese academics that were presented to a language consultant for revision prior to submission for publication. The corpus was interrogated for the presence of certain discourse features and compared with a control corpus of published articles by native-English academics in a similar field. Its purpose was to examine the hypothesis that not only lexical and syntactic features, but also phraseological and discourse features of L1 may be transferred into L2, thereby undermining the 'naturalness' of the writing and raising an (invisible?) obstacle to international publication. The results reveal significant overuse of certain features by Portuguese academics, and a corresponding underuse of others. This may be due to differences in epistemological outlook, which raises issues of both a practical and an ideological nature for the reviser of those texts.

15.1. Introduction

Texts written by foreign academics for publication in international English language journals typically undergo a series of interventions before their final polished form is achieved. Amongst the various 'literacy brokers' (Lillis and Curry 2006) that make their mark on the text, one of the most crucial is the language reviser, who is recruited primarily to correct grammar and spelling mistakes, and ensure that the register is suitable for the journal in question.

While foreign researchers are usually quite happy for their prose to be doctored in this superficial way, there exists another dimension of revision that is more controversial. Senior academics with established reputations in their own countries do not always take kindly to having their work meddled with at the *discourse* level – that is, when the reviser takes it upon herself to reformulate whole sentences or paragraphs, perhaps even excising chunks of text. Yet such radical surgery is sometimes necessary to bring the work into line with the norms of English academic discourse. That is to say, cultural differences at the discourse level are often unacknowledged by both foreign authors and Anglophone editors, leading to unfortunate misunderstandings. At worst, this may result in the text being rejected out of hand as 'badly written' (Frankenberg-Garcia 1990a).

The question of L1 transfer has of course been widely discussed within the EAP context, and in recent decades, this has gone beyond mere grammar and lexis to include aspects such as text organisation and cohesion. Since Kaplan (1966) first suggested that there are cultural differences in discursive or expository writing patterns, there has been a plethora of comparative studies from a variety of cultural perspectives (e.g. Duszak (ed.) 1997; Smith (ed.) 1987; Ventola and Mauranen (eds) 1996), culminating in the formal constitution of the discipline that is today known as Contrastive Rhetoric (Connor 1996). Hence, English academic writing has been compared to 'teutonic, gallic and nipponic' styles (Galtung 1981), German (Clyne 1987a, 1987b, 1988), Indian languages (Kachru 1987), Czech (Cmejrková 1996), Finnish (Mauranen 1993), Polish (Duszak 1994), Norwegian (Dahl 2004) and Russian/Ukrainian (Yakhontova 2006), to name but a few. Despite the undoubted value of these studies, none of them have gone so far as to suggest that there may actually be a different epistemological framework underlying the scholarly discourse of non-Anglophone cultures. Yet in the case of Portugal and Spain, the powerful influence of the Catholic Church, supported by conservative political regimes, ensured that the Scientific Revolution – which radically altered attitudes to knowledge in seventeenth-century England, with far-reaching consequences for discourse (Halliday & Martin (eds) 1993: 2–21, 54–68; Martin 1998) – did not happen. Instead, an older text-based humanities tradition remained central to the education system right through to the late twentieth century.[1]

As a result, the kind of discourse typically used in humanities writing in Portuguese displays features that are quite different from those prescribed in English academic discourse style manuals (Bennett 2009).[2] While English values succinctness, clarity and objectivity, much Portuguese humanities writing is characterised by a general 'wordiness' and redundancy, a preference for a high-flown erudite register over the demotic (evident in both syntactic and lexical choices) and a tendency towards abstraction and figurative language. There are also important differences as regards textual organisation, such as a propensity for indirectness, with the main idea often embedded, adorned or deferred at all ranks (Bennett 2010).[3]

It would not be surprising, then, if some of these features were to get transferred into Portuguese authors' English texts, even when those authors are very proficient in that language. For as with other kinds of social semiotic, questions of value frequently operate at the subconscious level and are 'taken for granted' in a way that grammar and spelling are not. Hence, it is not easy for the language reviser to convince her client that fewer words are better than many in English, or that a simple straightforward sentence is valued above a complex ornate one. Similarly, the editors of English-language journals may not realise that the presence of such features may be due to cross-linguistic transfer, rather than to ineptitude.

This chapter uses corpus analysis to procure empirical evidence of cross-cultural transfer at the discourse level in English-language research articles produced by Portuguese scholars. The study involves the comparison of two corpora, one consisting of English academic articles in the humanities written by Portuguese academics, and the other, similar articles from published journals by English L1 authors.

The project resulted from a collaboration between two language professionals from somewhat different backgrounds: a corpus linguist, and a professional language consultant/translator (who is also a researcher specialising in the critical study of academic discourse). This collaboration led to a few methodological tussles. For example, the corpus linguist, in accordance with accepted practice in his field (Sinclair 2004; Tognini Bonelli 2001), was in favour of approaching the data without preconceptions, following wherever it might lead; the language consultant, on the other hand, was interested in testing certain hypotheses that had been formulated over the course of her professional practice. Ultimately this problem was resolved by dividing the study into two distinct phases, as described below.

15.2. Corpora and procedures

Each of the two corpora contained around 113,000 running words. The corpus of texts by Portuguese authors, dubbed Portac, was essentially opportunistic, as it was made up of texts that had been presented to the language consultant for revision prior to submission for publication in English-language journals. These were all articles in the Humanities or Arts, and the authors were all senior Portuguese academics with a certain reputation in their home culture. Naturally, the authors' agreement was obtained prior to their inclusion in the corpus.

The control corpus (Controlit) consisted of published articles from journals which the Portuguese authors hoped to be or had been published in, and which were available electronically from our university library. We included only articles written by single authors who were native speakers of English, and which dealt with similar areas of interest to those of our Portac writers.[4]

Two software suites were used in a complimentary fashion. Wmatrix2 (Rayson 2003)[5] enables the investigator to compare two corpora and continually shift focus as trends become apparent; that is to say, researchers may quickly compare lexical and grammatical dimensions from the perspective of one or other corpus. Wordsmith Tools (Scott 2004) was used to carry out analyses not available in Wmatrix2, such as frequency counts of word clusters, and word/n-gram searches using wildcards (for example, for polysyllabic noun forms, a frequency list of all words ending in *ion). Results of corpus comparisons are expressed in terms of Log Likelihood (henceforth LL).[6]

The analysis was undertaken in two phases. The first phase set out to test the intuitions of the language reviser and therefore focused on particular features that had been noted during the course of her professional practice. The second phase explored issues that had arisen unexpectedly during the first phase and was therefore more properly corpus-driven.

15.3. Results

The results of the first phase have already been described elsewhere (McKenny and Bennett 2009) and will thus be merely summarised here. They include the following:

(a) Overuse of nominalisation:

The writing of the Portuguese academics showed a high degree of nominalisation compared to the control corpus. At the level of individual words, there was an overuse of nouns, both singular (LL 25.17) and plural (LL 69.81), and, concomitantly, a greater use of indefinite and definite articles (LL 43.81 and LL 36.13 respectively).

(b) Underuse of most pronouns:

There was marked underuse of pronouns in Portac, 6,154 (6.11% of all text) vs. 8,671 in Controlit (8.49%), giving a surprising LL of -394.98. This underuse of pronouns is more likely to be a consequence of nominalisation for, as Biber et al. (1999: 92) point out, after analyzing written corpora totalling 40 million words, 'a high frequency of nouns . . . corresponds to a low density of pronouns'. In particular, *he* (LL -232.00), *she* (LL -104.00), *him* (LL -96.00), *I* (LL -39.00), *me* (LL -37.00), *it* (LL -25.74) were all underused.

(c) Overuse of 'we' and 'us':

On the other hand, *we* (LL 39.41) and *us* (LL 16.85) were overused. This cannot be attributed to multiple authorship, as all the articles in our corpora were written by a single author. This would seem to directly result from the transfer of L1 discourse habits.[7]

(d) Overuse of the genitive:

There was also a startling overuse of the genitive, both singular and plural (*'s* and *s'*) (LL -211.64), and also of the alternative construction using *of* to express the same relationship (LL -34.03). In many cases, this seemed to be directly related to the tendency to over-nominalise, as in the example *a comment on the possibilities of the play's staging*, which was reconstrued by the reviser using a clausal form (i.e. *a comment upon how the play might be staged*).

(e) Underuse of subordination:

Using Wmatrix2 and the POS tagged versions of the corpora it was found that Portac writers underuse the subordinating conjunctions *if, because, unless, so, for, although, while* (LL -8.16). They greatly overuse coordinating conjunctions, such as *and, or, nor,* (LL 26.17), with the exception of *but* which is tagged separately in CLAWS7 as CCB, adversative coordinating conjunction (LL -14.74). This apparent underuse of subordination was somewhat surprising, and ran counter to the language reviser's intuitions. More corpus investigation, however, is needed of other subordinate structures such as non-finite, verbless, relative and correlative clauses.

(f) Overuse of embedding structures:

On the other hand, the Portac writers tend to make greater use of certain kinds of embedding or matrix structures (*We can see that . . .* ; *It should* *be pointed out that . . .*), particularly to carry epistemic stance. Searches using Wordsmith Tools for four variable structures (*It * * that, It is * * that, We * that, We * * that*) all yielded higher frequencies for Portac than for Controlit.

(g) Preference for Latinate vocabulary:

Portuguese authors favour polysyllabic abstract nouns of Latinate origin. Using Wordsmith Tools to search for *-ion*, 2,184 instances were found in Portac compared to only 1,458 in Controlit (LL 163), while the results for *-icity, -isation* and *-ation* gave LL 7.07, LL 14.16 and LL 50.71 respectively. There was also a high frequency of the indefinite article *an* (LL 18.65), which, according to Hofland and Johansson (1982: 22), indicates a high proportion of Latinate word tokens. This is perhaps to be expected given the derivation of their mother tongue from Latin.

(h) Overuse of reformulation markers:

This particular search was stimulated by a study by Cuenca (2003) into the usage of reformulation markers in academic English compared to similar writing in Spanish and Catalan. A comparison of our two corpora revealed a higher occurrence of reformulation markers (*namely, i.e., e.g., that is, in other words*) in the writing of the Portuguese academics (LL 67.76). This is likely to result directly from the transfer of discourse conventions from the L1.

(i) Overuse of prepositions:

In the initial Wmatrix contrast of the two corpora, significant overuse of prepositions by the Portac writers was apparent (LL 46.32). As noted above, *of* was a main contributor to this overuse (LL 31.31). A closer scrutiny revealed that multi-word prepositions (Granger and Meunier (eds) 2008) also showed a difference between the two corpora (LL 13.19), of which the most significant were *with regard to, by means of, with reference to, in spite of, in view of, in connection with, by way of, in front of, in conjunction with, in common with*. As these multi-word prepositions bear a fairly close resemblance to compound prepositions frequently used in Portuguese, it is likely that this overuse results from a simple process of cross-linguistic transfer.

(j) Overuse of multi-word expressions:

Wmatrix automatically extracts what it calls multi-word expressions (MWEs) from corpora by using a large-scale semantically classified multi-word expression template database. The definition of MWE is fairly straight-forward. Only word sequences in or predicted by the dictionary of the semantic tagger will count as an MWE. The decisions therefore have been taken in advance. Users of Wmatrix have the option of customising their MWE dictionary. One source of such enrichment is from perusing lists of N-grams extracted automatically by Wmatrix. N-grams are recurrent sequences of words (N>2) with a frequency of three or more as the default in Wmatrix. Wordsmith Tools uses the term *cluster* for the same notion.

More than 1,600 types of such MWEs were detected in both corpora. *Portac* had 5,756 tokens of MWEs as opposed to 4,772 tokens in *Controlit* (LL 92.10). This suggests that there are significant differences in the balance between novel and formulaic language in the two groups of writers. The more well-stocked the Wmatrix MWE dictionary becomes, the more accurate will be the automatic measure of the formulaicity in a corpus.

These initial findings on multiword expressions led us to believe that *Portac* authors may be less creative in their language use than the native speakers, and more dependent upon ready-made or formulaic expressions. Hence, the second phase of our study focused upon the phraseology used by our two groups of writers. We looked, firstly, at the lexical choices made by these authors in the light of word frequencies, and secondly, at some of the collocational patterns, as reflected in the N-grams found in the two corpora.

15.3.1. Lexical choices

Other corpus studies of the lexical choices made by advanced learners of English have suggested that they tend to underuse the most frequent words of the language. Fox and her colleagues on the COBUILD team found that the language of advanced foreign students 'is often too stilted, too formal and too high-level; and when it is analysed it is seen that the most common words are used less frequently and in fewer contexts than they would be by native speakers of English' (Fox 1998: 27).

Suspecting that the same phenomena might be found in the writing of our Portuguese authors, we compared frequencies in our two corpora of the most frequent words in the BNC using Leech et al.'s (2001) frequency lists. The results are shown in Table 15.1:

Table 15.1   Distribution of the most frequent words in the BNC in Portac and Controlit

	Portac	Controlit
100 most frequent words	59,618	65,892
101st–201st most frequent words	11,653	12,914
Total	71,271	78,806
Coverage	72%	79%

This would seem to seem to confirm Fox's claims. However, it is unclear whether this is due to the language learning career of Portac authors (in the sense that core words were only given attention at elementary and intermediate level of instruction and then neglected at higher levels) or to the transfer of discourse habits from the L1. That is to say, as Portuguese writing in the humanities tends to be very recondite and formal, it is possible that this underuse of everyday words reflects a deep-rooted sense that such vocabulary is inappropriate to the academic register.

15.3.2. Collocational patterns

When the collocational patterns in the two corpora are examined, the strength of the corpus-driven approach is clearly demonstrated. Wmatrix2 delivered a clear picture of the frequency of recurrence of N-grams. The results given in Table 15.2 show the startling discrepancy between the word sequencing of L2 writers and their L1 counterparts.

Table 15.2   N-gram tokens in the two corpora

Ngram	Portac	Controlit	Log Likelihood
5 grams	330	272	6.01
4 grams	1661	1058	134.85
3 grams	10050	7288	304.85
2 grams	47263	43174	184.94

It seems that the Portac writers are using more recurrent sequences (of two, three, four words and so on), making their writing more predictable and less creative than that of the native writers in Controlit.

However, we must be careful, when talking about N-grams or clusters, not to make assumptions about the formulaicity of the language or the use of multiword expressions (MWEs). N-grams do not provide a direct measure of the degree of 'chunkiness' (de Cock 2000) contained in a text or corpus. An N-gram is merely a sequence of consecutive words generated by the syntax or is a fragment thereof. To get from N-gram lists to formulaic sequences, it is necessary to apply a sequence of filtering rules, the strictness of which will determine the number of N-grams which are pronounced to be prefabricated or formulaic sequences. In this case, the following criteria were used to filter N-grams to obtain formulaic sequences.

- Obvious non-idiomatic sequences were eliminated: e.g. most sequences beginning with *and, a, an, he, the* and *they* (with some exceptions such as *a lot* and *the world*);
- Free combinations bound only by morphosyntactic rules were retained if they had some additional pragmatic or textual function. *I think (that)* was retained whereas *they are* was not;
- Recurrent sequences ending in *a, an,* and *the* were eliminated (This differs from Biber et al.s' (1999) lexical bundle approach);
- Substitution tests of constituent words were used to ascertain whether there was a degree of fixity or formulaicity in a sequence;
- Sequences with syntactic unity and a clear grammatical function in their context (e.g. compound verbs, nouns, adjectives, adverbs, prepositions, connectives, quantifiers) were counted.

Taking the fifty most frequently occurring 4-grams from Portac and applying these filtering rules, we were left with eighteen sequences in Table 15.3 which might be considered formulaic.

Table 15.3 Most frequent four-word formulaic sequences in Portac after filtering is applied

~~the end of the~~	~~17~~
~~one of the most~~	~~17~~
on the other hand	16
i would like to	14
at the same time	13
at the end of	~~13~~
~~as one of the~~	~~12~~
~~in the sense that~~	~~12~~

(Continued)

Table 15.3 (Cont'd)

~~the return of the~~	~~11~~
~~with regard to the~~	~~11~~
~~the beginning of the~~	~~10~~
~~the extent to which~~	~~10~~
in the light of	10
in the case of	9
~~the middle of the~~	9
on the one hand	8
~~as well as the~~	8
~~return of the caravels~~	8
~~in the mysteries of~~	8
~~be found in the~~	8
can be said to	7
~~by a sense of~~	~~7~~
~~the history of the~~	~~7~~
~~the title of the~~	~~7~~
~~the work of art~~	~~7~~
~~as much as in~~	~~7~~
in the form of	7
~~un coup de d~~	6
~~the fact that the~~	6
~~the figure of the~~	6
~~the representation of the~~	6
for the first time	6
in the middle of	6
mill on the floss	6
as we have seen	6
~~the latter part of~~	6
~~of some of the~~	6
~~the mill on the~~	6
~~in the course of~~	6
~~the light of the~~	6
neither here nor there	6
~~as much as of~~	6
~~can be found in~~	6
at the beginning of	6
the way in which	6
in the work of	6

(*Continued*)

Table 15.3 (Cont'd)

~~the case of the~~	6
~~of the work of~~	6
with a sense of	5
it is common to	5

Moreover, when the semantic tagger was used to extract the MWEs in the two corpora, the frequencies shown in Table 15.4 were obtained.

Table 15.4 Comparison of multi-word expressions

	Portac	Controlit
MWE tokens overused in Portac	3861	1527
MWE tokens underused in Portac	1661	3253
Total in each corpus	5522	4470

The twenty MWEs overused by Portac writers in comparison to Controlit authors (all with LL > 8) are listed in Table 15.5. It is noticeable that they include a number of phrasal verbs.

Table 15.5 Twenty MWEs overused by Portac authors

	Portac	Controlit
in_fact	87	14
with_regard_to	23	0
according_to	44	11
as_much_as	22	2
as_regards	13	0
in_the_picture	11	0
carried_out	10	0
in_question	17	2
due_to	14	1
brought_about	7	0
in_view_of	7	0
made_up	7	0
by_means_of	11	1
in_order_to	44	19
in_the_end	10	1
at_stake	6	0

(Continued)

Table 15.5   (Cont'd)

put_forward	6	0
stand_for	6	0
sum_up	6	0
vantage_point	6	0
such_as	42	20

These are just the preliminary results of an area of study that could even-tually prove to be very fruitful. They indicate that these Portuguese scholars tend to use more formulaic expressions in their L2 writing than their L1 counterparts, which could have important repercussions for language revisers and EAP professionals, as well as for the authors concerned.

15.4. Discussion

Our results clearly suggest that the English writing of established Portu-guese academics in the humanities differs in many respects from that of native speakers in the same field. In particular, the overuse of features such as nominalisation, embedding structures, Latinate vocabulary and reformulation markers, combined with the underuse of pronouns and everyday vocabulary, may have the cumulative effect of causing the prose to sound dense and abstract to native ears, while the prevalence of formulaic sequences may make it sound stilted and unnatural. In this section, we will discuss the extent to which such features may jeopardise these writers' chances of getting published in international journals, and how corpus linguistics might help remedy this situation.

It is important to distinguish between academic writing in science and in the humanities. Responding to the question of linguistic imperialism raised by Phillipson (1992), Pennycook (1994) and others, Tribble (2008: 308) contends that 'in professional and academic writing, both authorship and gate keeping authority have shifted and the production and evaluation of these texts is no longer a native speaker monopoly'. That is to say, in situations where English is being used as a *lingua franca*, native speaker accuracy is no longer an issue. Instead, Tribble argues, what counts is acceptability in the eyes of peers in the discourse community.

This claim may well be true for the sciences, where language is used as a transparent medium for transmission of a content that may be presented primarily in non-linguistic form (graphs, tables, diagrams, mathematical formulae, etc). But in the humanities, where the content is frequently inseparable from the words used to convey it, the matter is much more complex, and failure to comply with the stylistic norms of the target culture will often be taken as a sign of intellectual ineptitude or sloppy thinking.

The problem is compounded by the fact that, unlike the discourse of science, which in most languages of the world is calqued from English, the discourse of the humanities may vary dramatically between cultures as a result of long native traditions. In the Romance cultures, as we have seen, there is evidence that quite different values govern the production of scholarly texts; hence, authors who blindly transfer discourse features from their own languages into English may unwittingly be striking a blow at the target-culture's whole epistemology, provoking in some cases an equally blind response from the gatekeepers of that culture.

Comparative corpus studies such as this one may be useful in raising awareness of the culturally contingent nature of academic discourse conventions. Within the ELT environment, such analyses have traditionally been used to make learners aware of the ways in which their prose differs from that of native speakers, with a view to instituting corrective pedagogies (see, for example, Biber et al. 1999; Fox 1998; Frankenberg-Garcia 1990b). However, there may also be a place for such studies within the critical tradition, which resists the Anglo-American academic hegemony in the interests of epistemological pluralism. Corpus-driven research can offer hard empirical evidence of cultural differences that may otherwise be conveniently overlooked by the gatekeepers of the hegemonic culture, and can perhaps open up the way towards less rigidly prescriptive attitudes to the construction of knowledge.

How does this affect the reviser of the academic text, caught as she is between two worlds? If, as has been suggested in this case, there are distinct discourse norms operating in the source and target cultures, should her role be to ruthlessly domesticate the foreign author's text, bringing it into line with the Procrustean demands of the target culture in order to ensure publication at all cost? Or should she rather seek to produce a kind of palimpsest that allows the thought patterns of the original to be glimpsed beneath the surface of the revised text? These are issues that have preoccupied translation scholars for some time now, and which are unlikely to be resolved while the Anglo-Saxon world maintains its hegemony over academic production.[8] However, corpus studies may have a part to play in raising awareness of hitherto-unperceived cultural differences, thereby encouraging greater acceptance of alternative ways of construing knowledge.

Notes

[1] Scientific ideas only began to filter into Portugal in the second half of the eighteenth century via a loose network of exiled intellectuals living abroad, known as the *estrangeirados* (Carneiro et al. 2000; Gomes 1995; Nunes 2002). Indeed, in Portugal, there were only two very brief periods before 1974 when Enlightenment views were implemented – the period in office of the Marquis of Pombal in the eighteenth century and the brief Republic of 1910–1926. For a more detailed exploration of the historical circumstances conditioning the development of Portuguese academic writing, see Bennett (forthcoming).

[2] Contrastive studies by Martín Martín (2003), Moreno (1997), Mur Dueñas (2007a, 2007b) and Cuenca (2003) suggest that Spanish contains similar characteristics. This is to be expected, given the cultural proximity between the two countries.

[3] See also Bennett (2006, 2007a, 2007b) for detailed analyses of excerpts of Portuguese humanities texts.

[4] This was done on the basis of authors' names, which, though fallible, reduces the likelihood of using L2 writers in a corpus designed to represent L1 writing.

[5] Available at http://ucrel.lancs.ac.uk/wmatrix2.html.

[6] LL measures the likelihood that a difference between the observed frequency of an item and its expected frequency is not random. The higher the LL value, the more significant the difference between two frequency scores. An LL value of 3.8 or higher is significant at the level of $p < 0.05$ and an LL of 6.6 or higher is significant at $p < 0.01$. See http://ucrel.lancs.ac.uk/llwizard.html.

[7] Mur Dueñas (2007a) reports a similar phenomenon in Spanish.

[8] For a discussion of these issues in the context of Translation Studies, see Venuti (1995).

References

Bennett, K. (2006), 'Critical language study and translation: the case of academic discourse', in J.F. Duarte, A.A. Rosa and T. Seruya (eds), *Translation Studies at the Interface of Disciplines*. Amsterdam and Philadelphia: John Benjamins, pp. 111–127.

Bennett, K. (2007a), 'Galileo's revenge: ways of construing knowledge and translation strategies in the era of globalization'. *Social Semiotics*, 17, (2), 171–193.

Bennett, K. (2007b), 'Epistemicide! The tale of a predatory discourse'. *The Translator*, 13, (2), 151–169.

Bennett, K. (2009), 'English academic style manuals: a survey'. *Journal of English for Academic Purposes*, 8, (1), 43–54.

Bennett, K. (2010), 'Academic discourse in Portugal: a whole different ballgame?' *Journal of English for Academic Purposes*, 9, (1), 21–32.

Bennett, K. (forthcoming), *Academic Discourse, Hegemony and Translation*. Manchester: St Jerome Press.

Biber, D., Johansson, S., Leech, G., Conrad, S. and Finegan, E. (1999), *Longman Grammar of Spoken and Written English*. London: Longman.

Carneiro, A., Simões, A. and Diogo, M.P. (2000), 'Enlightenment science in Portugal: The *Estrangeirados* and their communication networks'. *Social Studies of Science*, 30, (1), 591–619.

Clyne, M. (1987a), 'Cultural differences in the organization of academic texts in English and German'. *Journal of Pragmatics*, 11, (2), 211–247.

Clyne, M. (1987b), 'Discourse structures and discourse expectations: implications for Anglo-Germanic academic communication in English', in L. Smith (ed.), pp. 73–83.

Clyne, M. (1988), 'Cross-cultural responses to academic discourse patterns'. *Folia Linguistica*, 22, (3–4), 457–475.

Čmejrková, S. (1996), 'Academic writing in Czech and English', in E. Ventola and A. Mauranen (eds), *Pragmatics and Beyond*. Amsterdam and Philadelphia: John Benjamins, pp. 137–153.

Connor, U. (1996), *Contrastive Rhetoric: Cross-Cultural Aspects of Second-Language Writing*. Cambridge: Cambridge University Press.

Cuenca M.-J. (2003), 'Two ways to reformulate: a contrastive analysis of reformulation markers'. *Journal of Pragmatics*, 35, (7), 1069–1093.

Dahl, T. (2004), 'Textual metadiscourse in research articles: A marker of national culture or of academic discipline?' *Journal of Pragmatics*, 36, (10), 1807–1825.

De Cock, S. (2000), ' "Repetitive phrasal chunkiness" and advanced EFL speech and writing', in C. Mair and M. Hundt (eds), *Corpus Linguistics and Linguistic Theory*. Amsterdam and New York: Rodopi, pp. 51–68.

Duszak, A. (ed.) (1997), *Cultural Styles of Academic Discourse*, Berlin and New York: Mouton de Gruyter.

Duszak, A. (1994), 'Academic discourse and intellectual styles'. *Journal of Pragmatics*, 21, (3), 291–313.

Fox, G. (1998), 'Using corpus data in the classroom', in B. Tomlinson (ed.), *Materials Development in Language Teaching*. Cambridge: Cambridge University Press, pp. 25–43.

Frankenberg-Garcia, A. (1990a), *Second Language Writing Instruction: a study of the effects of a discourse-oriented programme upon the ability of skilled writers to improve their written production*. Unpublished PhD thesis. Edinburgh University, UK.

Frankenberg-Garcia, A. (1990b), 'Do the similarities between L1 and L2 writing processes conceal important differences?' *Edinburgh Working Papers in Applied Linguistics*, 1, 91–102.

Galtung, J. (1981), 'Structure, culture, and intellectual style: an essay comparing Saxonic, Teutonic, Gallic and Nipponic Approaches'. *Social Science Information* 20, (6), 817–856.

Gomes, J.F. (1995), *Para a História da Educação em Portugal: Seis Estudos*. Porto: Porto Editora.

Granger, S. and Meunier, F. (eds) (2008), *Phraseology: An Interdisciplinary Perspective*. Amsterdam and Philadelphia: John Benjamins.

Halliday, M.A.K. and Martin, J.R. (eds) (1993), *Writing Science: Literacy and Discursive Power*. Pittsburgh and London: University of Pittsburgh Press.

Hofland, K. and Johansson, S. (1982), *Word Frequencies in British and American English*. Bergen: The Norwegian Computing Centre for the Humanities.

Kachru, Y. (1987), 'Cross-cultural texts, discourse strategies and discourse interpretation', in L. Smith (ed.), pp. 87–100.

Kaplan, R.B. (1966) , 'Cultural thought patterns in inter-cultural education' in K. Croft (ed.), *Readings on English as a Second Language*, Cambridge MA: Winthrop (2nd edn. 1980), pp. 399–418.

Leech, G., Rayson, P and Wilson A. (2001), *Word Frequencies in Written and Spoken English: Based on the British National Corpus*. London: Longman.

Lillis, T. and Curry, M.-J. (2006), 'Professional academic writing by multilingual scholars: interactions with literacy brokers in the production of English-medium texts'. *Written Communication*, 23, (1), 3–35.

Martin, J.R. (1998), 'Discourses of science: recontextualisation, genesis, intertextuality and hegemony', in J.R. Martin and R. Veel (eds), *Reading Science: Critical and Functional Perspectives on Discourses of Science*. London and New York: Routledge, pp. 3–14.

Martín Martín, P. (2003), 'A genre analysis of English and Spanish research paper abstracts in experimental social sciences'. *English for Specific Purposes*, 22, (1), 25–43.

Mauranen, A. (1993), 'Contrastive ESP rhetoric: metatext in Finnish-English economics texts'. *English for Specific Purposes*, 12, (1), 3–22.

McKenny, J. and Bennett, K. (2009), 'Critical and corpus approaches to academic text revision: a case-study of articles by Portuguese humanities scholars'. *English Text Construction*, 2, 228–245.

Moreno, A.I. (1997), 'Genre constraints across languages: causal metatext in Spanish and English RAs'. *English for Specific Purposes*, 16, (3), 161–179.

Mur Dueñas, P. (2007a), '"I/We focus on . . .": A cross-cultural analysis of self-mentions in business management research articles'. *Journal of English for Academic Purposes*, 6, (2), 143–162.

Mur Dueñas, P. (2007b), 'Same genre, same discipline; however, there are differences: a cross-cultural analysis of logical markers in academic writing'. *ESP Across Cultures*, 4, 37–53.

Nunes, M.F. (2002), 'Opinião pública, ciência e tecnologia em Portugal XVIII–XX'. *Cultura: Revista de História e História de Ideias*, vol. XV (2nd series), 211–223.

Pennycook, A. (1994), *The Cultural Politics of English as an International Language*. New York: Longman.

Phillipson, R. (1992), *Linguistic Imperialism*. Oxford: Oxford University Press.

Rayson, P. (2003), *WMatrix: a statistical method and software tool for linguistic analysis through corpus comparison*. Unpublished PhD thesis. Lancaster University, UK.

Scott, M. (2004), *Wordsmith Tools 4*. Oxford: Oxford University Press.

Sinclair, J. (2004), *Trust the Text: Language, Corpus and Discourse*. London and New York: Routledge.

Smith, L. (ed.) (1987), *Discourse Across Cultures: Strategies in World Englishes*. London: Prentice Hall.

Tognini Bonelli, E. (2001), *Corpus Linguistics at Work*. Amsterdam and Philadelphia: John Benjamins.

Tribble, C. (2008), 'In this paper . . . Some emerging norms in lingua franca English writing in the sciences?', in *Proceedings of the 8th Teaching and Language Corpora Conference*. Lisbon: ISLA.

Ventola, E. and Mauranen, A. (eds) (1996), *Academic Writing: Intercultural and Textual Issues*. Amsterdam and Philadelphia: John Benjamins.

Venuti, L. (1995), *The Translator's Invisibility: A History of Translation*. London and New York: Routledge.

Yakhontova, T. (2006), 'Cultural and disciplinary variation in academic discourse: the issue of influencing factors'. *Journal of English for Academic Purposes*, 5, (2), 153–167.

Index

Page numbers in **bold** denote figures and tables.